RANDOM HOUSE
COMPACT ATLAS
OF
WORLD HISTORY

RANDOM HOUSE
COMPACT ATLAS
OF
WORLD HISTORY

RANDOM HOUSE
NEW YORK

Random House
Compact Atlas of World History

All inquiries should be addressed to Reference and Information Publishing, Random House, Inc., 201 East 50th Street, New York, NY 10022.

Published in the United States by Random House, Inc., New York and simultaneously in Canada by Random House of Canada Limited, Toronto.

Originally published in Great Britain by Times Books, London in 1997.

The Random House compact Atlas of world History/edited by Geoffrey Parker
         p.   cm.
ISBN 0-375-70505-8
1. Historical geography--Maps. I. Parker, Geoffrey, 1933--.
G1030 .R39 1998 <G&M>
911--DC21   98-31173
                        CIP
                        Maps

Random House Reference & Information website address:
www.randomwords.com   ·

0 9 8 7 6 5 4 3 2
January 2000

ISBN 0-375-70505-8

New York   Toronto   London   Sydney   Auckland

CONTENTS

INTRODUCTION

This volume, like *The Times Atlas of World History*, first published in 1978 and now in its fourth edition (and available in 16 languages), attempts to cover the whole story of humankind from its origins, when our ancestors first emerged from the tropical forests of Africa, to the complex, highly articulated world in which we now live.

It differs, however, from the original *Atlas of World History*, and also from *The Times Concise Atlas of World History*, first published in 1982, in three important ways. First, as its name makes clear, it presents the data in a more compact form. Although it includes 76 spreads – one more than the *Concise* – each contains fewer, simpler maps and (proportionately) more text. Second, every map has been reviewed in order to highlight the salient trends and facts it features. Third, the topics selected for treatment include far more material from the modern period: 20 spreads concentrate on the period since 1914 (as against 16 in the *Concise*) and no less than 13 of them cover the half-century since 1945.

Nevertheless, although the present volume incorporates new material and differs in other important ways from its two predecessors, it rests upon the same principles. Above all, it tries to break away from a concentration on Europe and to offer instead a view of history that is world-wide in conception and presentation and which does justice, without prejudice or favour, to the achievements of all peoples, in all ages and in all quarters of the globe. It thus remains true to the vision of Geoffrey Barraclough, who planned and edited both the *Atlas* and the *Concise Atlas:*

"When we say this is an atlas of world history, we mean that it is not simply a series of national histories loosely strung together. In other words, it is concerned less with particular events in the history of particular countries than with broad movements – for example the spread of the great world religions spanning whole continents... In singling out topics for inclusion we have adhered to the principle of selecting what was important then rather than what seems important now."

The essence of history, as Geoffrey Barraclough realized, is change and movement over time; and the historian's principal mission is therefore to discern the static from the dynamic, the aberration from the trend, and the contingent from the constant. So instead of presenting a series of individual snapshots, *The Times Compact Atlas of World History* seeks to emphasize change, expansion and contraction. It aims to convey a sense of the past as a continuing process and thus to provide a fresh perspective on today's world which will meet the requirements and interests of present-day readers in all parts of the globe.

This revised edition incorporates several new features. First, all the later spreads – both maps and text – have been updated to cover events since the original edition went to press. Second, several other maps have been revised and improved and physical bases added. Third, errors brought to our attention by readers have been corrected.

GEOFFREY PARKER
October 1996

Human origins

All major developments in the evolution of the human species took place in tropical Africa. Although life on earth, in the form of single-celled organisms, can be traced back some 4,600 million years, ape-like species only emerged 15 million years ago. Despite obvious physical differences, the great apes of Africa (chimpanzees and gorillas) are genetically almost identical to humans. The divergence of the human line occurred there between 5 and 8 million years ago (diagram 1).

Remains of the earliest hominids, *Australopithecus* or 'southern ape', dating from about 4 million BC have been found in both the limestone caves of southern Africa and in the Great Rift Valley. About four feet tall, they lived almost exclusively on fruit and nuts, with a brain size of about 700 cubic centimetres (not much different from a modern ape); but they walked on two feet and had complex social lives which stimulated the development of a larger brain. They already operated in nuclear family groups. Around 2.5 million years ago a new species appeared in east Africa known as *Homo habilis* or 'handy man', with a rounder skull. These were the first hominids to make and use tools (chipped stones and flakes), and perhaps also the first to scavenge for meat as a regular part of their diet. Their brain size was still only 800 cubic centimetres, but with *Homo erectus* ('upright man'), who developed around 1.7 million years ago, this increased to 1000 cc and sometimes more. These creatures made more sophisticated tools (above all stone handaxes and cleavers worked on both faces), used shelters (both caves and simple houses) and clothes, and learned to make and control fire – three developments that, between 1.5 million and 500,000 years ago, enabled their descendants, known as *Homo sapiens* ('thinking man'), to spread beyond their original tropical homeland and colonize less hospitable environments in Europe and Asia (map 1).

The spread of human groups beyond Africa was a gradual process – halting or even reversing as the glaciers advanced, more rapid in interglacial periods. *Homo erectus* was already in Java by at least 1.3 million years ago. The first fossils in Europe, some 500,000 years old, are of an archaic type of *Homo sapiens*, but the dominant form in Europe and western Asia

was, by around 100,000 BC, a specialized form of *Homo sapiens* known as Neanderthal Man. Their brain size approached 1500 cubic centimetres, but their cold-adapted bodies were heavily built and so their brain as a proportion of body weight was less than that of modern man. Several of their settlements include careful burial sites in which some male skeletons lie with animal remains, unusually well-made stone tools, and even flowers (implying belief in an after-life), while others bear marks of previous disabling injury or disease (so the men must have been supported by other group members). They also hunted in groups and there is evidence they may have employed some form of speech, although this is disputed.

The earliest anatomically modern humans, *homo sapiens sapiens*, date from around 100,000 BC and also originated in east and south Africa. They co-existed with Neanderthal Man for tens of thousands of years, but eventually prevailed. They too spread to other parts of the Old World, bringing with them composite tools which combined the use of stone for the cutting edge and organic materials for the rest, such as spear-throwers and (probably) arrows, making it possible to kill animals some distance away. This enabled human groups to hunt more efficiently, following particular herds on their annual migrations and even perhaps taming a few horses and reindeer. By 30,000 BC, of the many species of hominid which had walked the earth during the past 5 million years, only one – *homo sapiens sapiens* – remained.

The Ice Age

The first Ice Age began some 1,500,000 years ago, and the pattern of alternating glacial advance and retreat has been the dominant feature of the global environment ever since. At intervals of around 90,000 years, temperatures on earth fell by up to 15°C and ice-sheets covered the northern parts of the Asian, American and European continents – almost one-quarter of the earth's present land surface lay under glaciers – preventing human settlement. Further south, however, the tropical regions remained warm, although much drier than today: about half the land between the tropics of Capricorn and Cancer became arid desert. In between the glaciations came warmer periods characterized by temperatures similar to those of the present day; but whenever the ice advanced, the animals suited to temperate conditions – such as humans, a species of tropical origin – had to move southwards.

The last Ice Age began some 80,000 years ago. As the ice advanced and more water became frozen at the poles, sea levels fell and caused the appearance of land bridges which linked most of the major land areas and many present-day islands (including the British Isles) into one vast continent (map 1). In the midst of this period a new species of human, *Homo sapiens*, began to spread from Africa, replacing or interbreeding with existing hominid populations in Europe and Asia (page 10). These modern humans, using an extensive range of bone, antler, and stone tools, and capable of creating imaginative art in several media (cave paintings, carvings, sculptures), spread throughout the habitable world. They took advantage of the shorter sea crossings caused by falling sea levels to colonize Australasia in about 50,000 BC. A little later, perhaps as early as 40,000 BC, they also reached Japan, across a land bridge from Korea. At about the same time they began to populate the Americas, either by crossing the land bridge which joined the two sides of the Bering Strait or by using boats. Within a few thousand years groups of hunters and gatherers had traversed the entire continent, reaching New England in the east and Chile in the south by 9000 BC (map 2).

Humankind's development of the skills, equipment and behavioural patterns to permit survival in such inhospitable environments constitutes a remarkable achievement. The mastery of fire and the invention of clothing and shelter, as well as new social and communication skills, all stem from this period. The human species is the product of the long process of adaptation to the harsh conditions of the Ice Age. The onset of warmer conditions around 10,000 BC, ushering in the interglacial period in which we now live, caused sea levels to rise and cut off America from further contact with Eurasia. Henceforth, these regions and their people pursued their own independent lines of development. By then, however, a total of perhaps 10 million humans engaged in hunting and gathering almost everywhere and had already become the world's most widespread and successful mammal.

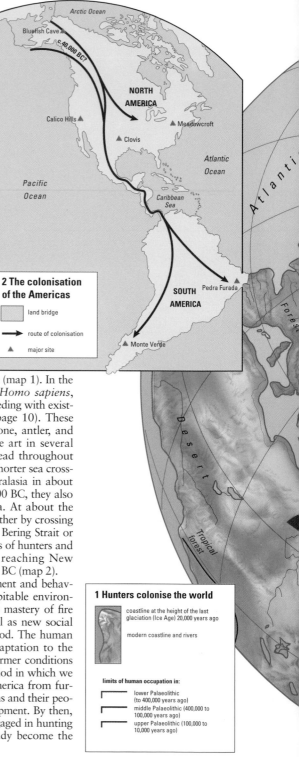

2 The colonisation of the Americas

- land bridge
- → route of colonisation
- ▲ major site

1 Hunters colonise the world

coastline at the height of the last glaciation (Ice Age) 20,000 years ago

modern coastline and rivers

limits of human occupation in:

- lower Palaeolithic (to 400,000 years ago)
- middle Palaeolithic (400,000 to 100,000 years ago)
- upper Palaeolithic (100,000 to 10,000 years ago)

North American ice sheet

Greenland ice sheet

Pacific Ocean

Ocean

p a c k   i c e

80° 100° 120°
60°   140°
40°   160°
20°   180°
0°
20°   160°
40°   140°
60° 80°   120°
       100°

Scandinavian
ice sheet

T a y m y r
i c e   s h e e t

T u n d r a

Black Sea

Caspian Sea

Steppe

Steppe

C o n i f e r o u s   f o r e s t

Sea of Japan

?

L. Balkhash

D e s e r t

Tarim Basin

Oriental
forest

I n d i a n   O c e a n

13

The origins of agriculture

By 8000 BC, when present-day climatic conditions began to prevail, humankind consisted of bands of hunters and gatherers who, although more numerous than ever before, pursued a lifestyle that differed little from that of their predecessors up to 100,000 years before. But within the next 2,000 years substantial villages appeared in certain regions; and in another 3,000 years there were towns and cities.

This decisive quickening in the pace of human development can be attributed largely to the beginning of agriculture: the deliberate alteration of natural systems to promote the abundance of an exploited species or set of species. Many parts of the globe, especially those between latitude 10° South and 50° North, have contributed to the present-day repertory of domesticated plants and animals (map 1). Among the earliest and most important centres of cereal cultivation were the Near East, where the wild ancestors of wheat and barley grew; China and South-East Asia, where millet and rice thrived; and Mesoamerica, which developed maize as a staple crop. In Africa, people in the lands south of the Sahara and in the high grasslands of North-East Africa domesticated a wide variety of native plant species. On the whole, cereal cultivation characterized temperate regions and root crop cultivation – potatoes, yams, bananas – predominated in tropical zones.

At the same time, useful local animal species were domesticated to provide meat, milk, hides or wool, and (except in the Americas, which lacked suitable animals) an important source of power for ploughing and other agricultural tasks. On the dry steppe-lands of central Eurasia, animal-keeping was more important than plant cultivation and the domestication of the horse gave rise to a specialized life-style based on nomadic herding.

The exact origins of agriculture remain unknown. The end of the Ice Age was certainly accompanied by an abundance of plant and animal food. This may have encouraged hunting and gathering communities to grow until their numbers made it necessary to find another subsistence strategy. Once chosen, however, farming developed a momentum of its own: once adopted, there was no easy turning back,

and the very success of the new lifestyle induced other fundamental changes. The increase in food resources which followed made possible a spectacular growth of human population, which may have multiplied several times between 8000 and 4000 BC. It also required cooperative effort, particularly after the introduction of irrigation led to the establishment of settled organized societies, at first in villages and later in towns and cities, and the development of new technologies, social systems and ideologies.

The transformation from hunting and gathering to agriculture, from a migratory to a sedentary life, was a decisive event in world history. Hunting and gathering peoples survived but, as farming spread, they became increasingly confined to the marginal world environments where agriculture could not secure a foothold (map 2). Both absolutely and relatively, their numbers declined until today their representatives survive only in hot deserts such as the Kalahari and central Australia, in the dense rain forests of the Amazon basin, central Africa and South-East Asia, and in the frozen wastes of the Arctic. Even there traditional lifestyles – followed by mankind for millennia – now face the threat of extinction.

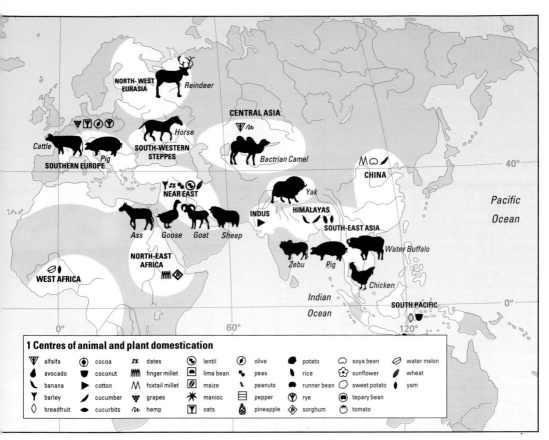

1 Centres of animal and plant domestication

⋎ alfalfa	🍫 cocoa	≈ dates	🌱 lentil	🫒 olive	● potato	◡ soya bean	⬭ water melon
🌶 avocado	● coconut	⋈ finger millet	◩ lima bean	⬧ peas	◗ rice	◯ sweet potato	◭ wheat
⌣ banana	▶ cotton	Ⲙ foxtail millet	◪ maize	⬦ peanuts	● runner bean	● tepary bean	◗ yam
⋎ barley	◢ cucumber	⁂ grapes	✳ manioc	▤ pepper	⋓ rye	◉ tomato	
◊ breadfruit	● cucurbits	∿ hemp	⍓ oats	🍍 pineapple	◈ sorghum		

2 The decline of hunting and gathering

world distribution of hunter-gathering peoples

15,000 BC

world population: 10 million
% hunters: 100

AD 1500

world population: 350 million
% hunters: 1.0

1960

world population: 3 billion
% hunters: 0.001

The first farmers of Asia

The first economies to be based on the husbandry of animal and plant staples came into being in the Near East. In the upland areas around the Zagros and Taurus mountains, and in Palestine, moister conditions as the ice-sheets released water that had been frozen led to the spread of large-seeded grasses – the ancestors of modern wheat and barley – which early hunters quickly appreciated for their nutrition and ease of storage. By 10,000 BC small villages of circular stone-walled huts developed, whose inhabitants lived from both the hunting and herding of gazelle and the harvesting of wild wheat. About 9000 BC, in northern Syria, some communities began to cultivate cereals outside their natural habitat while sheep were domesticated in Mesopotamia. By 7000 BC wheat and barley cultivation was established, as was the herding of goats, from Anatolia to the Zagros mountains, and this agricultural revolution spread shortly afterwards to Greece. Much of the Near Eastern lowland area, however, was too dry for cultivation. Only the development of irrigation – by spreading water from the rivers that drained from the mountains – allowed settlements to extend to the Mesopotamian plain in the sixth and fifth millennia .

Plants and animals were independently domesticated in many other parts of the world. Sedentary farming began in South Asia on the Kachi Plain of north-west India around 7000 BC. The early settlers cultivated barley and wheat, domesticated sheep, cattle and goats, and buried their dead with elaborate grave goods. From 6000 BC onwards, mud-brick storehouses divided into small compartments served as the focal point for food, tools and trade goods. By 5000 BC rice farmers had also established villages in the hills just south of the Ganges valley (map 3). In northern China the cultivation of millet, another cereal, began on the great loess plain around the Yellow River and its tributaries around 6000 BC. It remained the staple crop of the region for many centuries. Further south the principal cereal was rice, first cultivated in the Yangtze delta before 4000 BC (map 2). In addition, the ox-drawn plow began to be adapted throughout much of Eurasia, enlisting animal traction to increase the efficiency of farming. Villages acquired defensive walls, from

2 Early Chinese agriculture

- area of loess soil
- redeposited loess
- early millet cultivation
- approximate northern limit of wild rice distribution
- early wet rice cultivation

Chinese settlement
- ▲ 6000-5000 BC
- ■ 6000-4000 BC
- ● 5000-2500 BC

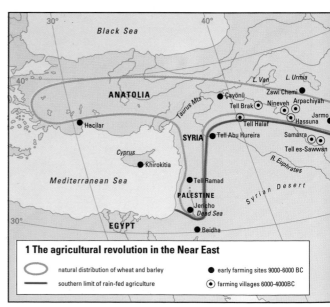

1 The agricultural revolution in the Near East

- natural distribution of wheat and barley
- southern limit of rain-fed agriculture
- ● early farming sites 9000-6000 BC
- ◉ farming villages 6000-4000BC

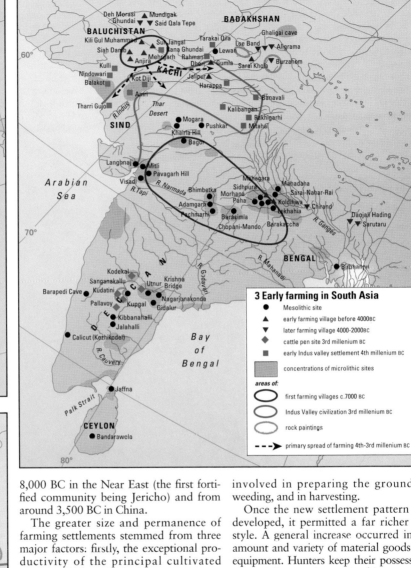

3 Early farming in South Asia

- ● Mesolithic site
- ▲ early farming village before 4000BC
- ▼ later farming village 4000–2000BC
- ◆ cattle pen site 3rd millenium BC
- ■ early Indus valley settlement 4th millenium BC
- concentrations of microlithic sites

areas of:

- first farming villages c.7000 BC
- Indus Valley civilization 3rd millenium BC
- rock paintings
- - - ▶ primary spread of farming 4th–3rd millenium BC

8,000 BC in the Near East (the first forti-fied community being Jericho) and from around 3,500 BC in China.

The greater size and permanence of farming settlements stemmed from three major factors: firstly, the exceptional pro-ductivity of the principal cultivated species, which could feed large concentra-tions of people all year round – something hunting and gathering can never do; sec-ondly, the ability of plant foods to survive storage over many months, allowing the community to stay in one place and live off the previous harvest while a new crop grows and ripens. Finally, farmers need to live near their fields, both to protect them against human and animal predators and to minimize the travel and transport

involved in preparing the ground, in weeding, and in harvesting.

Once the new settlement pattern had developed, it permitted a far richer life-style. A general increase occurred in the amount and variety of material goods and equipment. Hunters keep their possessions to a minimum, since everything must be carried around; but sedentary communities can produce and accumulate a wide range of items, both utilitarian and for ritual and pleasure – pottery and tools, ornaments and display items. The pace of change accelerated, and around 3000 BC a new threshold was reached, a critical stage in humankind's progress towards the modern world: the emergence of the first cities, and of the first ordered civilizations.

The rise of civilization

The first civilizations arose in the alluvial basins of four major rivers which drain from the mountain fringes where agriculture began: the Tigris and Euphrates in Mesopotamia, the Nile in Egypt, the Indus in India, and the Yellow River in China. Each proved capable of supplying the high, regular yields needed to support large urban populations. Cities of thousands, and then tens of thousands, evolved. In Mesopotamia, a number already existed by 3500 BC. Egypt adopted urban civilization in about 3200 BC and the Harappan civilization arose in the Indus plain from about 2500 BC. Civilization in north China appears to have developed, again wholly or largely independently, around 1800 BC.

These societies shared many common features: the development of cities; writing; large public buildings; and the political apparatus of a state. The large agricultural surpluses produced by irrigation – some Mesopotamian communities harvested 60, 70 or even 80 grains for each grain sown – made it possible to employ a large segment of society in activities other than farming, such as manufacture and trade. This in turn led to the emergence of a ruling class which accumulated wealth through the exploitation of labour and the imposition of taxes. In Mesopotamia the ruler was also the chief priest and the temple centre provided a vital element of the political system, its monumental structure forming a visual reminder to all

1 The rise of civilization

- fertile land
- centres of urban civilization
- areas of pastoral nomadism

citizens of the power that governed their daily life. The centralized control found in these societies fostered a special legal system, a standing army, a permanent bureaucracy, and the division of society into distinct classes. The state also supported scribes, who were usually trained and employed within the temples. The earliest writing was used as a means of keeping track of commodities, wages and taxes; but it soon served other purposes: to preserve religious traditions, which thereby became sacred books; to register social customs, which thereby became codes of law; and to record myths, which thereby developed into history and literature.

Since, apart from agricultural produce, the alluvial plains lacked most other natural resources, an extensive trading activity exchanged luxury goods and raw materials from other areas with the textiles and other manufactured goods of the cities and thus helped to develop other trading centres in a great arc from the eastern Mediterranean to the Indus valley and in China. The cities therefore exercised an influence out of all proportion to their comparatively small geographical extent. True, not all areas were affected: Australia, Africa, Europe and large parts of Asia had no cities; the first civilizations of the Americas did not emerge until about 1500 BC (and, when they did, owed nothing to ideas introduced from outside). Nevertheless the growth of the first urban centres, with their technology, literacy, and class divisions began a new phase in the development of human society.

The Near East 3600-605 BC

The earliest of all known civilizations, Sumer, rested upon some 12 city-states in southern Mesopotamia. At first, pre-eminence passed from one to another, but the growing concentrations of people on the fertile plain eventually called for greater management than a single city could provide. In 2371 BC, a centralized authority spanning the whole valley grew up under the first of a series of legendary conquerors: Sargon of Agade (c.2334-2279 BC). Before long, his power extended far beyond Mesopotamia to Elam and the Zagros mountains in the southeast, and all the way to Syria and the Mediterranean coast in the north-west, while his grandson Naram-Sin extended the empire eastwards to the Iranian plateau. But Sargon's empire proved to be short-lived and its collapse, due both to external invasions and to internal strains, gave way to a new empire with Ur as its centre, its hegemony stretching from the Persian Gulf to Nineveh. But Ur also fell after little more than a century, and a kaleidoscope of shifting alliances brought new cities to prominence, most notably Mari and Babylon on the Euphrates. Under its powerful king Hammurabi, Babylon created another empire that covered the whole of southern Mesopotamia; but, once more, it did not long survive the death of its founder (map 1).

Even before Sargon unified Mesopotamia, Egypt was under the sway of a single ruler. Around 3100 BC an Upper Egyptian ruler, his power based on the exploitation of goldfields near the Red Sea, conquered the Nile delta and established a new capital at Memphis, which for almost 2000 years served as the administrative centre for a densely populated region of some 15,000 square miles running from the first cataract at Aswan to the Mediterranean coast (map 2). At about the same time, writing in hieroglyphic script commenced. During the 'Old Kingdom' period (2685-2180 BC) the rulers of Egypt built a series of massive pyramid-tombs along the desert edge opposite Memphis which emphasised their power and prestige. Then, after a century of invasion and anarchy, the Egyptian state entered a second period of cultural achievement under the able rulers of the Middle Kingdom (2040-1783 BC); and another era of expansion under the XVIIIth and XIXth dynasties (1570-1200 BC). At home they undertook vast building projects, like the rock-cut temple at Abu Simbel created by Ramesses II (1290-1224 BC); abroad they advanced through Palestine into Syria and created an empire that extended almost to the Euphrates.

The continuity of Ancient Egyptian history, although not unbroken, stood in marked contrast to developments in Mesopotamia. The two civilizations also differed in other respects. First, because of the annual Nile flood, Egypt did not depend to the same extent on irrigation canals and dams; second, although it possessed some cities, they lacked the geographical concentration found in southern Mesopotamia, so that its rulers tended to arise from rural rather than urban power bases. Third, and most important, Egypt rarely suffered foreign invasion. Admittedly the Hyksos, an Asiatic people, overran most of the country in the 18th century BC, but a new native dynasty expelled them c. 1570 BC and then pursued the invaders northwards to the upper Euphrates. Egypt's Asiatic empire lasted until about 1200 BC when the 'Sea Peoples', marauders from the Aegean and Asia Minor, attacked all the major civilizations of the Near East and initiated a 'Dark Age', concerning which very few historical sources survive, until about 900 BC and the emergence of Assyria.

The power of Assyria was based on the prosperous farming communities of the northern Mesopotamian plain. As early as the 11th century BC, Assyrian kings were campaigning as far to the west as the Mediterranean, but the greatest expansion of Assyrian power began in the 9th century BC, during the reign of Ashurnasirpal II (883-859 BC). Under Shalmaneser III (858-824 BC) Assyrian armies reached the Mediterranean, Lake Van and the Persian Gulf, and incorporated the Aramaean and other states east of the Euphrates into the Assyrian empire, although the heart of the state remained the upper Tigris and Euphrates.

Shalmaneser's reign ended in civil war, and a temporary set-back followed in Assyria's fortunes, but under Sargon II (721-705 BC) the empire expanded dramatically once more and, from his capital at Nineveh on the Tigris, Ashurbanipal (668-627 BC) ruled the whole of Mesopotamia,

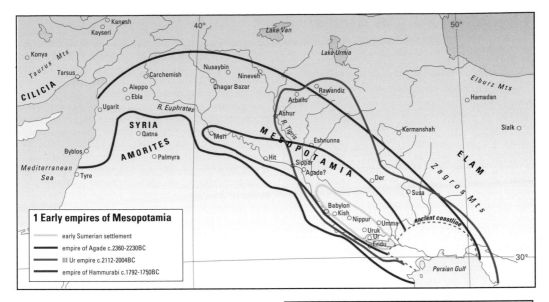

1 Early empires of Mesopotamia

- early Sumerian settlement
- empire of Agade c.2360-2230BC
- III Ur empire c.2112-2004BC
- empire of Hammurabi c.1792-1750BC

Syria and Palestine, and even (for a short time) the Nile delta (map 3). The Assyrians possessed a well-disciplined army and an efficient bureaucracy; to the Old Testament prophets, at least, they appeared invincible. Yet civil war, succession disputes and rebellions, particularly by the Babylonians, dogged the last century of Assyrian rule. In 612 BC Assyria fell before a coalition of her enemies: the Babylonians and Medes, aided by Scythian horsemen from the steppe. Nineveh was sacked and abandoned for ever.

2 Old Kingdom Egypt c.3000-2000 BC

- ● town or city c.3250-2000 BC
- ■ royal tomb c.3250-2650 BC
- ▲ pyramid c.2650-2000 BC
- cultivable land

3 The growth of the Assyrian Empire

- Assyria c. 1500 BC
- under Tiglath-Pileser I (1114-1076 BC)
- under Shalmaneser III (858-824 BC)
- under Sargon II (721-705 BC)
- under Ashurbanipal (668-627 BC)

The Americas to AD 800

The Americas, like Australia (page 24) were colonized from Asia during the last Ice Age, when lowered sea levels turned the Bering Strait into dry land. Then, the melting of the ice cut off the continent from Eurasia (page 12). It is one of the remarkable facts of human history that despite their geographical separation, development in Old and New Worlds followed much the same path: the adoption of agriculture; the creation of cities and empires; the invention of writing. These two geographical zones continued on parallel paths until the New World was invaded by Europeans after 1492 (page 68). The New World civilizations were highly inventive in their own right and in some ways in advance of their western counterparts. They produced – quite independent of the Old World – magnificent art, remarkable mathematical and astronomical skills, and monumental architecture.

The inhabitants of Mesoamerica and the central Andes began to experiment with plant cultivation around 7000 BC and by 1500 BC farming had allowed a rapid increase in population. By 800 BC the Olmecs on the Gulf of Mexico, the Zapotecs at Monte Albán, and the people of Chavín in Peru had developed complex societies with populations that numbered tens of thousands, with a hierarchy of social classes, an efficient civil service, a professional priesthood, and specialists in all kinds of tasks, from manufacturing to commerce and government.

Around and between these civilizations, other communities remained at the chiefdom level. Maize, beans and squash cultivation spread from Mexico to north America, and their arrival initiated a period of rapid development. In Ohio and Illinois, between 300 BC and AD 550, Hopewell chiefs built elaborate burial mounds and maintained trade contacts from Florida to the Rockies. Most American chiefdoms were agricultural, based on plant cultivation, but along the north-west coast rich fishing grounds and an abundance of whales and seals supported large villages and a complex ceremonial life by hunting and gathering alone. Towards the extremities of the continent, however, harsh conditions precluded farming, settlement remained sparse, and nomadic lifestyles persisted (map 1).

In Mesoamerica, new influences, especially among the Maya of Yucatán, complemented the early Olmec and Zapotec civilizations from the 4th century BC. Around AD 250 the Maya began to develop their own hieroglyphic writing and to erect carved stones bearing calendrical or historical inscriptions. They became preoccupied with the passage of time and their astronomers calculated the exact length of the solar year, the lunar month, and the revolution of the planet Venus, and predicted eclipses. To assist their calculations, they invented the idea of place value and the concept of zero.

Mayan civilization did not remain isolated. Important regional cultures developed elsewhere in Mexico: along the Gulf Coast (especially at El Tajín), in the valley of Oaxaca (where Monte Albán became a great city), and at Teotihuacán in the valley of Mexico. In its prime, around AD 600, the city of Teotihuacán, laid out in a precise grid plan, covered 8 square miles (20 km^2) and housed 125,000 people. Its wealth came from agriculture, crafts and trade, and it maintained diplomatic and commercial exchanges with the other civilizations of Mexico and with the Maya. But this prosperity did not last. Teotihuacán was destroyed and abandoned around AD 730; Monte Albán fell into disrepair during the 10th century; and Classic Mayan civilization collapsed, for reasons still not fully understood, between AD 800 and 900 (map 2).

A separate group of interrelated civilizations grew up in the central Andes, supported by spectacular irrigation systems in the lowlands and by ingenious raised fields in the highlands. The Andean peoples discovered sophisticated skills in working gold, silver and copper, and used these metals for tools as well as for jewellery. Although its vast distances and harsh topography made this region difficult to unify, the centuries between AD 600 and 1000 saw the rise of a truly imperial power based on Huari in the Peruvian Andes. Many elements of Huari religion and art originated at Tiahuanaco, further south, but were quickly adopted by Huari and then spread by force to many parts of the coast and highlands. For a short time Huari was the capital of a state embracing most of Peru, but around AD 800 the city was sacked and abandoned for ever. The fragile unity soon collapsed and not until the Inca conquests of the 15th and 16th centuries would the central Andes be reunified under a single government.

2 The Classic period in Mesoamerica, AD 300-800

- Teotihuacán civilisation
- classic Gulf coast civilisation
- Zapotec civilisation
- Maya civilisation
- ▲ city or ceremonial centre AD 250-850

Olmec States 800-400BC

OAXACA

Tuxtla Mts — Gulf of
Tres Zapotes — San
Laguna de los Cerros — La Venta
Lorenzo
Olmec contacts with San José Magote
San José Magote

Pavón ▲ — 95°
HUASTEC

pots and clay figures exported to west Mexico

Gulf of

obsidian mines of Pachuca
Teotihuacán ▲
VALLEY OF MEXICO
obsidian mines of Otumba
Cholula ▲ — Cacaxtla — *Maya-style murals*
resident Zapotecs occupy their own quarter of Teotihuacán
Xochicalco ▲
Teotihuacán stone figurines and masks

Comalcalco ▲
OLMEC STATES
Maya pottery to Teotihuacán
Teotihuacán influence

MIXTEC STATES

100° — *Pacific Ocean* — 15°

ASIA

Bering Strait

ARCTIC LITTORAL HUNTERS

GREENLAND

(ESKIMO)

HUNTERS OF THE SUB-ARCTIC FOREST

L'Anse aux Meadows
(Norse colony, founded by
Icelanders AD 1001
but soon abandoned)

PLATEAU
FISHERMEN
PLANT GATHERERS
HUNTERS

Huff Village

PLAINS HUNTERS
farming introduced
along river valleys
from eastern
woodlands

Hogup Cave
Danger Cave

FISHERMEN
MONTANE
GATHERERS

DESERT
GATHERERS

Simonsen

PUEBLO
INDIANS

Hopewell

1 American peoples and cultures, c. AD 500

S.W.
FARMERS

Tyuonyi
Pueblo Bonito

WOODLAND
FARMERS

Poverty Point

Hardaway

Etowah

DESERT
GATHERERS
FISHERMEN
SHELLFISH
COLLECTORS

DESERT
GATHERERS

Atlantic Ocean

- farming peoples
- chiefdoms
- civilized states
- hunters and gatherers
- ■ archaeological site

Gulf of
Mexico

El Tajín
Teotihuacán

Pacific Ocean

Monte Albán

Tikal

CARIBBEAN

FARMERS

MESOAMERICAN
CIVILIZATION

MAYA

MAIZE AND MANIOC
CULTIVATORS OF
CARIBBEAN LOWLANDS

60°

40°

20°

NORTH
ANDEAN
CHIEFDOMS

SAVANNAH
FARMERS

San Agustín

FARMING TRIBES
(manioc cultivators)
of the Amazon Rain Forest

Teso dos Bichos

Mexico

90°

Chichen Itzá
(900-1100)

Komchen
Dzibilchaltún

Teotihuacán influence in
temple architecture

Cobá
Tancáh

Acanceh

Uxmal

Kabáh

Teotihuacán style
pottery

Mexico

Becan
Santa Rita

Nohmul

fortifications of
Teotihuacán period

Altun Ha

figurines in Teotihuacán
style made from Pachuca
obsidian

Tikal

stelae slabs carved with
Teotihuacán figures

Palenque

Yaxchilán

Dos Pilas

Quiriguá

Bonampak

decipherment of
inscriptions has
documented ruling
dynasty

Chiapa de Corzo

Chinkultic

Copán

in pottery and frescos

offerings of
Teotihuacán pottery

Kaminaljuyú
Teotihuacán colony

Abaj Takalik
Olmec style pottery

Lake Atitlán

El Baúl Teotihuacán pottery

20°

Moche
Chavin
Las Haldas
La Florida
Huari

Pedra Furada

CENTRAL
ANDEAN
CIVILIZATION

Nasca

Tiahuanaco

SAVANNAH
FARMERS

about AD 500
farming introduced
from Amazon Basin
into Brazilian forest
and savannah

immigration of
Tupi-Guarani tribes

HUNTERS
OF THE
CHACO
SAVANNAH

0°

20°

Monte Verde

MARITIME
HUNTERS

GRASSLAND,
STEPPE HUNTERS

SHELLFISH
COLLECTORS

80°

60°

40°

23

Prehistoric Africa and Australasia

Both Australia and Africa were isolated from the rest of the Old World for most of prehistory, the former by sea, the latter by desert. Although the inhabitants of North Africa began the transition from hunting and gathering to farming around 8000 BC, the desiccation of the Sahara after about 4000 BC cut off Africa south of the Equator for centuries. In Australia, the aborigines mostly remained hunters and gatherers adapted to living in a large range of environments from tropical forest to harsh desert. They enjoyed a rich symbolic life, as evidenced by the decoration of their rock shelters with prolific designs. The colonization of the islands of Melanesia occurred considerably later, when settlers from New Guinea, associated with the distinctive Lapita pottery, reached Fiji around 1300 BC and then made their way into Polynesia via Tonga and Samoa, reaching the Marquesas islands in about AD 300 (map 2). From there they spread north to Hawaii (c. AD 800) and south-

west via the Cook islands to New Zealand between 850 and 1100. But populations remained small: about 300,000 in Australia and 100,000 in New Zealand when the Europeans arrived there in the 18th century.

The geographical isolation of southern Africa was never complete. In the east settlers spread down the Rift Valley from Ethiopia during the first millennium BC, while trans-Saharan trade increased in importance after the introduction of the camel from Asia, around 100 BC, which facilitated the spread of iron tools and weapons, introduced earlier in the north by the Greeks and Carthaginians, but also arriving from the south via Nigeria. Aided by the new technology, Bantu-speaking farmers and cattle-herders began to colonize southern Africa in the early centuries AD. By the 13th century powerful Bantu chiefdoms had emerged, such as that centred on Great Zimbabwe, and on cattle-raising communities engaged in long-distance trade, long before the Portuguese arrived off both the south-east and south-west coasts of the continent at the close of the 15th century.

2 Early settlement in the South Seas

Ψ prehistoric rock art

The Lapita potters:

☐ Lapita pottery area

• sites with Lapita pottery

→ settlement of Eastern Polynesia 150BC-AD1000

1 Africa: the Stone Age to the Iron Age

▲ bone harpoon site   ▲ early agricultural site

▨ area of Saharan rock painting c. 6000-1000 BC

limits of cattle domestication   ● site of cattle domestication

▨ area of megalithic monuments and tombs

➤ spread of iron   ▲ early iron-working site

major Iron Age sites:

● Mediterranean   ● Sudan-Ethiopia

● sub-Sahara   ▼ late Stone Age hunters and herders of southern Africa

▨ area of southern African rock paintings, from 1000 BC

Mediterranean Sea

Sahara Desert

N. African megaliths 2nd and 1st millenium BC

Utica
Carthage
Capeletti
Greek and Phoenician colonists
Cyrene
Lepti (Homs)

4500 BC
4000 BC
Naucratis
Merimde *4200 BC*
Sais
Memphis
Fayum *4300 BC* **EGYPT**

Meniet
Adrar Tiouiyne
Immidir
Adrar Bous
Arlit
Hoggar
Massif
Uan Muhaggiag
Tassili Massif
3000 BC
Tibesti Massif
Jebel 'Uweinat
Thebes
R. Nile
NUBIA

Karkarchinkat
Gao
2000 BC
Agadez
copper working in 2nd millenium BC
1500 BC
Ennedi
Nuri
Napata
Meroe *500 BC*
KINGDOM OF MEROE 900 BC-AD 400
Shaheinab *3200 BC*
Kadero
Adulis

S a h e l
Jenne-jeno
proto-urban settlement by 1st century AD
Daima
R. Benue
Jebel Moya
Axum
KINGDOM OF AXUM AD 100-1000

Ntereso *1400 BC*
Kintampo
Nok
Taruga *440 BC*
Ife
Atwetwebooso
Igbo Ukwu
shrines AD 840
Ethiopian Highlands
Ethiopian megaliths 1st and 2nd millenium AD
Ileret

iron and cattle
500 BC
1500 BC

possible spread of cultivation to lower Congo Basin 1st millenium BC

R. Congo
Funa River *270 BC*
Western Stream Iron Age sites
Katuruka *5th century BC*
Rift Valley
Urewe
Lake Victoria
Elmenteita
Narosura
Crescent Is.
Manda
East African 'pastoral neolithic' sites
Kwale

iron and cattle

ports involved in Indian Ocean trade by 8th century AD. SE Asian foodstuffs (bananas, taro) introduced

Lake Tanganyika
Sanga
late 1st millenium AD cemetery of 144 graves
Kalambo
Kilwa
Lubusi
Lake Nyasa
Kamnama
Nkope
Kapwirimbe
Kalundu
Ziwa
Gokomere
Zimbabwe
Mabueni
Malapati
Kalahari Desert
Phalaborwa

Arab traders and colonists

Madagascar
Indonesian colonists

AD 500
AD 1000

domestic sheep obtained by 1st century AD, perhaps from Iron Age source
Castle Cavern
Shongweni
Blackburn
Zaayfontein
Bonteberg
Wilton
Nelson Bay
Die Kelders

Indian Ocean

Marquesas Is.

Tuamotu Archepelago
Pitcairn I.
Easter I.

25

South and South-East Asia to AD 500

The first civilizations of the Indus valley (page 12) collapsed around 1500 BC. When the picture becomes clear once again the population of northern India had been transformed, with a Hindu religion, a Sanskrit literature, a caste system and (by about 800 BC) iron working, which enabled the spread of farming communities eastward into the rich plain of the Ganges. By 600 BC at least 16 political units had grown up along the Ganges, the subcontinent's new centre of gravity. By 400 BC war had reduced the states to four, and no doubt the resulting social tensions helped to spread new ethical and religious systems, for in the 6th century Gautama (Buddha), founder of Asia's most pervasive religion, was born in one of these states, while in another Mahavira formulated the teaching of Jainism (see page 32).

A further turning point came in 320 BC when Chandragupta Maurya seized the state of Magadha on the lower Ganges, and occupied large parts of central India, and in 305 BC annexed the province of Trans-Indus from the successors of Alexander the Great (see page 30). Chandragupta's grandson Asoka (273-232 BC) expanded this Mauryan empire southwards, bringing the greater part of the sub-continent under his rule and inscribing edicts on pillars and rock-faces all over India as a permanent reminder of his power (map 1). The death of Asoka introduced a troubled period, punctuated by invasions of both Greeks and nomads who founded states in the north-west, such as the Kushan empire, where Hellenistic and Indian influences

1 India's first empires, 297 BC-AD 150

(approximate limits shown)

▬▬▬ Chandragupta Maurya's empire 297 BC	▬▬▬ Western satraps AD 150
▬▬▬ Bindusara's empire 272 BC	▬▬▬ Kushan empire AD 150 (eastern limit)
▬▬▬ Asoka's empire 232 BC	▬▬▬ Satavahana kingdom AD 150
▲ rock and pillar edicts	

2 Prehistoric sites in South-East Asia

● Neolithic/Bronze Age settlements

○ Dong Son drums

● Early Iron Age and urn burial sites

3 Gupta India

- empire of Chandragupta I
- added by Samudragupta
- temporarily tributary to Samudragupta
- added by Chandragupta II
- tributary tribes and states
- under Gupta influence (c. AD 380–410)

mingled. Further south, the Satavahanas of the Deccan ruled a state that straddled the peninsula by AD 150. Then, in the 4th century, the Gupta dynasty, again based on Magadha, created an empire which by AD 400 almost extended from the Indus to the bay of Bengal, and projected north Indian values and religions far beyond (map 3).

The barbarian invasions of the 5th century (see page 38) caused the collapse of Gupta power, but it was precisely during this period that Hindu and Buddhist influences began to spread to South-East Asia. The cultivation of rice in this area, beginning as early as 3000 BC, allowed the development of prosperous farming villages. Bronze came into use after about 1000 BC, reflected in distinctive bronze Dong Son drums, and iron followed after about 500 BC (map 2). By AD 300 trading links with India had burgeoned, and Buddhist images appeared by AD 500, notably in Burma, Cambodia, and Java. By AD 700 the construction of Hindu temples in the same three areas had begun.

27

Early Europe 6000-1000 BC

Farming spread from the Near East to Europe about 6500 BC, beginning with Greece and Bulgaria. Agriculture in these regions involved wheat and barley, sheep and goats, just as in western Asia; but as farming spread north and west into more temperate zones, major adjustments became necessary. New, more robust types of cereal developed, and cattle and pigs became the dominant livestock. By about 5500 BC agricultural communities had developed along the Danube valley, and their descendants spread north-west from there until they reached the Paris basin around 4750 BC – an advance in the farming frontier of over one mile each year. After a brief pause, the final phase saw the spread of farming to the northern fringes of Europe, including Scandinavia and the British Isles, where it was adopted by existing hunter-gatherer communities by about 4000 BC (map 1).

Eventually these European farmers, like their Near Eastern counterparts before them, began to experience the difficulties caused by a shortage of suitable agricultural land to feed their growing population. The solution they adopted was not irrigation – temperate Europe, unlike the Middle East, never lacked rainfall – but the introduction, around 4000 BC, of the plough. This device required the maintenance of draught oxen which, although costly, provided a much more efficient way of breaking the ground than hoes and spades and allowed new areas to be farmed that would otherwise not have proved economic.

Meanwhile, in the Balkans, copper-working also began around 4500 BC and by 2500 BC it had become common to alloy the copper with tin to produce bronze.

1 The spread of agricultural settlement

main route of agrarian expansion

dates of agricultural settlement (based on tree-ring corrected radiocarbon dating)

- 7000-6000 BC
- 6000-5000 BC
- 5000-4000 BC
- 4000-3000 BC
- 3000-2000 BC

bowl cultures — early farming groups

○ Hembury — site of excavated farming village

2 The Aegean, 2500-1200 BC

— frontiers of Mycenaean world c. 1300 BC

Ⓜ major Mycenaean palaces (c.1500-1200)

Ⓜ major Cretan palaces

◪ smaller Cretan palaces

● other important settlements

● finds of Linear A tablets

● finds of Linear B tablets

The need to acquire these two raw materials led to the development of extensive trade networks, which also conveyed other materials, such as amber from the Baltic, which is found as far afield as Mycenae, in southern Greece, where graves filled with sumptuous funerary offerings of gold and jewellery appeared from 1600 BC.

Mycenae was not the earliest European civilization: that honour belongs to the island of Crete where from about 2000 BC 'Minoan' culture, based on palaces decorated with colourful frescoes and equipped with advanced sanitary and drainage systems, developed. Bureaucracy and trade flourished, and an alphabetic script known as Linear A developed around 1600 BC. Two centuries later, however, the Mycenaeans, who take their name from the fortress of Mycenae in the eastern Peloponnese, conquered Crete and became the principal military and economic power in the Aegean (see map 2). They

adapted the Minoan culture, including its script which they modified (to a form known as Linear B, clearly an early version of Greek) and used to administer their own empire. Mycenaean Greece was divided among a number of independent leaders, each of whom ruled a small kingdom, in much the same way as Greece in the classical period was divided into city-states (see page 30). The legend of the Trojan War, recorded centuries later in Homer's Iliad, is thought to recall a Mycenaean campaign of c. 1250 BC against the city of Troy, strategically situated at the entrance to the Dardanelles, and controlling access to the trade of the Black Sea. But this success, if indeed it occurred, must have been the final fling of the Mycenean warlords because by 1200 BC most of their palaces were in ruins, overthrown perhaps by rebellion or by outside attack, and a 'Dark Age' which left very few records ensued all over Greece for the next four centuries.

The Greek world 750-300 BC

After the fall of Mycenae, Greece dissolved into a mosaic of small farming communities and chiefdoms dominated by local Greek-speaking tribes. By the 8th century BC, however, a new order had evolved, centred on about 150 city-states, each one a limited, independent self-governing community. Their emergence depended upon geography: 80 per cent of Greece is rock and mountain, but the coasts are studded with comparatively small plains. By 800 BC the main city-states had been founded, and new colonies of Greeks had been established on the Aegean islands and on the Anatolian coast at Ephesus and Miletus (map 1). Writing was reintroduced, coinage invented around 650 BC, the first temples founded, and new styles of sculpture, architecture and vase-painting developed.

There was an amazing explosion of Greek influence during the 8th and 7th centuries BC, with the foundation of far-flung colonies around the coast of the Mediterranean and the Black Sea. These included many cities which have remained famous to the present, such as Marseilles and Naples. In the central Mediterranean the Greeks came into conflict with the Carthaginians, who for many centuries disputed control of Sicily with them. In Asia Minor, however, the Greeks came up against the Persian empire, which first sought to annex the city-states of Anatolia and in 490 and 480-479 BC invaded the peninsula itself. The Persians met with defeat and the next 50 years marked the great age of Greek culture: the tragic drama of Aeschylus, Sophocles and Euripedes; the comedy of Aristophanes; the histories of Herodotus and Thucydides; the splendour of the Parthenon; the sculptures of Phidias. 50 years after the defeat of the Persians, however, Greece found itself embroiled in a desperate struggle between the city-states. The principal protagonists were Sparta, the militarized power in the Peloponnese, and Athens, which had built up a formidable fleet and used it to create an Aegean empire. The Peloponnesian war lasted over 25 years, from 431 to 404 BC. Despite victories on both sides, Athens fatally overstrained her resources with a disastrous expedition against Syracuse in Sicily (415-13) and in 404 BC succumbed (map 2).

The 4th century saw more jockeying for power, while Persia sought to intervene in Greek affairs, until the well-trained Macedonian army of King Philip II (359-336 BC) subdued the city-states and imposed the ambitious aim of invading Persia upon them. Philip's remarkable son Alexander (336-323 BC) invaded Asia Minor with an army of 35,000 men, both Greeks and Macedonians, in 334; moved on to annex Egypt (332) and the Persian empire (331); and campaigned successfully in India and Central Asia (map 3). Alexander's death in 323 and the ensuing struggles between his leading generals created three major powers: Macedon, Egypt, and the Seleucid kingdom (comprising the bulk of the Persian empire).

Although politically the empire of Alexander the Great proved ephemeral, in other respects its consequences endured. Alexander himself founded some 70 cities, not merely as military strongholds but as cultural centres and thus carried Greek civilization far to the east. Greek culture infused and Hellenized the whole *oikumene* (civilized world) as far as India and China.

1 Greek colonization 750-550 BC

- extent of Greece 750 BC
- coast under Greek influence (approximate)
- coast under Phoenician/Carthaginian influence
- Greek parent state or region
- Ionian colony
- Achaean colony
- Aeolian colony

Atlantic Ocean

Ibero-Celts

BALEARIC ISLANDS

NUMIDIA

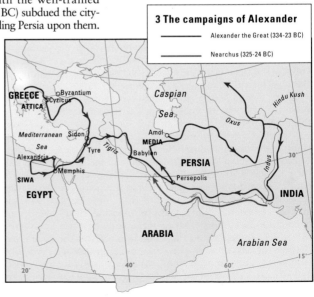

3 The campaigns of Alexander

— Alexander the Great (334-23 BC)

— Nearchus (325-24 BC)

GREECE / ATTICA / Byzantium / Cyzicus / Caspian Sea / Hindu Kush / Oxus / Mediterranean Sea / Sidon / Amol / MEDIA / Alexandria / Tyre / Tigris / Babylon / PERSIA / Indus / SIWA / Memphis / Persepolis / EGYPT / INDIA / ARABIA / Arabian Sea

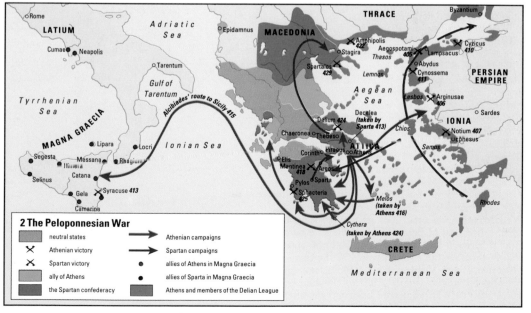

World religions

All the great world religions originated in Asia, and three of them – Judaism, Christianity and Islam – developed in the same small region. Moreover, several were either established or radically reformulated at much the same time: the outstanding prophets and reformers of Hinduism, Buddhism, Judaism, Confucianism and Taoism all lived in the 6th century BC. Their appearance perhaps reflected a need in the rising empires of the Old World for more universal creeds than local tribal deities could provide, and their diffusion – particularly the spread of the great missionary religions, Buddhism and Christianity – played an important role both in linking the different areas of civilization and in spreading the values of those advanced cultures to people living beyond the frontiers.

All the world religions shared, to some degree, a belief in a single spiritual reality. Hinduism, the oldest of them, although it reveres numerous gods emphasises the 'right way to live'; Buddhism, although it does not centre upon a god, instead stresses deliverance from suffering through the annihilation of desire. Originally a reformist movement within Hinduism, in its conservative, or Theravada, form, Buddhism soon spread throughout India and on to Sri Lanka, Burma, Thailand and South-East Asia. It later became perhaps the greatest of all missionary religions when it assumed the universalist, or Mahayana, form some 500 years after the death of its founder, Gautama (c. 565-483 BC). The first great landmark in Buddhist history was the reign of the Indian emperor Asoka (see page 26) in whose reign Buddhism spread to Sri Lanka. It had also reached China by the 1st or 2nd century AD, Korea in the 4th century, and Japan in the 6th century.

Judaism spread mainly as a result of the persecution of the Jews by more formidable neighbours, beginning with their forcible removal to Babylon (586-538 BC), which led to a change in the emphasis of the faith from observance and ritual to morality and righteous living. Oppressed by the Roman occupation (64 BC) and the destruction of the temple in Jerusalem (AD 70), Jewish groups spread far and wide until Judaism, too, became a worldwide religion. It also gave birth, directly or indirectly, to two other major creeds: Christianity (page 40) and Islam (page 46).

In the Far East the 6th century saw the rise of both the ethical system of Kung Fu-tzu or Confucius (551-479 BC) and the mystical religion of the Tao, or 'the Way', associated with the shadowy figure of Lao-tzu. Zoroastrianism, the other great religion of the period, which originated in Persia and saw life as a battleground between the forces of good and evil, spread widely through the Roman world in the form of Mithraism, with shrines as far afield as northern Britain. However, the decision of the Emperor Theodosius (379-95) to make Christianity the official

religion of the Roman empire doomed Mithraism. 'Heathen' temples were uprooted; rival creeds were condemned.

Most of the world religions spread along the trade routes, diffused by soldiers, administrators, merchants and ordinary travellers as well as by missionaries; and most tended to prosper under strong governments

1 The diffusion of world religions

- → dispersion of Jews to AD 500
- → spread of Christianity
- ▨ area converted to Christianity by AD 600
- → spread of Buddhism
- ▨ areas of Buddhist missionary activity
- ▨ area of rise of Mahayana Buddhism
- ● Buddist sites
- ▨ area embracing Hinduism
- ▨ area embracing Taoism
- ▨ area embracing Shinto
- ▨ area converted to Zoroastrianism
- → spread of Mithraism

*Map labels:* Pacific Ocean · JAPAN · Kyoto · Nara · Sea of Japan · Kyongju · KOREA · R. Amur · L. Baikal · Gobi Desert · Peking · Wutai Shan · Puto Shan · Tientai Shan · Chiuhua Shan · Yellow River · CHINA · Taiwan · Wanfohsiu · Dunhuang · R. Yangtze · Omei Shan · PHILIPPINES · Altai Mts · L. Balkhash · R. Jaxartes (Syr Darya) · CHINESE TURKESTAN · Takla Makan · A S I A · R. Volga · Aral Sea · R. Oxus (Amu Darya) · Pamir Mts · Hindu Kush · TIBET · Lhasa · South China Sea · ANNAM · R. Mekong · Caspian Sea · Rhagae · Merv · AFGHANISTAN · Himalayas · Kusinagara · Lumbini · NEPAL · Sarnath · R. Brahmaputra · BURMA · Pagan · Sukhothai · Angkor · PERSIA · R. Indus · R. Ganges · Benares · Bodh Gaya · Calcutta · Prome · Pegu · Rhangoon · SIAM · Sanchi · Karachi · Ajanta · Omei · Bombay · Karli · INDIA · Bay of Bengal · MALAYA · BORNEO · Arabian Sea · Madras · Borobudur · SUMATRA · SRI LANKA · Anuradhupura · Kandy · Indian Ocean · 60° · 80° · 100° · 120°

that brought peace. Of course, innumerable other creeds survived without making the transition to world religions. The Greek pantheon, adopted and adapted by the Romans, honoured a sky-god Zeus (Jupiter) and numerous other deities, each with a special function. The Scandinavians (whose gods Wotan, Thor and others provided names for the days of the week), and countless others, long retained their own eschatology. But the world religions provided the bonds that eventually linked areas of the world previously separate.

33

Rome 264 BC to AD 565

Rome's rise to power proved rapid and seemingly inexorable. In the 6th century BC the city was just a small fortress-town in central Italy commanding both the lowest crossing point on the river Tiber and a salt route between the mountains and the sea. By exploiting quarrels with its neighbours, the Roman Republic emerged as the dominant power first in central Italy and then in the whole peninsula. By 270 BC the entire area south of the river Arno lay under Roman control, and in 264 BC its army crossed into Sicily. This marked the beginning of Roman imperialism, for Sicily formed part of the Carthaginian empire, at the time the greatest sea-power of the Mediterranean. After three savage wars Rome acquired Sicily (241 BC), Spain (206 BC) and North Africa (146 BC). At the same time, conflict with the Hellenistic kingdoms further east resulted in the conquest of Macedon, Greece and Western Anatolia. In this way, almost by accident, Rome became an imperial power with far-flung possessions.

Administration of these provinces overstrained the Roman constitution, which had not been designed to manage an overseas empire, and the Republic finally collapsed in a series of civil wars. The last of these brought to power Octavian, who established himself as *Princeps* ('first citizen'), accepted the title Augustus (in 27 BC), and accumulated sufficient offices to allow him to reshape the constitution and extend the frontiers to a point where he hoped they would remain unchanged for ever. In fact, under his successors, Roman rule expanded further still until it stretched from Scotland to Egypt and from Spain to Assyria (map 1).

While maintaining undivided power in his own hands, Augustus allowed the Senate – the traditional government of Rome – to take a share in running the empire, with responsibility for several provinces. Thus, in theory, the Republican forms endured, and administration remained in civilian not military hands. Throughout the vast Roman world peace prevailed for over two centuries and population expanded, trade flourished and cities grew until, in the mid-3rd century AD, Germanic invasions in the west and Persian victories in the east brought the empire temporarily to its knees. A series of strong emperors between 268 and 284 restored a semblance of orderly government to the empire, but Diocletian (AD 284-305) realized that a single ruler could no longer hold the whole edifice together. He divided power between himself and a joint Augustus, with two deputies (Caesars), and split the empire into four prefectures and twelve dioceses (map 2). By now the military had triumphed over the civilian, and a new basis had to be found for imperial authority. Under the influence of eastern ideas, the Princeps became *Dominus* (lord), an absolute ruler, at the head of a vast bureaucracy. Gradually the centre of Roman power shifted towards the eastern part of the empire: Diocletian's successor Constantine (305-37) established a new capital at Byzantium (330), which he renamed Constantinople.

Although theoretically governed by joint rulers, the empire gradually broke into eastern and western halves, and when

2 The later Empire, AD 284-565

- Praefectus Praetorio Galliarum
- Praefectus Praetorio per Orientem
- Praefectus Praetorio per Illyricum
- Praefectus Praetorio Illyrici, Italiae, Africae
- - - Borders of Dioceses
- Empire at abdication of Diocletian AD 305
- Justinian's reconquests
- Empire at death of Justinian AD 565

the western defences crumbled before a new wave of Germanic invaders in the early 5th century, little help arrived from the east. Rome itself was sacked in 410 and 455, and the Ostrogoths created their own kingdom in Italy in 493. Justinian (AD 527-565) did briefly recover some of the western provinces but failed to reunite the empire.

Nevertheless, the Byzantine state survived for another millennium, and many Roman traditions continued in the West. The Latin tongue, although developing into the derivative 'Romance' languages, long remained the language of churchmen and scientists; Roman Law forms the basis of most modern Western legal systems; many feats of Roman engineering genius survive to this day; and the Roman church lives on as a direct link with the past.

1 The Roman Empire, AD 14-284

- under administration of the Senate
- imperial provinces in AD 14
- public provinces in AD 14
- provinces added after AD 14 with date

China: the first empires

From the 16th to the 11th century BC China's first historical dynasty, the Shang, presided over a confederation of clans in the Yellow River valley. Around 1027 BC the Chou replaced them and extended their authority over the Yangtze valley as well, investing their supporters with fiefs to create a feudal hierarchy sustained by the services, food and clothes produced by peasant communities. Then in 771 BC western invaders sacked the Chou capital, and the feudatories seized the opportunity to break away. Over 100 belligerent political units sprang up. In the 5th century BC, however, bronze technology gave way to iron, animal power and irrigation transformed agriculture, increasing both food production and population, while warfare reduced the number of states. By 300 BC seven states still competed for hegemony; by 221 BC only one of them remained – Ch'in.

The Ch'in organized their subjects into groups which bore collective responsibility to maintain public order, and to provide manpower both for construction works (above all roads, canals and fortifications) and for the army (which was composed primarily of infantry). The defeated nobles suffered demotion and, instead of performing labour services to their lord, the peasants now paid taxes to the conqueror. A savage penal code, administered by a professional bureaucracy, enforced the new system.

In 221 BC Prince Cheng of Ch'in, took the title Shih Huang-ti (meaning 'first emperor'); ordered the construction of a national network of roads and canals, centered on his new capital at Hsiengyang; rebuilt and strengthened the Great Wall; introduced a uniform coinage whose distinctive shape (circular with a square hole in the centre) remained standard until 1911; and took steps to standardize the written language throughout the empire. Small wonder that his dynasty gave 'China' its name.

The burdens imposed by the autocratic first emperor provoked civil war shortly after his death in 206 BC; but before long a new dynasty, the Han, reunited China. At first they worked through feudal principalities allocated to their family and supporters, but by 100 BC the fiefs had again come under strong central control. The Han also extended the Great Wall far to the north-west, undertook several military expeditions against the nomad Hsiung-nu in the north, invaded northern Vietnam and Korea, and for a brief period after 59 BC controlled the Tarim basin. They also consolidated control over the Canton region, eliminating the Min-Yueh kingdoms of the south-east coast. A lively export trade, mainly in silk, began to Parthia and to the Roman empire (see map 1).

2 Han China in AD 2
- ◉ imperial capital
- enfiefed principalities
- commanderies
- —— highways
- ⊓⊓⊓ canals

A census in AD 2 revealed some 57 million people in the empire. Great cities abounded, the largest – Changan, the capital – housing 250,000 people. The heart of the empire remained the Yellow River plain, where population densities in some areas approached 150 per square mile, and numerous fiefs survived (see map 2). Shortly afterwards, however, court families and great feudatories increased their influence, while agrarian unrest mounted. Real power lay in the hands of the regional commanders and warlords and the last Han emperor abdicated in 220. The Han empire fragmented into three regional states and a century later the Hsiung-nu burst through the Great Wall and overran northern China (see page 38). China was to remain politically fragmented until 589.

1 The expansion of the Han Empire

China in 206 BC

boundary of Former Han empire

territory added under Former Han

boundary of Chinese protectorate of Western regions

journey of Chang Chien, envoy of Han Emperor 138-126 BC

HSIUNGNU TRIBES

residence of the Hsiungnu King

Li Ting's expedition

western extension to wall built by Han emperors 117-100 BC

Li Kuang-li expedition 92 BC
Wei Ch'ing's expedition 128 BC
Ho Ch'u-ping and Wei Ch'ing 119 BC

Gobi Desert

Conquered and put under Chinese administration 109-106 BC

men Kuan

Chuyen

Great Wall rebuilt and strengthened by Ch'in emperors 220 to 210 BC

KOREA

Changyah

Kiuchan

Tunhwang

Wuwei

rought under Chinese dministration 117-115 BC

Yellow Sea

Yellow River (Huang Ho)

CH'IN EMPIRE

(221 to 206 BC)

LOLANG

R. Yangtze

(first explorations from 136 BC) expeditions against Tien: 109 BC kingdom suppressed

86 BC
82 BC } expeditions to far south-west

MINYUEH

defeated 100 BC but not assimilated

VIETNAM

INDEPENDENT KINGDOM OF NANYUEH 206-113 BC

under Chinese administration after 111 BC

South China Sea

The Great Wall

routes opened to trade by Former Han

administrative centres under Later Han

centre of Later Han protectorate, AD 73-127

territory added under Later Han

new route opened by General Pan Ch'ao for Later Han

expeditions against Hsiungnu (Huns)

The collapse of the ancient world

By the 3rd century AD, a continuous web of complex, advanced societies stretched across the southern half of the continents of Europe and Asia. In the West, Rome ruled the whole Mediterranean world and much of Europe; in China, the Han ruled a state that equalled the Roman empire in population and extended from the Pacific to the Takla Makan desert in central Asia; in between lay the Persian empire. The co-existence of these great states brought to vast areas of the Old World internal peace and efficient government, conditions that made possible commercial and cultural interchange on an unprecedented scale.

But most of this 'civilized world' formed only a narrow corridor, flanked to the north by the domain of nomadic tribes, expert horse archers who lived off their herds of sheep and cattle and possessed in war a speed and striking power that their sedentary neighbours could rarely match. In the 4th and 5th centuries AD, for reasons that remain mysterious, numerous nomad groups – although lacking central direction – launched devastating attacks against all the major civilizations. A confederation known as the Hsiung-nu from Mongolia broke through the Great Wall of China in 304 and within a decade reached the Yellow River, sacking the ancient Han capital Ch'ang-an (316). A succession of invaders from the steppes dominated northern China for the next three centuries.

At the same time another branch of the Hsiung-nu, the Huns, swept south-westwards through Asia, causing a chain reaction among the Germanic peoples along the Black Sea and the Danube. To escape them the Visigoths, perhaps 80,000 strong, forced their way into the Balkans and in 378 defeated a large Roman army outside Adrianople. Next, they moved into Italy and in 410 captured and sacked Rome itself. Meanwhile other Germanic tribes crossed the Rhine. The Vandals, the Alans and the Suevi invaded Gaul in 406 and plundered it for three years before passing on to Spain and north Africa. In their wake, the Franks, the Burgundians and the Alemanni also invaded Gaul, while the Picts from Scotland and marauders from the continent ravaged Britain. The empire's only success came in 451 when, with the aid of the Franks and Visigoths, a Roman army defeated and drove back a further onslaught by the Huns, led by Attila.

In 480 another branch of the Huns invaded India and destroyed the Gupta empire (page 27) before attacking the Persian empire, where they defeated and killed the ruler in 484. Finally, around 550, another group of warlike nomads from central Asia – the Juan-juan or Avars – moved west and within a generation ravaged Gaul and the Balkans, followed by the Slavs and Bulgars, who also invaded the Balkans, and the Lombards, who occupied northern Italy.

By AD 600 the great cities of Eurasia – Rome, Changan, and countless others – were in serious decline and the empires that built them had perished. Persia and southern China weathered the storm relatively intact, while in India and northern China, the invaders adopted native methods of government and co-operated with local elites, taking on their customs and culture as they did so. In all these areas, classical

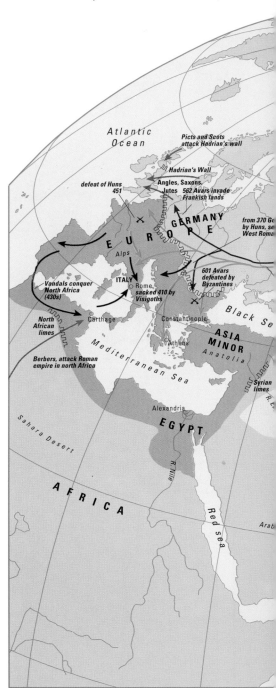

civilization emerged impaired but not extinguished. In Europe, too, the Roman tradition was modified rather than supplanted by the imposition of rulers of Germanic origin: the Franks in France; the Visigoths in Spain; the Ostrogoths in Italy. The deposition of the last Roman emperor in the west in 476 marked a further stage in the transformation of the west from classical to medieval. The Latin tongue survived, too, while knowledge of classical culture was transmitted through a handful of monasteries.

1 The collapse of the ancient world

→ Hsiung-nu and Huns
→ Juan-juan (Avars)
→ Goths and Vandals
→ other peoples

Roman Empire c.AD 454
Gupta Empire c.AD 410
Sassanian Empire c.AD 261
Han Empire c.AD 100
⊓⊓⊓⊓ fortified frontiers

R. Lena

R. Yenisey

R. Ob

L. Baikal

R. Volga

Ural Mts.

R. Amur

MANCHURIA

Don

0 Black Huns pear in rope

A

S

I

MONGOLIA

Great Wall of China in AD 220

Caspian Sea

Aral Sea

R. Jaxartes (Syr Darya)

L. Balkhash

SINKIANG

Hsien-pi invade north China by 440

Yellow R.

550 Juan-juan (Avars) drive westwards out of Mongolia by Blue (Celestial) Turks

A

Takla Makan

1st century AD Hsiung-nu broken by Han China and move westwards

Changan

Loyang

north China reunified under Toba Wei

Hsiung-nu renew attacks on China, sacking capital Loyang 311, Changan 316

Zagros Mts.

R. Oxus (Amu Darya)

Hindu Kush

Kabul

484 White Huns (Ephthalites) kill Sassanian emperor, but Persian empire survives

R. Indus

TIBET

expansion of Tibetans

H i m a l a y a s

PERSIA

Persian Gulf

Mathura

Pataliputra

R. Ganges

R. Yangtze

C H I N A

R. Mekong

480 White Huns destroy Gupta empire

sert

INDIA

Indian Ocean

The spread of Christianity to 1500

Christianity began as a Jewish splinter movement in Roman Palestine. Its founder, Jesus of Nazareth, claimed to be the Messiah, or Saviour, sent to prepare the Jews for 'the kingdom of God' but, after an initial, short-lived success, he was executed as a revolutionary (AD 29). Jewish orthodoxy rejected his message, but his followers turned instead to the conversion of non-Jews and by AD 200, despite repression and persecution, communities of Christians (as the followers of Jesus came to be called) flourished in several cities of the Roman empire (especially Antioch and Edessa). In 313 the Emperor Constantine granted the new faith toleration and in 325 at Nicaea presided over the first ecumenical council, representing the whole church, which defined beliefs for all Christians. A full ecclesiastical organization developed, with a hierarchy of bishops and a framework of patriarchates, provinces and dioceses throughout the empire (map 2).

The council of Chalcedon (451) attempted to enforce orthodoxy on the Christian world, but instead alienated the Monophysite (or Coptic) Christians of Egypt, Syria and Armenia, and the Nestorians who, expelled from Edessa, took refuge in Persia. Meanwhile the disintegration of the Roman empire in the West (page 34) undermined the position of the church. But salvation came from the periphery. The Coptic church of Egypt, with a strong monastic tradition, sent missionaries down the Nile from the 4th century, converting the peoples of Nubia and Ethiopia; while from the 7th century, the Nestorians of Persia expanded south into Arabia and east to China. In the west, the impetus for revival came from the monastic missionary church of Ireland, which evangelized first its Celtic neighbours in Britain and Brittany, and then in the 7th and 8th centuries the pagan tribes of continental Europe (map 1).

As the Muslim onslaught devastated the Christian Mediterranean (page 46), both Rome and Constantinople launched missions northwards among the Slavs. Russia opted for Orthodox Christianity, and in 988 the Russian prince Vladimir was baptized, while Poland (966) and Hungary (1001) chose Catholic Christianity. Although rivalry between the two patriarchates resulted after 1054

1 Christianity in Europe

- Monophysite Christians
- Orthodox Christians
- Catholic Christians
- original Catholic core
- Celtic churches
- Islam
- heathen peoples
- ☦ metropolitan see
- bishopric
- ⊕ monastery/hermitage
- ○ other churches
- → routes of missionaries

2 The spread of Christianity

- areas strongly Christian by 325
- areas largely Christian by 625
- ⚲ patriarchate
- ⚲ archbishopric
- ⊕ ecumenical council (with date)
- ☉ council
- ☻ the Seven Churches of Asia

in schism, the popes increased their authority by sponsoring Christian counter-offensives, in Iberia, the Baltic and the Near East: the crusades (page 44). The attempt to restore Christianity to Palestine proved a costly failure, but the militant crusading spirit remained alive. Meanwhile, within Europe, monks and (from the 13th century) friars joined the expanding network of parish clergy in Christianizing the countryside and combating heresy. In 1387 Lithuania, the last remaining heathen state in Europe, converted to Catholicism, just as persecution by Timur and other rulers (page 58) extinguished the faith in Asia, the continent of its birth.

China 581-1279

After the barbarian invasions of the 4th and 5th centuries (page 38) the Sui dynasty (581-617) reunified China. They consolidated their empire through standardized institutions, a state-supported broad-based Buddhism, and the construction of a canal system linking the Yangtze with the Yellow River and the Loyang region. The T'ang dynasty (618-907) continued the process, creating a uniform administrative organization of prefectures, in which officials recruited through an examination system replaced the traditional aristocracy. The T'ang also extended their control to the Tarim basin and northern Korea: in the 660s, the Chinese empire reached its greatest extent and 88 Asiatic peoples recognised Chinese overlordship, adopting its culture, its written language and its political institutions (map 1).

In 751, however, at the Talas River, an Arab army defeated the Chinese, while a major rebellion rocked T'ang power in 755-62, causing many of the new conquests to be abandoned. Within the empire, power began to pass to the provinces until in 907, following a wave of peasant uprisings, China split into ten separate regional states. Although the Sung dynasty reunified the country between 960 and 979, they failed to regain the new territories. Nevertheless, Chinese economic growth continued. A massive movement of population into the fertile Yangtze valley and southern China produced large agricultural surpluses which stimulated trade and economic development. Between 750 and 1100, the population of the

empire doubled; trade reached new heights; and a great concentration of industries arose around the capital, K'ai-feng, centre of the canal system and of the eastern road network.

In 1126-7 the Chin, a powerful nomadic state north-east of the Great Wall, invaded and conquered all of northern China, with terrible devastation. The Sung now controlled only the centre and the south, but stood constantly on the defensive, maintaining huge armies and paying vast subsidies to their aggressive neighbours (map 2). Even after the Chin invasion,

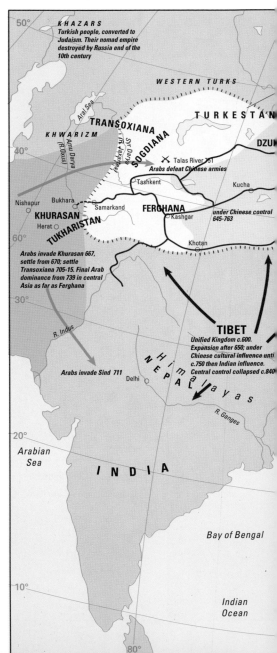

KHAZARS
Turkish people, converted to Judaism. Their nomad empire destroyed by Russia end of the 10th century

WESTERN TURKS

TRANSOXIANA

KHWARIZM

SOGDIANA

TURKESTAN

DZU

Talas River 751
Arabs defeat Chinese armies

Tashkent

Kucha

Nishapur   Bukhara   Samarkand   **FERGHANA**

KHURASAN   Kashgar   under Chinese control
645-763

Herat   **TUKHARISTAN**

Khotan

Arabs invade Khurasan 667, settle from 670; settle Transoxiana 705-15. Final Arab dominance from 739 in central Asia as far as Ferghana

R. Indus

TIBET
Unified Kingdom c.600.
Expansion after 650; under Chinese cultural influence until c.750 then Indian influence. Central control collapsed c.840

Arabs invade Sind 711   Delhi

NEPAL

Himalayas

R. Ganges

Arabian Sea

INDIA

Bay of Bengal

Indian Ocean

2 Sung China
○ provincial capitals
······· canals
—— principal roads
—— boundary between Southern Sung and Chin after 1127

LIAO   Chen-ting-fu   Po Hai

HSI-HSIA   T'ai-yuan   HO-PEI   TUNG

Lan-chou   HO TUNG   Ta-ming-fu   Ching-chou

CH'IN-FENG   YUNG-HSING   CHIN   CHING-TUNG   TUNG

Feng-hsiang-fu   K'ai-feng   CHING-TUNG HSI   Ying-t'ien-fu

Hsing-yuan   CHING-HSI PEI   HUAI-NAN TUNG   Yang-chou

LI-CHOU   CHING-HSI NAN   Hsiang-yang-fu   Shou-ch'un fu   Chiang-ning-fu

Ch'eng-tu-fu   Tung-ch'uan-fu   HUAI-NAN HSI

K'uei-chou   Chiang-ling   CHIANG-NAN TUNG   Hang-chou

CH'ENG-TU-FU   TUNG-CH'UAN FU   CHING-HU PEI   Lung-hsing fu   LIANG-CHE

T'an-chou   CHIANG-HSI NAN

CHING-HU NAN   FU-CHIEN   Fu-chou

Ch'ing-chiang   KUANG-NAN HSI   KUANG-NAN TUNG

HOUTA-YÜEH   Kuang-chou

42

however, the Sung state remained immensely prosperous, since its southern territories proved far more productive than the old northern heartland of China. Population continued to increase rapidly; trade and industry boomed; and the new capital, Hangchou, became the world's largest city. This was also a period of great cultural achievement. The visual arts, literature, philosophy, science and technology all reached new heights; education became more widespread, aided by the dissemination of printing, which had been invented in T'ang times and now became commonplace. Merchants formed guilds and partnerships, setting up a complex commercial organization with banks, credit systems and paper money. The government was run by a mandarinate of career bureaucrats.

But their days were numbered. Between 1211 and 1234 the Mongols (page 56) had overrun the Chin empire, causing widespread devastation, and in the 1270s the forces of Kublai Khan – 'the most powerful man since Adam' according to a European visitor – annexed the entire Sung empire. For the first time, all of China lay under foreign rule.

KIRGHIZ

AMUR

SHIHWEI

MALGAL

Powerful unified Turkish Kingdom in 6th century, split into Eastern and Western groups c.585. Eastern Turks conquered by T'ang 630, but re-emerge from 681 and 699-715 are re-united with Western Turks. In 715 Western Turks break away: Eastern Turks finally destroyed 744

TURKS (to 743)

KHITAN (LIAO)

Proto-Mongol people raid Chinese border from 695, sometimes vassals of Turks. Set up own empire (Liao) in Manchuria in early 10th century

UIGHURS
Uighurs replace Turks in the steppe. 745-840, more stable, less anti-Chinese than Turks. Destroyed by Kirghiz

Gobi Desert

PARHAE
Powerful Kingdom on the Chinese model set up by remnants of Korean ruling clan of Koguryo. Independent from 710. Destroyed by Khitan 934

Still occupied by Ainu aboriginal peoples

Turfan

Hami

NINGSIA

Chinese occupation 668-676

Sea of Japan

GARIA

KANSU

Yellow R.

Tunhwang

to Tibet 763-843

Po Hai

SILLA

JAPAN

Kyoto

Nara

140°

Loyang

Changan

T'ANG EMPIRE

Yang-chou

CHINA

Ningpo

Hang-chou

Independent politically; increasing Chinese cultural influence from 6th century. In 7th century a strong centralized kingdom based on Chinese institutions

R.Brahmaputra

R. Yangtze

Before 660 there were three states in Korea: Koguryo, Paekche and Silla. The T'ang destroyed Paekche in 660, Koguryo in 668 and occupied N. Korea. Strong resistance led to Chinese withdrawal in 676, leaving all Korea under Silla, a powerful, centralized state on Chinese lines

Pacific Ocean

NANCHAO
Kingdom formed by federation of tribal groups organized on T'ang model

Canton

Chiachou

Pagan PYU

Sukhothai

Indianized Buddist Kingdom invaded by Nanchao in 8th and 9th centuries

ANNAM

South China Sea

KHMER
Kingdom under strong Indian/Hindu influence

CHAMPA

Kingdom centred on Hue. Strong Indian influence

1 T'ang China

▨ area under permanent T'ang civil administration

▨ area of temporary occupation during 7th century

▨ area under Chinese military control

▬ zone of Chinese cultural dominance

▨ Islamized areas by 750

→ Islamic penetration

— trade routes

⊥⊥⊥ canals

100°

120°

The Byzantine world
610-1453

Almost from its inception, the Roman empire's centre of gravity moved to the east, first pulled by the lure of economic wealth in Egypt and western Asia; then pushed by the loss of the western provinces to Germanic invaders (page 34) and by the pressure of Sassanid Persia on its eastern frontier. Except during the reign of Justinian (page 35), the west was neglected and the Roman empire became an eastern, Greek-speaking state – normally known, from the reign of Heraclius (610-641), as Byzantium.

Heraclius ended the long contest with Persia victoriously, capturing Nineveh in 628, but almost at once Byzantium faced two even more redoubtable foes: Islam (page 46) and the Slavs. However, after the failure of two long Arab sieges of Byzantium (673-8 and 717-18), the empire launched a succession of vigorous counter-offensives. Basil II (976-1025) even managed to advance the imperial frontiers close to their earlier limits: the Arabs retreated into Palestine; the Russians met defeat at Silistra on the Danube; the Bulgars, who had advanced to within 60 miles of Constantinople, became imperial subjects; plans were laid to recover the former Byzantine territories in Italy. However, the constant campaigns imposed heavy financial strains, as well as profound and debilitating social change, and in spite of further phases of recovery, the frontiers steadily shrank (map 1).

The crucial development was the emergence, in the 11th century, of the Seljuk Turks (page 46), whose crushing victory over Byzantine forces at Manzikert in 1071 induced Emperor Alexius I (1081-1118) to call on the west for help, thus initiating the sequence of events that led to the First Crusade (1096-9). It proved a disastrous move since the Franks were less concerned to aid Byzantium than to set up their own principalities in Palestine and Asia Minor; the Normans, already in control of Sicily and Byzantine Italy, coveted lands in Greece; and the Italian cities, led by Venice, strove to increase their share of Mediterranean trade. After a century of mounting tension, the soldiers of the Fourth Crusade in 1204 conquered and pillaged Constantinople, partitioned the Byzantine empire, and established Latin states all over the Balkans (map 2).

The Latin Empire proved short-lived – its Greek-speaking subjects resented it and a new dynasty, the Palaelogogi, restored the Greek empire in 1261 – but the new Byzantine state was only a shadow of its former self and when, shortly afterwards, the Ottoman Turks established themselves first in Asia Minor and then advanced into Byzantium's European territories, its fate was sealed. The capital of the east Roman empire fell in 1453 (page 66).

Nevertheless, the history of Byzantium includes both greatness and lasting achievements. For centuries it transmitted Roman culture back to areas from which the barbarian invasions had effaced it. It also passed on its culture and its religion to the Balkan peoples and to Russia. 'Two Romes have fallen', a Russian monk wrote shortly after 1453, 'but the third is still standing and a fourth shall never be.' He referred to Moscow (page 52), now emerged as the heir to the Byzantine inheritance.

1 The Byzantine Empire, 628-1143

〜〜〜 imperial frontier c. 628
〜〜〜 imperial frontier c. 1025
〜〜〜 imperial frontier c. 1143

special areas:

Exarchate of Ravenna
to Lombards 751

Exarchate of Africa
〜〜〜 to Arabs from 670
━━━ to Franks from 754
▪▪▪ to Arabs from 815

Catapanate of Italy
▪▪▪ to Normans from 1071

general territorial losses:
▨ to Arabs 636-641
▨ to Arabs after 641
▬▪▬ to Seljuk Turks from 1065
〜〜 Sultanate of Rum from 1071

temporary reconquests:
▨ Africa 685-710 ▨ Ani 1054
▨ Syria 975 ▨ Edessa 1052
▨ Sicily 1038-1043 ▨ Rum c. 1118

2 The Crusades and the decline of Byzantium

- ➤ the Norman attack 1084–5
- ➤ routes of the First Crusade 1096–9
- ·····➤ the Norman attack 1147
- - - ➤ the Norman attack 1185
- - - ➤ route of Fourth Crusade 1202–4
- —— imperial frontier 1180
- ▮ imperial territory in 1214
- ▮ Despotate of Epirus
- ▮ Latin Empire in 1204
- ▮ Venetian territory in 1214

PECHENEGS

Black Sea

WALLACHIA

SERBIA

DALMATIA

Adriatic Sea

Vidin
R. Danube
Mesembria
Sinope
Kastamuni
Theodosiopolis

Serdica
Philippopolis
Adrianople
Constantinople
Nicomedia
Sebastea
Manzikert

Ragusa
Dyrrhachium
Ochrida
Prilep
Vodena
Tzurulum
Nicaea
EMPIRE OF NICAEA
Dorylaeum
R. Halys
Caesarea

Bari
Brundisium
Avlona
Castoria
Berrhoea
Thessalonica
Cyzicus
Adramyttium
Prusa
Sardis
Smyrna
Samosata
Edessa
Marash
Iconium

Corfu
Larissa
Aegean Sea
Lesbos
Pergamum
Amorium
Philomelium
Tyana
Carrhae
R. Euphrates

NORMANS
Cephalonia
Negroponte
Chios
R. Meander
Sozopolis
Heraclea
Tarsus
Aleppo
Homs

MOREA
Zacynthus
Corinth
Athens
Chonae
Attalia
Antioch
Orontes

Modon
Monemvasia
Cerigo
Cos
RHODES
CYPRUS
Tripoli
Tyre
Acre

CRETE

Mediterranean Sea

SELJUKS OF RUM

Caspian Sea

Bosporus
ABASGIA
IBERIA
LAZICA
Tiflis

Cherson
Phasis
ALBANIA

Black Sea

Dorostolon
Marcianopolis
Sinope
Trebizond
Kars
Ani
Manzikert 1071

MOESIA
Singidunum
R. Danube
Nicopolis
PAPHLAGONIA
Neocaesarea
PONTUS
L. Van
Bitlis
L. Urmia

DACIA
Serdica
Anchialus
PERSIA
Ragusa
Scupi
THRACE
Arcadiopolis
Philippopolis
Adrianople
Constantinople
Ancyra
Sebastea
Mosul
Nineveh

Dyrrhachium
Heraclea
Pylea
Nicomedia
CAPPADOCIA
Arabissos
Samosata
R. Tigris

NEW EPIRUS
MACEDONIA
Gallipoli
Prusa
Helenopolis
Caesarea
Germanicia
Edessa

Avlona
Thessalonica
BITHNIA
Malagina
Zeugma
Carrhae
Zenobia

ANCIENT EPIRUS
Troy
Abydus
Cotiaeum
CILICIA
Hieropolis
Aleppo
R. Euphrates

THESSALY
Larissa
LYDIA
Iconium
Adana
Antioch
Circesium

Nicopolis
Demetrias
Sardis
PHRYGIA
Tarsus
Laodicea
Ionian Sea

Thebes
Ephesus
ISAURIA
Emesa
Palmyra
Zenobia

Athens
Miletus
PAMPHYLIA
Attalia
Tripoli
Damascus

Patras
Corinth
Halicarnassus
CYPRUS

Lacedaemon
RHODES
Laodicea
Tiberias

CRETE
PALESTINE
Jerusalem
Bostra

Sea
Gaza
Maan
Petra
Hebron

Apollonia
Damietta
Pelusium
ARABIA

PENTAPOLIS
Alexandria
Mareotis
Memphis

TRIPOLITANIA

Arsenoe
Tabuk

EGYPT
R. Nile

The Islamic world 632-1517

The rise and expansion of Islam ranks as perhaps the most significant development in world history between the fall of Rome and the European invasion of the Americas. Within a remarkably short time, a new world religion created a dynamic civilization which now embraces one-seventh of the global population: 600 million Muslims, spread from Morocco to Indonesia, and from Siberia to Zanzibar. 'Islam', which means 'submission to the will of God', was conveyed to humankind through the Koran, a volume of prescriptions on behaviour as well as belief, revealed by God to Mohammed his prophet, who was born in the religious and commercial centre of Mecca about 570. As Mohammed's followers grew in number, they aroused the hostility of the merchants of Mecca and in 622 the group withdrew to the neighbouring town of Medina (the *hijra*). But Mohammed returned to Mecca in triumph in 630, transforming it into the focal point for the new faith of Islam, and when he died in 632 his authority extended over much the Hejaz and much of central and southern Arabia.

For the next century Islam expanded rapidly: Arab armies defeated Latin Christian, Byzantine, Persian, Indian and Chinese armies to spread the new faith from the Himalayas in the east to the Atlantic in the west (map 1). In 711 they crossed over the Straits of Gibraltar and conquered Spain. Until 656 political control over the empire remained with Mohammed's relatives, but then a split occurred, with some Muslims following Ali, the Prophet's cousin and son-in-law (the Shi'ites), and others – the majority – accepting the rule of the Umayyad dynasty from Mecca who claimed to represent the Sunna or traditions of the Prophet. The Umayyads ruled from Damascus in Syria between 661 and 750, followed by the rival Abbasid dynasty, who created a new capital at Baghdad in Mesopotamia and opened government to non-Arab Muslims (known as *mawali*).

Gradually, the Muslim world lost its political unity and split into a number of local dynastic entities, some Sunnite and others Shi'ite (map 2). In 1055, however, the centre of the Islamic world was strengthened when the Seljuk Turks established themselves in Baghdad and shortly thereafter drove the Christians from most of Anatolia (page 44). Despite invasions from the west in the 12th century (the Crusades: page 45) and from the east in the 13th (the Mongols: page 56), Islam retained its hold over the Near East, while missionaries and merchants carried the faith eastwards to Malaysia, Indonesia and the Philippines, and southwards both to the sub-Saharan states and the cities of the Swahili coast of Africa (page 54). For a millennium after the birth of Mohammed, Islam remained the western hemisphere's leading and most extensive civilization.

1 The expansion of Islam

- empire under Mohammed
- growth under Abu Bakr (632-634)
- growth under Omar (634-644)
- growth under Othman (644-656) and Ali (656-661)
- expansion of Umayyad Caliphate (661-750)
- expansion 750-850
- → routes of advance
- ✕ battles

2 The Middle East and North Africa, 786-1260

R. Danube
Black Sea
Caucasus Mts. 45°
60° 75°
Kashgar

BYZANTINE
Constantinople
Derbent
Tiflis
Karakhanids
(992-1211)
KHWARIZM
Urgench
Bukhara
Samarkand
R. Jaxartes
(Syr Darya)

EMPIRE
Trebizond
Manzikert
(1071)
Caspian Sea
Turks
TRANSOXIANA

ANATOLIA
Konya
Turks AZERBAIJAN
Tabriz
Nishapur
Merv
R. Oxus (Amu Darya)
Balkh

Palermo
Sicily
(conquered by the
Normans 1090)
Crete
Antioch
Aleppo
Mosul
R. Tigris
SYRIA
Homs
Tripoli
Cyprus
Beirut
Acre
Damascus
Baghdad
Hamadan
Kermanshah
Seljuks
(1038-1194)
Isfahan
Yazd
IRAN
KHURASAN
Herat
Hindu Kush
Kabul
AFGHANISTAN
SEISTAN
Ghaznavids
(977-1186)
Ghazni
Kandahar
Lahore
R. Indus
Multan

Mediterranean Sea
Jerusalem
Alexandria
Cairo
Ain Jalut (1260)
R. Euphrates
Basra
Shiraz
Persian Gulf
INDIA

Tripoli
Fatimid caliphate
(909-1171)
EGYPT
Mamelukes
(1250-1517)
HEJAZ
R. Nile
Medina

ARABIA
Muscat
OMAN

Red Sea
Jedda
Mecca
Arabian Sea
30°

2 The Middle East and North Africa, 786-1260	Zaidi Imams
Abbasid Caliphate at greatest extent 786-809	Almohads 1130-1269
countries recognising Abbasid suzerainty c.1090	→ line of Turkish advance
territory disputed between Seljuks and Byzantine Empire	*Seljuks* Muslim dynasties with dates

Sana
YEMEN
Aden

KHAZAR EMPIRE
Aral Sea
R. Oxus
Talas 751
FERGHANA
40°
R. Don
Caspian Sea
Samarkand 710
Bukhara 710
Balkh 651
PUNJAB

R. Dnieper
R. Dnieper
Caucasus Mts
Derbent
AZERBAIJAN
Ardabil
GURGAN
Merv
Nishapur
Herat
KHURASAN
Hindu Kush
Kabul 664
Sulaiman Range
Multan
Sea
ARMENIA
Tiflis
Rai
PERSIA
30°
SIND

Tarsus
Erzurum
R. Tigris
Mosul 641
Tabriz
Jalula
Nehavend 642
Susa
Isfahan
SEISTAN
R. Indus
Antioch
Edessa
MESOPOTAMIA
Zagros Mts
Persepolis
(Istakhr) 648
FARS
KIRMAN
MAKRAN

SYRIA
Damascus 635
R. Euphrates
Kerbela 680
Ctesiphon
Baghdad
Kufa
Qadisiya 636
Basra 856
Persian Gulf
OMAN
Suhar
Arabian Sea

Ramla
Yarmuk 636
Fihl
Jerusalem 638
Qadisiya 636
BAHRAIN
YAMAMA
Hiji
20°

Ajnadain 634
HADHRAMAUT

Tabuk
ARABIA

HEJAZ
Medina
Badr 624
YEMEN
Mecca

NUBIANS
Red Sea
KINGDOM OF AXUM

40°
50°

Franks and Anglo-Saxons 714-814

Within a century of the Germanic invasions (page 38), settled kingdoms had grown up in western Europe, but not in Britain, where invaders from the continent met with resistance. During the 7th century, however, seven separate important kingdoms – which are traditionally known as the Heptarchy – emerged in England. Geographical obstacles seem to have prevented the states in the south-east (Sussex, Kent, Essex, East Anglia) from expanding, and leadership at first passed to Northumbria, whose progress benefitted from its early conversion to Christianity. Mercia led the opposition, sometimes in alliance with the 'Britons' on the periphery, and by the time of Offa (757-96) its pre-eminence was unquestionable: it controlled the four southeastern kingdoms, and even Wessex recognized Mercian overlordship (map 1).

On the continent, the Franks (whose original power base lay in what is now northern France, the Low Countries and the Rhineland) converted to Christianity under Clovis (486-511) and began to expand south and east. From their new capital at Paris, Clovis and his sons and grandsons defeated the Visigoths, conquered Burgundy and Provence, and extended their overlordship in Germany as far as the middle Danube.

Most of the new lands served to maintain the loyalty of the Frankish warriors, however, and when the conquests ceased in the mid-7th century the kings had to reward their followers and endow the Church by granting away their own estates and revenues. In doing so they diminished their resources and, in time, power passed to the families which had benefitted from royal favour. Eventually Pepin of Herstal, the leader of a prominent family from Austrasia achieved prominence, and at Tertry (687) defeated his chief rivals.

Pepin and his son Charles Martel (from whom the dynasty took the name 'Carolingian') restored Frankish fortunes and inaugurated a second surge of territorial expansion (map 2). Charles Martel (714-41) defeated the Arabs at Poitiers in 732, halting their rapid incursion into western Europe (page 46), while his son Pepin the Short (d. 768) expelled them from southern France. In 751, with the

2 Anglo-Saxon England c.AD 800
- Mercia and subordinate kingdoms under Offa (757-796)
- allied with Mercia
- British kingdoms

1 The Frankish Empire, 714–814
- Frankish realm 714
- extent of empire 814
- marches in 814 (with date of formation)
- Frankish royal residencies
- archbishoprics
- important monasteries
- GASCONY 769 province with date of acquisition

sanction and support of the pope, Pepin made himself king of the Franks. His son Charles the Great or Charlemagne (768-814) conquered Lombardy (774) and established Frankish rule in much of Italy. He won great victories over the Frisians (784-5), Bavarians (788), Avars (796) and Saxons (who were finally subdued in 804); and created a march, or boundary province, across the Pyrenees between 795 and 812. In 800 the pope in Rome crowned him emperor of the west .

However, Frankish custom called for the royal domain to be partitioned. Charlemagne's father had divided it between his two sons – Charlemagne only inherited the whole when his brother died in 771 – and the new emperor likewise planned in 806 to partition his possessions among his three sons, a scheme frustrated only by the early death of two of them,

making it possible for the survivor, Louis the Pious (814-40), to inherit the whole empire. After his death, however, the treaty of Verdun (843) created three kingdoms: one in the east, one in the west, and a 'middle kingdom' which ran from the Low Countries to Italy. .

The Carolingians ruled through direct agents, rather than through Gallo-Roman bishops and counts as their predecessors had done; and throughout the 8th century these men generally remained loyal. After Charlemagne's death, however, their descendants tended to identify with the particular interests of their own localities, at the expense of the whole. Frankish hegemony in western Europe was thus disrupted by fragmentation just as it came under attack from merciless invaders, including the Vikings and Magyars (page 50).

Europe 814-1250

The activities of three separate groups of invaders in the 9th century shattered the relative stability achieved by Charlemagne in western Europe and by Offa of Mercia in England (page 48). The Saracens occupied the islands of the western Mediterranean and raided Italy and France; the Magyars of Hungary devastated northern Italy and Germany; the Vikings from Scandinavia not only plundered settlements around the European coast as far as the Mediterranean, but also created trade routes through Russia to Byzantium (page 44) and settled substantial parts of Britain, Ireland, northern France, Iceland and even Greenland.

The invasions disrupted royal authority and caused political fragmentation. In the Carolingian empire, the Frankish kings virtually capitulated to the Vikings, leaving defence to the local magnates who swiftly created their own power bases. In England, although determined resistance by Alfred the Great of Wessex (871-99) held the Danes at bay, a second wave of Scandinavian invasions a century later proved irresistible. However

in the eastern half of the Frankish empire, Otto I's defeat of the Magyars at the Lechfeld (955) proved a turning point, and Germany became the first country in Europe to recover from the invasions. This achievement assured its predominance in Europe for almost three centuries.

German rulers rarely sought to assert control over the west Frankish lands but, as heirs to the Carolingians, they claimed the imperial title and the right to rule over Italy and the lands of the former "middle kingdom" (page 49). In 962 Otto I's coronation as emperor sealed the connection between Germany and Italy, and in 1034 his successors annexed Burgundy. However the emperors became increasingly dependent upon the wealth of Italy, and this embroiled Frederick I of Hohenstaufen (1152-90) with both the papacy and the populous fortified cities of the Lombard plain, all of whom saw Imperial power in Italy as a threat to their independence. The conquest of Sicily by Frederick's son Henry VI in 1194 made the Hohenstaufen the richest rulers in Europe; but the prospect of total encirclement once more alarmed the papacy and the

1 Viking, Magyar and Saracen Invasions

Lombard towns, leading to a long and costly struggle with Frederick II (1212-50). After his death, the Imperial position in Italy steadily deteriorated, and the last Hohenstaufen prince met defeat and death at the battle of Tagliacozzo in 1268.

Meanwhile, in Germany, the princes took advantage of their rulers' preoccupation with Italy both to consolidate their power and, on the eastern frontier, to direct a major expansion. The Slavs were driven out or enslaved, in favour of German settlers who, by 1250, had increased the German kingdom by about one-third and shifted its centre of gravity from the Rhine to the Elbe. The empire might no longer be the strongest or richest polity in Europe, but it remained the largest.

2 The Hohenstaufen Empire 1152-1250

- eastward spread of German peasant settlement 12th century
- German settlement by 1200-1250
- city with over 10,000 inhabitants
- member of Lombard Leagues of 1167 and 1226
- member of 1167 League only
- member of 1226 League only
- German invasions 1190-94
- Henry VI's Genoese and Pisan fleet 1194
- main Hohenstaufen palaces and castles
- mountain pass

Early Russia 862-1242

Three factors shaped the early history of Russia: the eastward movement of Slav settlers; the impact of the Vikings (who were known to the Slavs as Varyagi or Varangians) from the north; and, most important of all, the division of the region into forests (in the north and centre) and treeless steppe (in the south). Before the arrival of the Vikings in the 9th century, the Slavs had begun to settle the central river basins, clearing the forests and living by agriculture, hunting, trapping and the fur trade, while nomadic tribes from Asia, such as the Pechenegs, occupied the grasslands of the south.

At first the Slavs resisted the Varangians, but in 862 they called in 'Rurik the Viking' to protect them from Pecheneg raiders. Since most of the rivers of Russia follow a north-south axis, great potential existed for trade between the Baltic and the Black Sea, and the Vikings sought to dominate and exploit these waterways and the territories adjoining them (map 1). Rurik therefore occupied Novgorod, and his followers soon pushed south to Smolensk and then down the Dnieper to Kiev (882). The principal trade route established by the Vikings ran from the Gulf of Finland up the river Neva, through Lake Ladoga to the river Volkhov, thence by portages to the Dnieper and on across the Black Sea to Byzantium.

Grand Prince Svyatoslav (962-72) campaigned to the south and east, greatly extending the frontiers of the Kievan state, which forged strong links with Byzantium, its chief trading partner; and from Byzantium it received the Christian faith during the reign of Vladimir Svyatoslav (980-1015). At the same time Kiev retained numerous connections with the West: one of Vladimir's granddaughters married the king of France, another the king of Hungary and a third the king of Norway. Half a century later, however, dynastic conflict and administrative inefficiency brought weakness and a new wave of Asiatic nomads, the Polovtsy, broke through the defences built by Svyatoslav and Vladimir. In 1093 they sacked Kiev itself.

A great northward exodus ensued to safer regions between the Oka and the Volga, where many new towns were founded (such as Vladimir, Suzdal, Rostov and Tver) and several new states developed – notably Vladimir-Suzdal, which included the fast growing commercial centre of Moscow (first mentioned in 1147), and Novgorod, which built up a fur-trading empire that reached to the Arctic and the Urals. Meanwhile, further south, Novgorod-Seversk, Vladimir-Volynsk and Galich broke away from Kievan rule (map 2).

Mongol invaders struck the final blow to the old order (page 56). In 1237-8, moving along the frozen rivers, they struck north and sacked the wealthy towns of Vladimir-Suzdal; in 1239-40 they advanced through southern Russia, systematically destroying settlements, including Kiev. Meanwhile Novgorod, although it escaped the Mongol onslaught as the onset of spring thawed the frozen rivers, faced repeated attacks by both Swedes and Germans in the Baltic region until Prince Alexander decisively defeated the former in 1240 on the river Neva (thus earning the title 'Nevsky') and the latter in 1242 on the ice of Lake Peipus. Despite these successes, however, even Novgorod had to recognize Mongol overlordship, exercised by the Golden Horde on the lower Volga, while the Lithuanian state expanded into the old Kievan heartland).

The Mongol invasion had other lasting economic, social and political effects. The destruction of so many towns decimated both trade and industry, while the elimination of the urban middle class smoothed the path of an autocracy which imitated its overlords in ruthless terror and extortion. The fall of Kiev destroyed the cultural centre of medieval Russia, with its rich Byzantine-based literature and art, while the Mongol forces, controlling the grasslands around the Caspian and the Black Sea, prevented almost all contact with Byzantium. Russia therefore inevitably developed a distinctive culture, society and political system of its own.

1 Varangian Russia, 862-1054

- Varangian territory c.980
- *Ulichi* East Slav tribes
- **KHAZARS** Finno-Ugrian and Asiatic people
- → Varangian (Viking) trade routes
- ⇢ Varangian raids on Constantinople 907, 944
- → Svyatoslav's campaigns 964-71
- → Pecheneg raids

2 Kievan Russia, 1054-1242

○ towns and places of significance 1054

□ towns and places of significance 1054-1200

MARI tribes

→ movement of steppe nomads in 11th century

defensive works built against nomads

boundaries of Russian principalities c. 1200

waterway trade routes

tundra

coniferous and deciduous forest

steppe and desert

mountain vegetation

Arctic Circle

R. Pechora

70

SAMOYED

YUGRA

White Sea

Pinega

R. Mezen

KARELIA

Northern Dvina

R. Onega

NOVGOROD EMPIRE

CHUD

R. Vychegda

PERM

R. Sukhona

VYATKA TERRITORY

60

L. Onega

Beloozero

MARI

L. Ladoga

R. Volkhov

Ladoga

Galich

Gulf of Finland

R. Neva 1240

Baltic Sea

ESTS

L. Peipus 1242

Novgorod

Yaroslavl

Kostroma

Gulf of Riga

Yuriev

L. Ilmen

Rostov

Riga

Pskov

Izborsk

VLADIMIR-SUZDAL

KURS

Kukeynoys

R. Lovat

Torzhok

Tver

Pereyaslavl

Suzdal

LIVONIAN ORDER

Gertsike

Volok Lamsky

Dmitrov

Nizhniy Novgorod

R. Kama

LATVIA

Toropets

Vladimir

R. Klyazma

Murom

Bolgar

TEUTONIC ORDER

Polotsk

Vitebsk

POLOTSK

SMOLENSK

Moscow

R. Moskva

Bilyar

Gorodno

Orsha

Smolensk

Kopys

R. Oka

Kolomna

VOLGA BULGARS

Suvar

Minsk

Ryazan

Drogochin

Nesvizh

Koselsk

MORDVA

Berestye

Kletchesk

TUROV-PINSK

CHERNIGOV

MUROM-RYAZAN

Bryansk

R. Desna

VLADIMIR-VOLYNSK

Pinsk

Turov

Rechitsa

Karachev

Kholm

Listem

NOVGOROD-SEVERSK

Novosil

Vladimir

Cherveno

Vruchy

Lyubech

Novgorod-Severskiy

Belz

Korosten

Rylsk

Kursk

Peremyshl

KIEV

Gorodets

Galich

Terebovl

Kiev 1093

PEREYASLAVL

POLOVTSY

GALICH

Pereyaslavl

Donets

(in 1054)

Kolomyya

Kamenets

Rodnya

R. Don

R. Ura

Peresechen

Poltava

50

HUNGARIAN KINGDOM

PECHENEGS

P O L O V T S Y

TORKI

R. Volga

SAKSINY

R. Dniester

Belgorod

R. Dnieper

R. Danets

Sarkel

Itil

Carpathian Mts.

Pereslavets

Oleshe

R. Danets

Sea of Azov

Caspian Sea

Danube

Dristol

Khersones

Sugdeya

Tmutarakan

R. Kuban

R. Kuma

ULGARIA

Black Sea

KASOGI

YASI

African states and empires
900-1800

By the end of the first millennium AD great changes had taken place in Africa. The rise of a culture based on iron-working (page 24) led to the appearance of extensive states and empires based on trade. In the south, Zimbabwe, with its monumental stone buildings, exported gold and copper via the port of Sofala; in the west, the Kongo state carried on an important trade. Further north, Arab traders developed the trans-Saharan trade routes and so assisted the growth of major sub-Saharan states. Although Ghana rose to prominence before the Islamic era, its successors, Mali and Songhay, owed much of their wealth and culture – described in glowing terms by Arab travellers – to the impact of Islam. So did the Kanem-Borno empire around Lake Chad and the Hausa city-states. In the east Arab merchant colonies also spread down the Swahili coast as far as Kilwa and Sofala, bringing this part of Africa into an Indian Ocean trading complex. The staple exports in all cases were gold, ivory and slaves (map 1).

The arrival of the Portuguese in the 15th century at first had little impact on Africa. Their immediate object was to share directly in the gold trade, previously dominated by Muslim middlemen; the slave trade remained a secondary interest. However, with the development of labour-intensive sugar-plantations in the Americas (page 80), the slave trade attracted others. By the 18th century, nine European states maintained almost 50 fortified trading posts on the west coast, from Arguim to Whydah, to handle this burgeoning commerce, while the Portuguese continued to export slaves further south from Angola and Mozambique. Of some 15 million Africans shipped abroad by Europeans between 1450 and 1870, almost 90 per cent went to South America and the Caribbean, most of them during the 18th century. Muslim traders exported perhaps as many more again northward across the Sahara and from the Swahili coast. The effects on Africa of this appalling trade in human beings are hard to quantify, since the loss of population was not evenly divided. Some states, such as Kongo and Lunda, suffered disproportionately, while others seem to have profited. Thus, after the destruction of the powerful Songhay empire by Moroccan troops in 1591, the forest states of Asante, Dahomey and Benin, having direct access to the Atlantic and thus to European slave-traders, increased in importance and political power (map 2).

Apart from the Portuguese in Angola and Mozambique, and the fortified posts along the west coast, only the Dutch attempted to create a European colony in Africa before 1800: in the far south, around Cape Town. In the north-east, Islam continued to spread, but the Christian kingdom of Ethiopia still held its own. In the north, the Ottoman empire (page 66) maintained only nominal suzerainty over the states from Morocco to Egypt. In 1800, almost all of Africa thus remained independent of foreign control: a world unto itself, the 'dark continent'. However, precisely because of its autonomy, it would lack the ability to compete with the technological dynamism of the West in the 19th century (page 104).

1 Africa, 900-1500

- state nucleus
- Islamised c. 900
- Muslim colony
- major gold producing region
- Ghana 8th-12th century
- Mali 12th-15th century
- Songhay c. 1500

gold	N	cattle	
M musk	C	copper	
slaves		salt	
bananas		millet	

OTTOMAN EMPIRE

2 Africa, 1500–1800

→ movement of peoples
→ spread of Islam
▦ area of Islamic influence by 1800
→ trade routes
→ slave trade routes

→ Spanish offensives against Algiers and Tunis in the 16th century
→ Moroccan military expeditions
--- Saladian extension of Moroccan territory c. 1591
→ Portuguese voyages to Africa and India
━ areas of Ottoman control c. 1600

coastal settlements:

○ Dutch　● Ottoman
◑ French　◑ British
◑ Portuguese　◑ Spanish
◐ Danish　◑ Brandenburger

Mediterranean Sea

Granada, Bougie, Algiers, Tunis
Tangier, Fez, Oran, Tlemcen
MAGHREB, ALGIERS, *Corsair cities under Ottoman suzerainty 1516*, Tripoli
Sijilmassa, Wargla, Ghadames
Tuat, Ain Salah, Ghat
Taghaza, Murzuk
Sahara Desert

Alexandria
Arab trans-Saharan slave trade route
E G Y P T
Ottoman conquest 1517
Red Sea

SONGHAY, Tadmekka, Tamanrasset, AIR, Agades, Bilma
Timbuktu, Gao, Jenne
Nilotic Sudan
Suakin
Massawa
FUNJ 16th C
Sennar
ETHIOPIA 16th C
Zeila, ADAL, Berbera
SHOA

MOSSI STATES 15th C
BORGU STATES, NUPE
HAUSA STATES, Katsina, Kano, Zaria
KANEM, BORNO, WADAI, DARFUR
White Nile

ASSANTE 18th C, Accra
DAHOMEY 18th C, Badagri, Ife, OYO 17th C, BENIN
Whydah, Lagos, Brass, Slave Coast
NIGER DELTA STATES 18th C
KWARARAFA
TIKAR BAMUM BAMILEKE
BANDA
NZAKARA
AZANDE
NILOTES
PARANILOTES
NILOTES
GALLA
SOMALI

West Africa-arrival of Portuguese 15thC and 16thC. Dutch, English and French 17thC.
Fernando Po
Principe
São Tomé
NGBANDI, NGUMA, BABWA
R. Congo
MANGBETU
BUNYORO, BUGANDA
ANKOLE, KARAGWE
RWANDA
Lake Victoria
KIKUYU, Lamu
Mt Kilimanjaro, Malindi, Mombasa
Mogadishu, Brava
Zanzibar
Vasco da Gama to India April 1498–Dec. 1498

PYGMY, TEKE, MONGO
LUANGO, Luango
KONGO, Ambriz, Luanda
KUBA, LULUA, TETELA, KETE
CHOKWE, LUNDA 16th–17th C
LUBA 15th–16th C
BEMBA
Lake Tanganika
BURUNDI
Arab slave trade
Kilwa Kisiwani

Benguela
OVIMBUNDU
LUENA-LOVALE
SANGA, BEMBA
BISA
Lake Nyasa
Comoro Is.
LOZI
MARAVI
LAMBA
Mozambique

OVAMBO
SAAN
TONGA
LENJE
MWENEMUTAPA 16th C
Tete, Sena, Sofala
Quelimane

HERERO
TSWANA
KARANGA
ROZWI, Great Zimbabwe
settlements of mainland African slaves
HOVA MERINA
M A D A G A S C A R
Fort-Dauphin

KHOISAN
SOTHO
NGUNI
R. Orange
SOTHO
Cape established by Dutch East India Company in 1652. Gradual spread of white settlers inland. Occupied by Britain 1798.
Portuguese slave trade
Indian Ocean

CAPE KHOISAN
Cape Town
Bartholomew Dias rounds Cape of Good Hope, 1487
Cape of Good Hope

Inset (Arabia / East Africa):

Medina, Jedda, Mecca
Persian Gulf
Arabia
MAKURRA, Napata, ALWA
Dahlak Is., Aden
Meroë 3rdC–8thC
Sennar
FAGAU
AXUM
DANAKIL
ADAL, Zeila
SIDAMA
Ras Hafun, Berbera
PLAINS NILOTES
HIGHLAND NILOTES c. 1000
Mogadichu
Lamu, Malindi
Mombasa, Pemba Is., Zanzibar
Indian Ocean
Kilwa Kisiwani
Comoro Is.
MANGANJA
Sofala
M A D A G A S C A R
migrations of Bantu speakers to Madagascar bringing cattle and millet
Indonesian expansion from East Coast into interior bringing bananas and rice

The Mongol Empire
1206-1696

The Mongols, a nomadic people from the grasslands of Central Asia, staged a sudden and devastating irruption into world history in the first half of the 13th century (map 1). Theirs was not the first empire of the steppe, however. In the 7th century AD, in the wake of the upheavals that destroyed the ancient world (page 38), a confederation of Turkish tribes had managed to dominate the plains of Asia from the Great Wall of China to the Black Sea; but by 750 their rule had collapsed and the area disintegrated into feud and faction. Thus it remained for four centuries, when a charismatic leader, Temujin (1167-1227), gained recognition as supreme ruler and in 1206 took the title Genghis Khan, 'prince of all that lies between the Oceans'. Under his leadership the Mongols first invaded the Chin empire in north China and then turned

1 The Mongol Empire

- Mongol Empire
- area under loose Mongol control
- → campaigns of Genghis Khan
- → campaigns of his successors

against the Islamic states to the west. By the time of Genghis's death, his empire stretched from the Pacific Ocean to the Caspian Sea. His successors continued the tide of destructive conquests: Kievan Russia (1237-40); the Abbasid Caliphate (1256-60); Sung China (1271-9). Europe and Japan were also threatened: one Mongol army reached the gates of Vienna while another defeated a German-Polish army at Liegnitz in 1241; two amphibious expeditions unsuccessfully attacked Kyushu in 1274 and 1281.

However the vast empire lacked coherence and stability, and the Mongols failed to develop appropriate institutions. On hearing of the death of Genghis's successor Ogedei in 1241, the victorious commander of the Mongol forces in Europe withdrew eastwards with his army, in order to take part in choosing a successor. They never returned. Likewise in 1260, on hearing of the death of Ogedei's successor, the victorious commander of the Mongol forces in the Near East decided to return to the Mongol heartland,

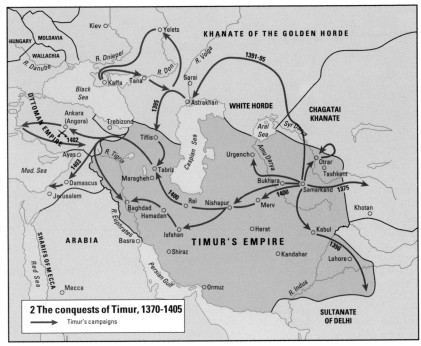

2 The conquests of Timur, 1370-1405

→ Timur's campaigns

leaving only a skeleton force behind him. This soon became known in Cairo, and the Sultan of Egypt marched to the defence of Islam, still reeling from the sack of Baghdad, the capital of the Caliphs, two years before. At Ain Jalut on 3 September 1260 the Mongols suffered a decisive defeat and withdrew to Persia.

The Mongol empire now fragmented. The title of Great Khan went to Kublai who, although never forgetting that he was the grandson of Genghis, spent most of his long reign (1260-94) seeking to reunify China and conquer Japan. The other Mongol states – the Golden Horde in the west; the Il-Khans in Persia; the Chagatai empire in the traditional Mongol heartland – went their own way.

Despite the widespread destruction of the Mongol onslaught, their temporary unification of Eurasia permitted the exchange of goods and ideas between the

far east and the far west on an unprecedented scale. For over a century the 'Silk Road' of ancient times revived: silver and gold from Europe and the Near East reached China while Chinese silks and porcelain circulated in Europe. But the Black Death (see page 62) and the rise of Timur, or Tamerlane (1336-1405) changed all that, for he destroyed the Chagatai khanate, dislocated the Golden Horde, defeated the Ottoman empire at the battle of Ankara in 1402 (page 66), and initiated a policy of religious intolerance. However Timur died in 1405 before he had created the institutions and traditions required to ensure the survival of his vast empire (map 2). Instead, Mongol power in the west steadily lost ground to Russia (see page 78), and crumbled in China with the rise of the Ming dynasty (see page 88). Mongolia itself came under Chinese dominion in 1696.

The Muslim Empires of India and Persia 1206-1707

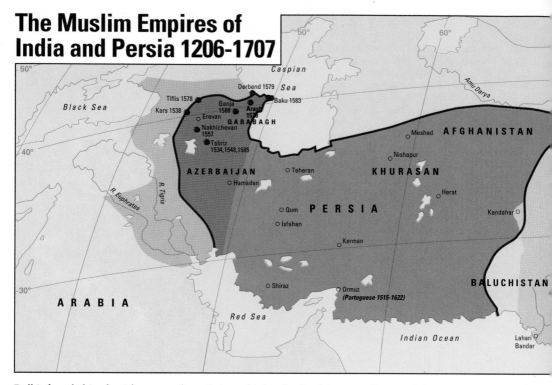

Delhi, founded in the 8th century by a Rajput chief, remained the focus of north Indian politics and also the centre of Muslim culture from the 13th to the 19th century. It served as the capital of the six Muslim dynasties, all of Turkish or Afghan extraction, who sought (unsuccessfully) to extend their rule into the Deccan between 1206 and 1526; and, after the defeat of the last of the Sultans of Delhi at Panipat (1526) by Babur – a descendant of Timur (page 56) – it became the headquarters of his descendants, the Mughals.

Babur's grandson, Akbar (1556-1605), extended the frontiers of the empire to Bengal in the east, to Gujerat and the river Godavari in the south, and to Kashmir in the north. New territories were added under Akbar's grandson, Shahjahan (1627-56) and his son Aurangzeb (1656-1707), who annexed Bijapur and Golconda in the south, and Orissa in the east. However, these achievements depended absolutely upon the acquiescence of the 150 million or so Hindu peasant farmers and petty landlords who paid the taxes that supported the Mughals' 4 million warriors, and the court grandees who commanded them. It was a delicate balance, for if the peasants and landlords were overtaxed, they would revolt; and if the grandees were not rewarded with office and wealth they would desert the court. Around 1700 the Hindu Marathas began to ravage southern regions, while some Rajput states and the Sikhs rebelled. All this reduced tax yields, and after the death of Aurangzeb several frontier provinces split off from the empire (page 90).

Meanwhile, to the West, after 1500 the leader of a fanatical sect of Shi'a Muslims, Ismail Safavi, re-unified Persia – which had been in a state of chaos since Timur's invasions – and proclaimed himself Shah. However the Sunnite Ottomans under Selim I (page 56) invaded in 1514, defeated Ismael at the battle of Chaldiran and captured Tabriz, thus initiating a duel between the two powers that lasted for over a century. The conflict centred around the key cities of Mesopotamia, and Baghdad, Tiflis, Derbend and Basra changed hands repeatedly; but its intensity stemmed from the religious division within Islam between Sunnite and Shi'ite (page 46), which excited the same passions as the split between Protestant and Catholic Christians at the same time. Eventually Shah Abbas (1587-1629) with assistance from both Russia and the Christian West, managed to regain most of the lost territories; but the Turks recaptured much of Mesopotamia in the 1630s.

Both empires boasted a rich civilization. Akbar and Abbas each built luxurious new capital cities – at Fatehpur Sikri and Isfahan respectively – and attracted to their courts local and foreign writers, artists and craftsmen. Shahjahan built the magnificent Taj Mahal outside Delhi. Nevertheless, two developments threatened these achievements. On the one hand, as in all autocracies, government authority could suddenly collapse under a weak ruler. Thus in 1739 Nadir Shah, who had usurped the Persian throne three years previously, invaded India and sacked Delhi, leaving the Mughal empire fatally weakened; but in 1747 Nadir was assassinated and Persia too suffered a period of anarchy. On the other hand, the armed forces of various European states established themselves around the fringes of the empires. In the north, the Russians in the 1550s advanced to the mouth of the Volga (page 78), gaining access to the Caspian. In the south, the Portuguese created fortified bases around the Indian Ocean in the early 16th century, followed after 1600 by the Dutch, English and French. Although the number of Europeans in each enclave remained relatively small, they served corporate entities – the East India Companies – that never died. Whenever Mughal or Safavid control faltered, the Europeans stood poised to take advantage (page 90).

1 The Safavid and Mughal Empires

extent of the Mughal empire

- at Akbar's death (1605)
- under Shahjahan (1627-58)
- under Aurangzeb (c. 1700)

extent of the Safavid state

- at the death of Abbas the Great (1629)

Ottoman conquests from Safavids

- from 1566-1639
- conquest of town, with date
- conquests of Suleiman I (1520-66)

South-East Asia to 1511

Situated at one of the world's main cross-roads, civilization developed early in South-East Asia: traces of 'Java man' date from the middle Pleistocene and remains of *homo sapiens* from c. 40,000 BC; rice cultivation in Thailand began about 6000 BC and bronze working in Thailand and Vietnam in 1000 BC or earlier (pages 10 and 16). Early trade routes linked India with ports along the coasts of Burma, Thailand, Cambodia and Vietnam; Hindu-Buddhist influences from India reached the area around the 2nd or 3rd century AD; and by the 5th century Buddhist images and votive tablets appeared, along with Sanskrit inscriptions. These influences never obliterated the unique character of South-East Asian civilization; instead, the next thousand years saw their assimilation to produce distinctive societies in the area. The culture of Java and southern Sumatra likewise became Indianized, but these areas also developed commercial and political links with China, which welcomed tribute missions from a growing number of states. From the 8th century temple complexes, each combining Hindu and Buddhist influences, evolved in four main areas: central Java (notably at Borobudur and Prambanan, from the 8th to 10th centuries), Cambodia (especially at Angkor, from the 9th to 13th centuries), Burma (Pagan, from the 11th to 13th centuries) and, associated with the Hindu-Buddhist kingdom of Champa, along the coast of central Vietnam. Meanwhile Palembang (a centre of Sanskrit culture from perhaps as early as the 7th century) emerged as the capital of the maritime empire of Srivijaya, which for centuries controlled international trade passing through the straits of Malacca and Sunda, and across the Isthmus of Kra (map 1).

The great temple-states fell into decline after the 12th century. In Java, the area of Prambanan was superseded in importance by eastern Java, where three states developed in succession: Kediri (12th century), Singhasari (13th century) and finally Majapahit (late 13th-early 16th century). On the mainland, first Mongols and then Shans sacked Pagan in the 13th century, while Angkor fell to Thai attacks after 1369. Sukothai, the first of the lowland Thai cities, was itself in decline by the late 14th century. New political centres replaced the old temple cities: in Burma,

2 Cultural divisions South-East Asia in 1500
distribution of major religions:

- Theravada Buddhism
- Mahayana Buddhism mixed with Confucianism and Taoism
- Hindu-Buddhism
- Islamic States
- places sending tribute to China between 1370 and 1440

1 South-East Asia, AD 500-1500

▲ Hindu-Buddhist remains and temples AD 500-1300

◉ major political centres of c.AD 1200-c. 1300

⟵ Mongol attacks 1257-92

Champa kingdom: independent from 10th century

Dai Viet kingdom: gradually absorbed by Dai Viet (11th-15th centuries).

Khmers: their temple kingdoms united under Angkor (9th-14th centuries).

Thai-Lao-Shan region: the Thai peoples expanded southwards from the 12th century, conquering the Mons of Dvaravati. Shan states later fell under Burmese domination.

Mons: their kingdoms of Thaton (11th century) and Pegu (14th-16th centuries) were later absorbed by the Burmese, and their kingdom of Dvaravati (7th-13th centuries) by the Thais.

Burmese: their empire of Pagan (11th-13th centuries) was succeeded by Ava and other states (14th-16th centuries)

Arakanese: their Muslim kingdoms independent in 14th and 15th centuries; later absorbed by Burma.

Toungoo (1347), Ava (1364), and Pegu (1369), capital of a new Mon kingdom in the south; in Thailand, Chiengmai (1296) and Ayutthaya (1350); in Cambodia, Phnom Penh and other cities along the Mekong; in Laos, Luang Prabang (1353). All were Theravada Buddhist in the Singhalese tradition, with stupas rather than temples. Meanwhile, in Vietnam, after the failure of Chinese attempts at reconquest (despite invasions in 1075-7 and 1285-8) a new kingdom, called Dai Viet, emerged and gradually absorbed Champa (annexing its capital, Vijaya, in 1471). Further south, Srivijaya declined and a powerful new Muslim state developed after 1400 at Malacca, commanding the narrow straits through which most east-west trade passed. By that time the east Javanese empire of Majapahit was in decline, and the west Javanese kingdom of Pajaran also collapsed before Muslim pressure from the northern coastal ports in the early 16th century.

Islam had began to influence northern Sumatra just before 1300; now it spread further, often under Malaccan influence, to the north Javanese trading ports, the Spice Islands, Borneo and, in the 16th century, the Philippines (map 2). When the Spaniards arrived, Mindanao had already been converted and the spread of Islam in Luzon was only halted by the Spaniards' capture of the Moorish fort at Manila in 1571 and their determined promotion of Christianity (page 74).

Meanwhile, in Vietnam, Confucian scholarship strengthened, despite the failure of another attempt at reconquest under the Ming; and all over southeast Asia the series of voyages made by the Muslim admiral Cheng Ho in the early 15th century revived and reinforced China's system of tributary relationships (page 70). From the 1430s, however, China abandoned its interest in the wider world and southeast Asia began to assume its modern pattern of cultures and polities which even the arrival of the Europeans, starting with the Portuguese capture of Malacca in 1511 (page 74) influenced little until the 19th century.

Europe 1250-1500

The 14th century brought to an end the rise and consolidation of national monarchies in western Europe (page 50). Though growth in population and productivity was steady until the later 13th century, both began to decline thereafter. Part of the problem lay in a sudden climatic deterioration which terminated the agricultural boom that had prevailed since 1150: crop yields fell, marginal areas brought into cultivation were abandoned. In 1315-17 Europe experienced the first of many famines; and the weakening of human powers of resistance through inadequate nourishment may have accelerated the spread of the 'Black Death', or bubonic plague, which killed perhaps 20 million Europeans between 1346 and 1353, wiping out in some areas as much as a third of the population within two years (map 1).

However, the impact of the plague was not even. Some areas escaped altogether, and Eastern Europe seems to have suffered relatively little: Bohemia under Charles IV (1333-78), Poland under Casimir III (1339-70) and Hungary under Louis the Great (1342-82) all made rapid strides – aided in part by skillful exploitation of their natural resources, such as the silver mines of Kutna Hora in Bohemia. Above all, in the wake of the Mongol invasions (page 56) Lithuania expanded into the former heartland of Kievan Russia and united in 1386 with Poland to form the largest state in Eastern Europe (map 2).

But elsewhere the setback proved more serious. All the western states had overextended themselves financially, and the new economic and demographic crisis exacerbated by the Black Death – combined with the tensions caused by the fragmentation of Italy and Germany after the end of Hohenstaufen rule in 1250 (page 51) or the Hundred Years' War between England and France – produced a series of popular uprisings in both cities and the countryside: the Jacquerie (1358) in France; the Peasants' Revolt (1381) in England; urban insurrections in Spain, Italy and the Low Countries. Few rebellions achieved their aims, but they all weakened state power even further.

2 Eastern Europe 1278-1389

growth of Lithuania 1300-1377:

- to 1300
- under Gedymin 1316-41
- under Olgierd 1345-77
- Lithuania under Jagiello and Witold from 1377
- Poland-Lithuania after union of 1386
- Habsburg lands
- Bohemian lands

62

1 Europe at the time of the Black Death

extent of spread of Black Death:

1346	end 1349
1347	1350
mid 1348	c. 1351
end 1348	c. 1353
mid 1349	little or no plague mortality

political changes:

Union of Kalmar 1397

Milanese territory under Giangaleazzo Visconti 1378-1402

territory under Florentine control, end 14th century

Luxembourg lands

Wittelsbach lands

Habsburg lands

social unrest:

| | | | | areas of disturbance during peasants' Revolt in England 1381

centre of urban revolt

rural uprisings   ✗ battles

religious unrest:

spread of Lollardy in England to death of Richard II, 1399

| | | | | area of Hussite influence

■ Hussite centre

RUSSIAN STATES

Orkneys

NORWAY

Novgorod

PRINCIPALITY OF MOSCOW

SWEDEN

Visby

Riga

Smolensk

OTLAND

Edinburgh

North Sea

DENMARK

Baltic Sea

Königsberg

TEUTONIC ORDER

Carlisle

Newcastle

Copenhagen

Danzig

York

Lincoln

ENGLAND

Chester

LES

Bury St Edmunds

Bristol

Norwich

Amsterdam

FRIESLAND

Lübeck

Hamburg

Bremen

POMERANIA

Warsaw

LITHUANIA

London

Winchester

Bruges

Antwerp

SAXONY

BRANDENBURG

Magdeburg

POLAND

Kiev

R. Dnieper

Ypres

Roosebeke 1382

FLANDERS

Ghent

Aachen

Cologne

R. Rhine

Brunswick

HOLLAND

Agincourt 1415

Crécy 1346

Amiens

Liège

HOLY

Frankfurt

SILESIA

R. Oder

Prague

Cracow

UKRAINE

Rouen

Mello 1358

Trier

Mainz

BOHEMIA

MORAVIA

Paris

Meaux 1358

Rheims

FRANCONIA

Tabor

R. Dniester

Chartres

1358

LORRAINE

ROMAN

Regensburg

Orleans

Troyes

Strasbourg

Augsburg

BAVARIA

Passau

R. Loire

SWABIA

Munich

Vienna

Buda

Pest

Poitiers 1356

BURGUNDY

Basle

Constance

AUSTRIA

Salzburg

MOLDAVIA

FRANCE

Lausanne

SWISS CONFED.

EMPIRE

CARINTHIA

HUNGARY

Bordeaux

R. Dordogne

Geneva

SAVOY

Turin

Trieste

Venice

Milan

R. Danube

Bucharest

NGLISH CONY

Cahors

DAUPHINÉ

REPUBLIC OF VENICE

Ravenna

WALLACHIA

Black Sea

Avignon

Genoa

BOSNIA

Belgrade

BULGARIA

Toulouse

PROVENCE

Pisa

Florence

Siena

Ancona

SERBIAN PRINCES

Narbonne

Marseilles

PAPAL

Ragusa

Adrianople

AGON

Barcelona

STATES

Rome

Adriatic Sea

PRINCIPALITY OF ALBANIA

Salonica

Constantinople

Corsica

KINGDOM OF NAPLES

Naples

Amalfi

OTTOMAN TURKS

Sardinia

Balearic Islands

DUCHY OF ATHENS

Athens

ACHAEA

Mediterranean

Palermo

Messina

KINGDOM OF SICILY

Rhodes

Crete

Sea

China and Japan 1279-1644

The Mongol invasion of China caused immense destruction. During the conquest of the north (1211-34: page 56) much of the land went out of cultivation, many cities and industries perished, and countless people died or became slaves. The conquest of the south (1270-9) brought similar hardships, and Mongol rule proved harsh. Popular resentment erupted in a wave of popular uprisings after 1335, exacerbated by disastrous floods in coastal regions in the 1350s. One of the rebel leaders, Chu Yüan-chang, gradually overcame his rivals and in 1368 established a new dynasty, the Ming.

The Ming rebuilt irrigation and drainage works in great numbers, reforested on a grand scale, and moved vast numbers of people to repopulate the devastated north. New crops were introduced and the canal system extended to transport produce: by 1421 the 'Grand Canal' stretched from Hang-chou to just south of Peking and carried some 200,000 tons of grain northwards every year. Thanks to these measures, the Chinese population rose from some 60 million in 1393 (40 per cent fewer than a century before) to about 130 million by 1580. The great cities of the Yangtze delta became major industrial centres, particularly for textiles, while the southern ports fitted out the enormous fleets sent by Chu's son, the Yung-lo emperor (1402-24), to the South China Sea and the Indian Ocean.

The Ming entrusted control over the vast population to a gentry class of degree-holders, who had passed through the examination system and shared the value of the bureaucracy without actually holding office. But the system discouraged innovation and was over-centralized, with all major decisions dependent upon the emperor; and few of Yung-lo's successors possessed the dedication necessary for such heavy responsibilities. Nevertheless, the early Ming engaged in an aggressive foreign policy. They restored Korea to vassal status in 1392, occupied Annam from 1407 to 1427, and invaded Mongolia (map 1). However, after a northern campaign in 1449 resulted in the capture of the emperor, the Ming reverted to a defensive strategy, strengthening the Great Wall until it ran for almost 2,500 miles, and increasing the garrisons in the north and north-west. China remained relatively stable for another century, but in the 1430s the government banned all overseas trade by sea, except under close supervision. Not surprisingly, by 1500 smuggling had become commonplace in the south-eastern provinces and by 1550 heavily-armed bands of smugglers and pirates infested the seas around China and terrorized the coastal regions from their bases in Japan.

Central authority in Japan had collapsed in the 1330s and the country became plagued by local and provincial wars – almost continuously in the century after 1467. By about 1560, some nine leading families had formed alliances that covered most of the country, and competed openly for supreme power (map 2). In

1568 Nobunaga, leader of the Oda clan, captured Kyoto, the imperial capital, and by the time he was assassinated in 1582 by a jealous rival he had forced almost all the other lords to accept his orders. Within a decade, his ablest general Toyotomi Hideyoshi had completely reunified Japan, reorganizing the tax system and redistributing land to provide sufficient funds for his ambitious policies – including the invasion of Korea in the 1590s. After his death in 1598 another of Nobunaga's generals, Tokugawa Ieyasu, assumed power and in 1603 established the dynasty of shoguns who ruled Japan until the 19th century (page 82).

The Tokugawa put an end to the pirate problem, thus easing the pressure on the Chinese coast; but at just this time a new threat arose in the north-east, where the Manchu gradually expanded their power into the areas immediately to the north of the Great Wall and (in 1637) into Korea. Ming authority now collapsed. After 1627 a wave of rebellions broke out in the wake of repeated crop failures in the north-west, and much of central and northern China soon came under rebel sway. In 1644, one of the rebel leaders captured Peking and the last Ming emperor committed suicide. Almost immediately the Manchus intervened, seized Peking, and began the conquest of China (page 88).

1 The Ming dynasty, 1368-1644

- Ming empire c. 1500
- Ming military campaigns
- northern defences
- provincial capitals
- frontier defence area
- Japanese military campaigns
- Japanese pirate invasions before 16th century
- coastal areas affected by Japanese pirate invasions
- Grand Canal

2 Civil War in Japan 1467-1590

spheres of influence of the most powerful Daimyo clans

boundaries of Daimyo domains

The Ottoman Empire
1300-1699

The overthrow of the Abbasid Caliphate by the Mongols in 1256-60 (page 56) left the Muslim world in disarray for half a century. One of the centres of recovery lay in north-west Anatolia where, around 1300, a Turkish leader named Osman founded a state which became the core of the future Ottoman empire (map 1). The damage to the structure of the Byzantine empire caused by the Fourth Crusade in 1204 (page 44) facilitated the Ottomans' rapid advance in the 14th century. By 1354 the Turks had crossed the Dardanelles to Gallipoli, and their victories at Kosovo (1389) and Nicopolis (1396) left them masters of the Balkans. The invasion of Timur (page 57) and his destruction of the Turkish army at Ankara (1402) gave the hard-pressed Byzantine empire some respite, but the renewal of expansion under Murad II (1413-51) and Mohammed II (1451-81) sealed its fate. In

(1574), although his fleet of galleys met with defeat at the hands of a Christian coalition at Lepanto (1571). However the wars of his successors against Persia (1578-90 and 1602-39) and against the Austrian Habsburgs (1593-1606) resulted in the loss of the Caucasus to the former and of annual tribute for Hungary from the latter.

The end of expansion, coupled with rapid price inflation (from 1584), a rising population and a static economy provoked a spate of popular and military uprisings between 1596 and 1610 in the Anatolian heartland of the empire (map 2). Nevertheless, Mesopotamia was regained from Persia in the 1630s and Crete conquered from the Venetians in the 1660s; and in 1683 a great army laid siege once more to Vienna. But it failed, and a Christian counter-attack drove the Turks out of Hungary by 1699 – although the Turks still remained a formidable power, controlling the entire Arab world east of Libya and most of the Balkans until the 19th century.

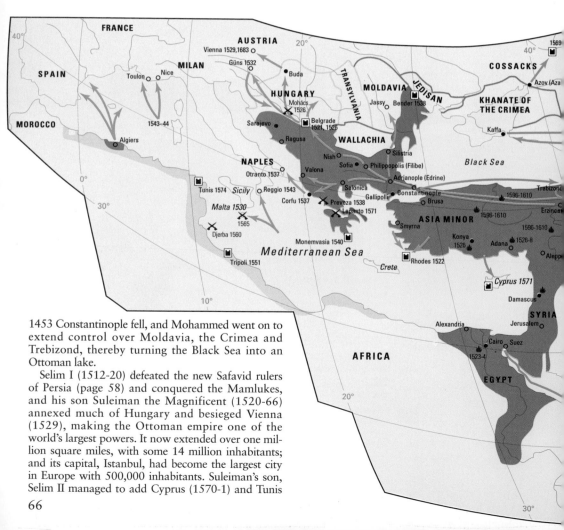

1453 Constantinople fell, and Mohammed went on to extend control over Moldavia, the Crimea and Trebizond, thereby turning the Black Sea into an Ottoman lake.

Selim I (1512-20) defeated the new Safavid rulers of Persia (page 58) and conquered the Mamlukes, and his son Suleiman the Magnificent (1520-66) annexed much of Hungary and besieged Vienna (1529), making the Ottoman empire one of the world's largest powers. It now extended over one million square miles, with some 14 million inhabitants; and its capital, Istanbul, had become the largest city in Europe with 500,000 inhabitants. Suleiman's son, Selim II managed to add Cyprus (1570-1) and Tunis

RUSSIA

10°   20°   30°   40°

Volga

Danube

45°

MOLDAVIA (BOĞODAN)
(1455)

KHANATE OF THE CRIMEA (VASSAL 1475)

Sea of Azov

Caspian Sea

HUNGARY

BUJAK
(1484)

TRANSYLVANIA

ÇERKES
(CIRCASSIA)

○ Belgrade

BOSNIA
(1463)

WALLACHIA (EFLÂK)
(1396)

Black Sea

HERZEGOVINA
(1463-83)

SERBIA
(1389)

DOBRUJA

REPUBLIC OF RAGUSA
(VASSAL 1463)

RUMELIA (BULGARIA) (1393)

EMPIRE OF
TREBIZOND (1461)

ÇANDAR 1393

Adrianople (Edirne)

1461

KARAKOYUNLU

○ Istanbul (1453)

AKKOYUNLU

○ Bursa

Salonica (Selenik)
(1430)

SIVAS
1398

Tigris

KARASI 1345

GERMIYAN
1380   1428

SARUHAN
1390   1405

35°

MOREA
(1460)

Athens

AYDIN
1396   1426

HAMID
1381

KARAMAN
1390

MENTEŞE
1396   1428

TEKE
1391   1427

1468

Euphrates

20°

1426

Mediterranean Sea

MAMELUKE EMPIRE
(1517)

30°   40°

DAGHESTAN

Caspian Sea

Derbend 1579

Tiflis 1578

Baku 1583

Ganja 1588

Arash 1578

Kars 1578

SHIRVAN
QARABAGH

Erzurum

Nakhichevan 1557

Van ○

Tabriz 1534, 1548, 1585

AZERBAIJAN

PERSIA

30°

1596-1610

IRAQ

Baghdad 1534

LURISTAN

Basra 1546

20°

ARABIA

Red Sea

● Medina

● Mecca

YEMEN   Aden ●

40°

Precolumbian America

Two major civilizations confronted the Spaniards when they arrived on the American mainland in the early 16th century: the Aztec Empire in Mexico, with a subject population of perhaps 12 million, and the Inca empire in Peru, ruling some 6 million. The rest of the continent remained sparsely inhabited – perhaps 1 million people lived north of the Rio Grande with another million in the rest of South America – divided among more than a thousand small tribal societies with distinct languages. Few regions, particularly in the north, had reached the stage of settled agriculture, despite some contacts in the north-east with Europeans around the year 1000 (map 1).

The Aztec and Inca Empires differed markedly in character, and no evidence exists of any contact between them. Like the Toltecs, who between 968 and about 1170 controlled much of the valley of Mexico from their capital at Tula, the Aztecs came from the north. In 1325 they arrived in the valley and settled on a group of islands in the swampy margins of Lake Texcoco, where they built their capital, Tenochtitlán (site of Mexico City). Serving at first as mercenary warriors for neighbouring towns, by 1428 they had overthrown them all and, led by a priest-king and an hereditary warrior aristocracy, embarked upon an ambitious programme of conquest. When the Spaniards arrived in 1519, the Aztecs controlled the greater part of Mexico and had entered Maya territory in Yucatán (map 2).

The Inca formed one of the numerous tribes of Quechua stock inhabiting the central Andes, but until the accession of Pachacuti Inca in 1438 they played only a

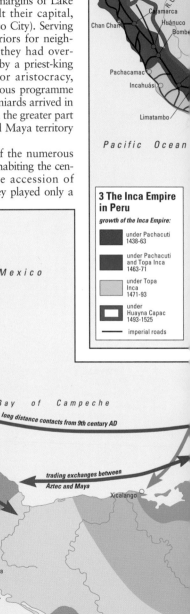

3 The Inca Empire in Peru

growth of the Inca Empire:

under Pachacuti 1438-63

under Pachacuti and Topa Inca 1463-71

under Topa Inca 1471-93

under Huayna Capac 1493-1525

— imperial roads

2 The Aztec Empire in Mexico

Maya cultural area

Post-Classic Maya Kingdoms

area of Aztec domination 1519

spread of Toltec influence from 9th century AD

Post-classic trading routes

La Quemada
NW outpost of Mexican culture

centre of Toltec military state 800-1000

Late Post-Classic Tarascan site

Aztec capital founded AD 1325

Tamuin
late Huastec centre

Gulf of Mexico

Tzintzuntzán

Tula

Castilo de Teayo

Azcapotzalco

El Tajín

major centre of Aztec allies

Bay of Campeche

Tenochtitlán   Texcoco
Tlacopán

Tlaxcala

Cacaxtla

long distance contacts from 9th century AD

Aztec period temple carved in rock

Malinalco
Xochicalco

Cholula

Cempoala

trading exchanges between Aztec and Maya

early Post-Classic site 800-1000 with Maya contacts

R. Balsas

Teotitlán

Xicalango

Monte Albán
tombs in old Zapotec ceremonial centre

Yagul

Oaxaca Valley

Tehuacán Valley

Mitla
early post-Classic Mixtec site

Guiengola

Pacific Ocean

XOCONUSCO

rich province supplying cacao to the Aztec capital

Zaculeu

Xoconocho

Iximché

1 Archaeological sites in North America, from AD 1000

minor role. Within 45 years, however, Pachacuti's conquests extended Inca control from Lake Titicaca to Huánaco in the north, while his son Topa pushed north into Ecuador and south to Chile, and from the Pacific coast to the Upper Amazon. This created an empire 200 miles wide and 2500 miles long, held together by an impressive system of highways, post-stations and relay runners (map 3).

The Incas created a genuine imperial system, with an hereditary dynasty of absolute, 'divine' Incas, a Quechua aristocracy, and a highly trained bureaucracy. All land was state-owned, with a complex system of irrigation. The ordinary Inca subject spent 9 months working for the state, but in return received protection from famine (through state-owned food stores) and support during sickness and old age. The Aztec Empire, on the other hand, exercised harsh military dominion over vassal peoples who enjoyed political autonomy provided they paid heavy tribute to Tenochtitlán in food, textiles and other goods – increasingly in humans for ritual sacrifice to the Aztec gods (up to 50,000 a year by 1510). These demands help to explain why so many people in the valley of Mexico welcomed the Spaniards, just as a recent succession dispute provided allies for the European invaders in Peru. Although both the Aztec and Inca polities expanded faster than any 15th-century state in Latin Christendom, neither empire proved as stable as it seemed. Mexico fell to a force spearheaded by under 2,000 Europeans in 1519-22, Peru to a band of less than 200 in 1531-3 (see page 80).

The world *c.* 1492

The central feature of world history since the 1490s has been the expansion of Europe and the spread of European civilization throughout the globe. Until then, the world had, on the whole, pressed in on Europe; thereafter the roles became reversed. In the 16th century, however, Europe continued to stand on the periphery of the civilized world, eclipsed by Ming China (the most powerful and advanced state of the period, with over 100 million inhabitants – equal to the whole of Europe) and by the rising Ottoman, Safavid and Mughal empires of the Middle East. Meanwhile Islam won converts in central and Southeast Asia, and among the peoples of sub-Saharan Africa.

The total area occupied by the major civilizations, roughly co-terminous with the area of plough cultivation, nevertheless remained relatively small. Almost 80 per cent of the world's surface was inhabited either by food gatherers or herdsmen (as in Australia and most of Siberia, North America and much of Africa) or by hand cultivators (especially in South-East Asia,

West Africa and Central and South America). But plough cultivators proved far more productive, and the relatively small area that had been brought under the plough probably housed between two-thirds and three-quarters of the global population (map 1).

Until the 1490s, worldwide racial segregation prevailed. Although Christians and Muslims from all over Eurasia made pilgrimages to their Holy Places in the Middle East, they seldom settled; and although merchants travelled widely across and around Asia, their numbers remained few. In the early 15th century a succession of Chinese voyages, commanded by the Muslim admiral Cheng Ho, secured tribute and extended recognition of the new Ming dynasty; but they led to no lasting interchange of population.

Until the 1490s, therefore, the Negroids remained concentrated in sub-Saharan Africa and a few Pacific islands; the Mongoloids in Asia and the Americas; the Caucasoids in Europe, North Africa, the Middle East and India; and the Australoids in Australia and South India (map 2a). By 1800, however, the pattern had fundamentally altered as the

1 Dominant economies and major civilizations, 1492

- food gathering
- pastoralism
- hand-cultivation
- plough-cultivation
- Chinese Admiral Cheng Ho's voyages 1405–33

result of six inter-continental migrations: from Europe and Africa to the Americas; from northern Europe to Africa and (later) Australasia; from Russia into Siberia; from China to South-East Asia; and from India to Africa, South-East Asia and the Caribbean. By far the greatest change occurred in the Americas, where the native population declined dramatically in the century following the first contact with the Europeans – in some cases by 90 per cent – to be replaced by Europeans, Africans, and in some parts of Latin America by a mixed race of mestizos (map 2b).

Nevertheless, the tempo of change must not be exaggerated. Although in America the Aztec and Inca empires collapsed suddenly in 1521 and 1533 respectively (page 68), elsewhere the political impact of Europe remained limited until the 18th century. China and Japan survived intact, and India kept the Europeans at arm's length for 250 years following the arrival of Vasco da Gama in 1498. There, as in Africa and South-east Asia, the European presence long remained confined largely to trading stations and fortresses along the coast. The cultural influence of

Europe was even more negligible: Christianity made little headway, except when imposed by the conquerors (as in the Americas and the Philippines), until it received the backing of western technology in the 19th century.

The comparative fragility of the Aztec and Inca civilizations in the Americas, and of the African kingdoms immediately south of the Sahara, despite their outstanding achievements, may be partially explained, first, by their geographical isolation and relative lack of external stimulus and, second, by their dependence on hand cultivation. After 1492, when all the continents came into direct contact with each other for the first time, many of these non-Eurasian civilizations proved unable to offer more than a feeble resistance to outside aggression. To be sure not until the 19th century, with the opening of the Suez Canal and the construction of the transcontinental railways in North America, Siberia and Africa, did areas that had previously been separate finally blend into a single world economy; but the first stages of global integration were completed in the three centuries following 1492.

2b Diffusion of races after 1492

2a Distribution of races, 1492

- ☐ Mongoloid
- ☐ Caucasoid
- ☐ Australoid
- ☐ Negroid

The great discoveries 1480-1616

In 1480 European shipping remained largely confined to the North Atlantic, the Baltic and the Mediterranean, while the West African coast had been explored cursorily, and only very recently by Europeans; Indian, Persian, and Arab vessels plied the northern Indian Ocean; Chinese and Indonesian junks sailed in the western Pacific, but rarely went beyond Japan, the Philippines and the Indonesian archipelago; and local craft navigated the Caribbean and the coasts of Peru and Ecuador. No shipping used the southern Indian Ocean, the South Atlantic, or the main basin of the Pacific. In the course of the next 150 years, however, European navigators opened all the seas, except in the regions of circumpolar ice and the South Pacific, to European ships. Initially, in the 15th century, two series of voyages sought a sea passage to southern Asia in the hope of initiating direct trade in spices. One series, mounted from Portugal, sailing by a south-eastern route and employing local navigators in the East, eventually reached their declared destinations: the entrance to the Indian Ocean (1488), Malabar (1498), Malacca (1509), and the Moluccas (1512-13). The other series, based on Spain and sailing west or south-west, proved less successful in its immediate purpose but

1 Voyages of discovery, 1480–1630

→ voyages intended for Southern Asia by South East route

→ voyages intended for Asia by North West and North East routes

→ voyages intended for China and Southern Asia by West or South West route

⇨ approximate prevailing winds (shown for the first quarter of the year)

⇨ alternating monsoons

Major European voyages of discovery from about 1480 to 1613 (above) Explorers seeking sea routes to Asia found, in addition, a continent hitherto unknown to Europe, and an ocean of unsuspected extent. They proved that all the oceans were connected, and that the world was much bigger then accepted authorities had taught.

more fruitful in incidental discovery: the Spaniards hit upon the West Indies (1492) and the Spanish Main (1498). Eventually they too reached South-east Asia (1521), but by a route too long and arduous for commercial use – for to reach the Pacific they had to circumnavigate an immense land-mass which, although it was initially thought to be a peninsula of Asia, by the 1520s had been recognized as a new world. They immediately began to settle the area (page 69). Taken together, the Spanish and Portuguese discoveries proved that all the oceans of the world, at least in the southern hemisphere, were connected.

For most of the 16th century, by the use and threat of force, the Iberian powers managed to prevent other Europeans from using the connecting passages, except for occasional raids. The third great series of voyages, therefore, mostly by English, French and Dutch navigators, searched for alternative routes to Asia in the northern hemisphere, in the west, north-west, and northeast. Although unsuccessful in their primary purpose, they revealed another continental land-mass with a continuous coast extending from the Caribbean to the Arctic, and opened the way for the European exploration and settlement of eastern North America (page 80).

3/Cabral 1500 (outward) the second Portuguese voyage to India, landed in Brazil.
4/First Portuguese voyage to Malacca, 1509.
5/Abreu 1512–13 visited Moluccas.
6/First Portuguese visits to Canton River, 1516.
7/Da Mota, Zeimoto and Peixoto 1542–43 Portuguese discovery of Japan.
8/Columbus 1492–93 (outward and homeward) discovered islands in Bahamas, explored north coasts of Cuba and Hispaniola; interpreted discoveries as part of Asia; found best return route.
9/Columbus 1493–94 (outward) explored south coast of Cuba; reported it as peninsula of mainland China.
10/Columbus 1498 (outward) discovered Trinidad and coast of Venezuela; recognized coast as mainland, surmised it to be terrestrial paradise.
11/Columbus 1502–4 explored coast of Honduras, Nicaragua and the Isthmus. Believed Honduras to be Indo-China.
12/Ojeda and Vespucci 1499–1500 (outward) reached Guiana coast, followed coast west to Cape de la Vela. First report of Amazon.
13/Coelho and Vespucci 1501 (outward) followed

16/Saavedra 1527 discovered route from coast of Mexico across Pacific to south-east Asia.
17/Urdaneta 1565 found feasible return route Philippines to Mexico in 42N. using west winds.
18/Schouten and Le Maire 1616 discovered route into Pacific via Le Maire Strait and Cape Horn.
19/Cabot 1497 (outward) rediscovered Newfoundland, first sighted by Norsemen in 11th century; believed it NE extremity of Asia.
20/Corte-Real 1500 rediscovered Greenland.
21/Verazzano 1524 traced east coast of North America from (probably) 34N. to 47N; revealed continental character of North America.
22/Cartier 1534 and 1535 explored Strait of Belle Isle and St Lawrence as far as Montreal.
23/Willoughby and Chancellor 1553 rounded North Cape and reached Archangel.
24/Frobisher 1576 reached Frobisher Bay on Baffin Island, which he took for a 'strait'.
25/Davis 1587 explored west coast of Greenland to the edge of the ice in 72° N.
26/Barents 1596-7 discovered Bear Island and Spitsbergen and wintered in Novaya Zemlya.
27/Hudson 1610 sailed through Hudson Strait

1/Dias 1487–88 (outward) discovered open water south of Cape Agulhas; entered Indian Ocean; reached Great Fish River.
2/Vasco da Gama 1497–98 (outward) made best use of Atlantic winds on the way to Cape of Good Hope; reached India, guided by local pilot.

coast south from Cape São Agostinho to (possibly) 35S.
14/Solis 1515 entered River Plate estuary and investigated north bank.
15/Magellan and Elcano 1519–22 discovered Strait of Magellan, crossed Pacific, reached Moluccas via Philippines. First circumnavigation.

to the southern extremity of the of Hudson Bay, which he and others took to be the Pacific.
28/Button 1612 explored the west coast of Hudson Bay, concluded Bay landlocked by the west.
29/Baffin and Bylot 1616 explored whole coastline of Baffin Bay and came to the conclusion that no navigable NW passage existed in that area.

European overseas expansion 1492-1713

By 1492, Portugal already possessed several archipelagos in the Atlantic and the Gulf of Guinea, some fortresses in Morocco, and a few trading stations in West Africa (above all the castle at Elmina). In the next half century she established some 50 forts and trading posts around the shores of the Indian Ocean, as well as coastal enclaves in Angola and Brazil. Strategically, the most important bases were Mozambique (1507), a port of call for fleets sailing to India; Goa (1510), headquarters of Portuguese Asia; Malacca (1511), a major market on the strait connecting the Indian Ocean with the South China Sea; and Ormuz (1515), a key entrepot of the international spice trade. East of Malacca the position of the Portuguese was far more precarious and their activities remained purely commercial. A few bases, some fortified, grew up in the Moluccas; a clandestine settlement developed at Macao on the Chinese mainland after 1557; and from 1580 Jesuit missionaries held a lease on the Japanese port-city of Nagasaki (map 1).

In Africa and Asia the Portuguese generally sought to control trade rather than production; and though they could not eliminate the commerce of others in the Indian Ocean, they forced many ships to use harbours under their control, and extorted tolls or duties from the rest. The Spaniards in the Americas, by contrast, embarked on a deliberate policy of conquest and colonization: from the 1490s in the Caribbean islands; from the 1520s in Mexico; from the 1530s in Peru; and from the 1570s in the Philippines.

Few dared to challenge the Iberian monopoly – apparently enhanced by the union of Portugal and Spain in 1580 – before the 17th century. However, the foundation of East India Companies by the Dutch, the English and (later) the French brought the Portuguese under increasing attack. Dutch forces first established independent bases in the East (above all at Batavia, the heavily fortified headquarters of the Dutch East India Company) and then between 1640 and 1660 wrested Malacca, Ceylon, most South Indian ports and the lucrative Japan trade from the Portuguese. In 1652 they also created a useful south African base on the route to the East at Cape Town. The English and French also established modest settlements in India, and developed a promising trade with China. Even the Spaniards undermined the Portuguese, exporting Chinese goods after 1572 through their colony in the Philippines (map 2). Elsewhere in Asia, however, Europeans during this period traded in competition with local merchants on terms laid down by local rulers, and their efforts constituted but a fraction of Asia's total commerce.

1 Spanish and Portuguese trade and settlement by c. 1600

← principal Spanish trade routes

← principle Portuguese trade routes

■ areas under effective Spanish control

■ areas under effective Portuguese control

□ important towns in the 16th century

● Spanish towns

● seat of *Audiencia* (Spanish administrative division)

● Portuguese towns

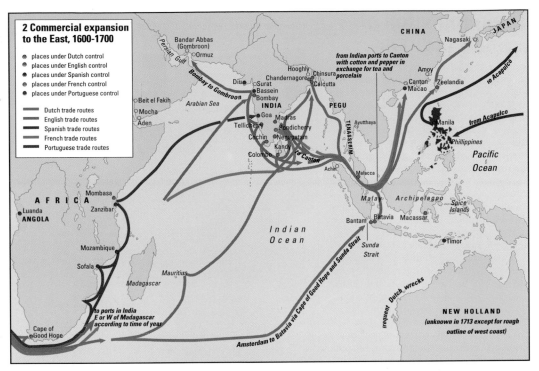

2 Commercial expansion to the East, 1600-1700

- places under Dutch control
- places under English control
- places under Spanish control
- places under French control
- places under Portuguese control

— Dutch trade routes
— English trade routes
— Spanish trade routes
— French trade routes
— Portuguese trade routes

Persian Gulf
Bandar Abbas (Gombroon)
Ormuz
CHINA
Nagasaki
JAPAN

Hooghly
Bombay to Gombroon
Diu
Chandernagore
Chinsura
Calcutta
Surat
Bassein
Bombay
INDIA
PEGU
from Indian ports to Canton with cotton and pepper in exchange for tea and porcelain
Canton
Macao
Amoy
Zeelandia
to Acapulco

Arabian Sea
Beit el Fakih
Mocha
Aden

Goa
Madras
Tellicherry
Pondicherry
Cochin
Negapatam
Kandy
Colombo
to Canton
Achin
Malacca
TENASSERIM
Ayutthaya

Manila
from Acapulco
Phillippines
Pacific Ocean

AFRICA
Mombasa
Zanzibar
Luanda
ANGOLA

Indian Ocean

Malay
Archipelago
Spice Islands

Mozambique
Sofala

Mauritius
Madagascar

Bantam
Batavia
Macassar

Sunda Strait

Timor

frequent Dutch wrecks

NEW HOLLAND
(unknown in 1713 except for rough outline of west coast)

to ports in India E or W of Madagascar according to time of year

Cape of Good Hope

Amsterdam to Batavia via Cape of Good Hope and Sunda Strait

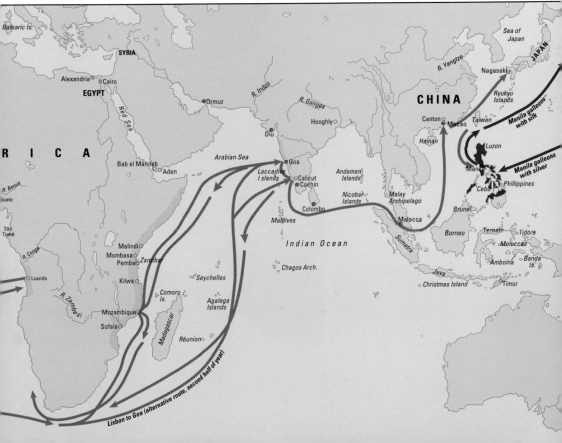

Balearic Is.

Sea of Japan

SYRIA
Alexandria
Cairo
EGYPT

Ormuz
R. Indus
R. Ganges
Hooghly
Diu

CHINA
R. Yangtze
Nagasaki
JAPAN
Ryukyu Islands
Canton
Macao
Taiwan
Hainan
Manila galleons with silk

RICA

Red Sea
Bab el Mandeb
Aden
Arabian Sea
Goa
Laccadive Islands
Calicut
Cochin

Andaman Islands
Nicobar Islands
Malay Archipelago

Luzon
Manila
Cebu
Phillippines
Manila galleons with silver

R. Benue
Guato

São Tomé

R. Congo

Luanda

R. Zambesi

Malindi
Mombasa
Pemba
Zanzibar

Kilwa

Comoro Is.

Seychelles

Agalega Islands

Mozambique
Sofala
Madagascar
Réunion

Colombo
Maldives

Chagos Arch.

Indian Ocean

Malacca
Sumatra

Brunei
Borneo
Java
Christmas Island

Ternate
Tidore
Moluccas
Amboina
Banda Is.
Timor

Lisbon to Goa (alternative route, second half of year)

The expansion of France 1440-1789

In 1415 English troops invaded France and by 1429 had established suzerainty over almost half the kingdom (map 1). In the 1440s, however, with the aid of a powerful artillery train, Charles VII (1422-61) began a rapid reconquest which by 1453 had expelled the English from all but the port-city of Calais, and doubled the size of the royal domain. His successors annexed Burgundy (1477), Brittany (1491) and Bourbon (1527) by force, and inherited Anjou and Provence (1481). Several other semi-independent fiefs came to the crown at the accession of Louis XII (1498), Francis I (1515) and Henry IV (1589).

After Henry's death in 1610, continuing religious division, costly foreign wars and aristocratic faction, culminating in the Fronde revolt (1648-53), brought France to the brink of dissolution again. However Henry's grandson Louis XIV (1643-1715) restored order and made France the dominant state of Europe. During the relatively peaceful years between 1659 and 1672 the king and his ministers struggled to develop the French economy (agriculture, manufacture and trade), to extend overseas possessions, and to expand the army and navy. They also developed commercial harbours and sponsored public works, such as the Languedoc Canal connecting the Atlantic and the Mediterranean. The richness of resources available to the French, including a population of perhaps 20 million (the largest of any 17th-century European state), undoubtedly played a part in these achievements; but so did the ceaseless efforts, directives, and resources emanating from the Court (map 2).

Despite France's gains at the peaces of Westphalia (1648) and the Pyrenees (1659), Louis still feared Habsburg encirclement (page 86). He sought both to secure territories that might plug the gaps in his frontier (in wars fought in 1667-8 and 1672-8 which brought the acquisition of territory from the Spanish Netherlands and of Franche-Comté), and to create an 'iron frontier' of state-of-the-art fortresses, thickest on the ground in the north and east, to create a defence in depth that would prevent any enemy forces from penetrating to the heart of the realm as the English and the Habsburgs had done in the past. Perhaps his success in this endeavour

1 The reunification of France, 1440-1589

- frontier of France 1493
- Royal Domain c. 1475
- lands annexed from Burgundy 1477
- lands of René of Anjou, annexed 1481
- lands of the Duke of Brittany, annexed 1491
- lands brought to the crown by Louis XII, 1498
- lands brought to the crown by Francis I, 1515
- lands of the Duke of Bourbon, annexed 1527
- lands brought to the crown by Henry IV, 1589
- other fiefs annexed with date
- fiefs still independent at end of 16th century
- lands recognising English suzerainty 1429

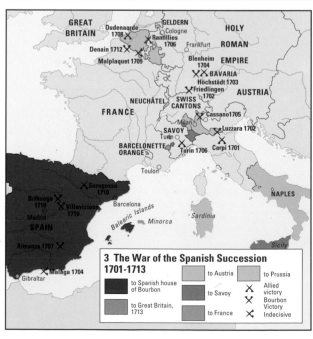

3 The War of the Spanish Succession 1701-1713

- to Spanish house of Bourbon
- to Great Britain, 1713
- to France
- to Austria
- to Savoy
- to Prussia
- X Allied victory
- X Bourbon Victory
- X Indecisive

made him too bold, for in 1700 he accepted the will of the childless Spanish Habsburg Carlos II which bequeathed to Louis's grandson Philip the entire Spanish empire – Spain, Spanish America, the South Netherlands and half of Italy – even though he knew this sudden concentration of territory in the hands of the Bourbon dynasty would provoke a general European war. After some French initial victories (1702-3), followed by a string of searing defeats (1704-9), the 'iron frontier' showed its worth and forced France's exhausted enemies to conclude the compromise peaces of Utrecht (1713) and Rastatt (1714), by which Philip retained Spain and Spanish America, while Savoy, Britain and the Austrian Habsburgs partitioned the rest (map 3).

Louis had thus secured the integrity of France's frontiers, and ended for ever the threat of Habsburg encirclement; but the ruinous cost of his wars created a legacy of financial disorder and internal discontent which served to hamstring his successors. Although Louis XV (1715-74) managed to incorporate Lorraine in 1766, and his successor Louis XVI (1774-93) assisted the successful rebellion of the American colonies against Great Britain (page 98), both monarchs sacrificed (as Louis XIV had done) France's overseas possessions and accumulated such monstrous public debts that, in 1789, the government summoned a representative assembly, the States-General, to solve the financial crisis. In doing so, it unleashed revolution (page 93).

2 France under Louis XIV

Frontiers and administration:

Frontier of France 1713-14
administrative units of Louis XIV's reign, the *généralités* (generalities)

⊙ seat of intendants, Louis XIV's royal commissioners

⊕ *parlement* (law courts)

defence:

▮ fortifications (the so-called *barrière* or *frontière de fer*)

▣ fortifications built by Vauban but ceded during reign of Louis XIV

➤ fortification gap, possible invasion route (*porte*)

⚓ galley port

⊞ naval port

economic:

‡ commercial harbours

The expansion of Russia 1462-1815

After the Mongol invasion of the 13th century (page 56), the lands which had formed part of Kievan Russia fragmented. Lithuania expanded in the west, while the east and south became subject to Mongol overlords, in whose service the principality of Muscovy rose to prominence. Ivan III (1462-1505) opened another phase of expansion: in 1478 he annexed the city republic of Novgorod and in 1480 proclaimed independence from the Mongols. In 1510 his son Vassily (1505-33) overran the republic of Pskov, bringing Muscovite control close to the Baltic; and his grandson Ivan IV (1533-84) conquered the Tatar states of Kazan (1552) and Astrakhan (1556), gaining control of the Volga down to the Caspian Sea. In addition, from the 1580s, the lucrative fur trade lured enterprising Russians deep into Siberia. Crossing the Urals, they followed the River Ob until they came within portage of the Yenisey, where they built and fortified Turukhansk (1607); thence they reached the Lena river system, where they built Yakutsk (1632), and finally the Pacific, where they built Othotsk (1649) – some 6,000 miles (9,700km) east of Moscow (map 2).

However Ivan IV failed to realise his principal territorial ambition, the acquisition of Livonia and direct access to the Baltic, while his attempt to break the power of the traditional nobility by creating a 'private domain' (the *oprichnina*) around Moscow resulted in massive depopulation. Muscovy was also still not entirely safe from the Crimean Tartars, who sacked Moscow in 1571. Then succession disputes following the extinction of the old Muscovite ruling house (the

'Time of Troubles', 1598-1613) caused the loss of much territory to Poland and Sweden.

Recovery came only in the mid-17th century, when successful wars with Poland (1632-4 and 1654-67) brought substantial gains, including Kiev and the Ukraine. Meanwhile the settlement of Siberia continued: 23,000 Russians lived there by 1622, 105,000 by 1662 and 230,000 by 1709. However the Amur Basin, acquired in the 1650s, had to be ceded to China in 1689 (albeit in return for useful trading concessions: map 2) and attempts to force access to the Black Sea failed. Instead, Peter I ('the Great', 1682-1725) concentrated on achieving a 'window on the west', wresting Estonia and Livonia from Sweden in 1721, acquiring the ancient port of Riga and founding the new one of St Petersburg (1703). Peter's successors reverted to his policy of expansion on the Black Sea. Catherine II ('the Great', 1762-96) annexed the Tatar khanate of the Crimea and also acquired large parts of Poland – although the cost of her campaigns, on top of the oppressive social system which required serfs to spend almost all their time labouring on the lords' lands, provoked a major peasant uprising under Emelyan Pugachev (1773-5). The period 1772 to 1815 saw the Russian land frontier expand 600 miles (970 km) at the expense of Poland. Finally, despite a French invasion which reached Moscow in 1812, the Congress of Vienna in 1815 confirmed Russia's acquisition of Finland, Poland, Bessarabia and Transcaucasia (page 110).

The population ruled from Moscow had grown, both by territorial acquisition and by natural increase, from some 10 million in 1600, to over 15 million in 1725 and to almost 43 million in 1812, and the empire – the largest in the world – now stretched over 11 of the world's 24 time-zones.

1 Muscovy and the Russian Empire, 1462-1815

- ∿ boundary of Russian territories in 1462

the expansion of Muscovy:

- Moscow territory at end of 13th century
- *1478* date of acquisition by Muscovy
- acquisitions to 1462
- acquisitions under Ivan III, 1462-1505
- acquisitions during 16th century
- acquisitions during 17th century
- acquisitions during 18th century
- acquisitions 1801-15
- territory lost 1617-18 and recovered during the 17th century
- ∿ area affected by Pugachev uprising 1773-4
- Orel 1564 date of foundation of new town

2 Russian Expansion in Siberia, 1581-1800

- Russian territory in 1581
- territory added 1581-98
- territory added 1598-1618
- territory added 1618-89
- territory added in 1650s; returned to China 1689
- territory added 1689-1725
- territory added 1725-62
- territory added 1762-1800
- *YAKUTS* native peoples
- ○ Batsk 1630 forts and trading posts (with date of foundation)

Barents Sea

Obdorsk 159-

Kola Peninsula

R. Ob

Berezov 1593

R. Pechora

PECHORA

1478

1501

R. Mezen

White Sea

Archangel 1584

Kholmogory

Northern Dvina

R. Onega

R. Vychegda

1478

NOVGOROD TERRITORY

Kargopol

Solvychegodsk

Ustyug

R. Sukhona

1472

Solikamsk

YUGRA MTS.

Ural Mts.

FINLAND *1809*

L. Onega

1478

Vologda

Soligalich

R. Vyatka

R. Kama

Nizhniy Ta- *1724*

KARELIA

1743

1721

L. Ladoga

Vyborg

Gulf of Finland

Kronstadt 1704

St. Petersburg 1703

Narva

Galich

1489

Vyatka

Perm 1724

Yekaterinb-

Kungur

Yekaterinb 1725

ESTONIA *1721*

L. Peipus

1478

Novgorod

L. Ilmen

Kostroma

Yaroslavl

MARI

UDMURTY

Baltic Sea

LIVONIA

Pskov

1510

R. Lovat

Tver

Dmitrov

Nizhniy Novgorod

KHANATE OF KAZAN *1552*

Kazan

R. Belaya

BASHKIRS

Ufa 1586

Riga

Western Dvina

1772

1503

Velikiye Luki

1514-21

1494

Mozhaysk

Moscow

Vladimir

Arzamas

Simbirsk 1648

Memel

COURLAND

LITHUANIA

Polotsk

Vitebsk

Vyazma

Smolensk

Serpukhov

Kaluga

Murom

MESHCHERA

CHUVASHI

MORDVA

R. Niemen

Minsk

Mogilev

1772

1494

Kolomna

Ryazan

Tula

1521

Penza 1650

R. Sura

Samara 1586

Syzran 1683

Kalish

R. Vistula

Warsaw

1807

1793

Pinsk

Gomel

Bryansk

Orel 1564

Yelets *1592*

Voronezh 1586

Tambov 1636

Saratov 1590

R. Volga

Orenburg 1743

R. Ural

POLAND *1815*

Lublin

R. Pripet

Chernigov

Kursk 1586

1503

Belgorod 1593

Kamyshin

NOGAI TARTARS

Port Alexander

R. Dniester

Kamenets

1793

Bratslav

Kiev

Pereyaslavl

R. Dnieper

1667

Kharkov 1654

Poltava

R. Don

R. Donets

Tsaritsyn 1589

KHANATE OF ASTRAKHAN

KALMUKS

Guryev 1645

Novgorod-Volynskiy

BESSARABIA

MOLDAVIA

1791

Kishinev

ZAPOROZHYE

Sech

Yekaterinoslav (Kodak)1786

1739

R. Donets

DON COSSACKS

1739

1556

Aleutian Is.

Nikolayev 1789

Ochakov

Akkerman 1812

Odessa

Kherson 1774

KHANATE OF

1783

Taganrog

Azov

Cherkassk

R. Don

KALMUKS

Astrakhan

CRIMEA

Yevpatoriya

Sea of Azov

Koroh

Simferopol 1784

KUBAN COSSACKS

1783

R. Kuma

Sevastopol 1783

Yekaterinodar 1792

Stavropol

Caspian

Pyatigorsk

R. Terek

1784

1810

Sukhum-Kale

Vladikavkaz

DAGHESTAN

Sea

Poti

1804

1806

Kutaisi

1801

Derbent

Tiflis

GEORGIA

R. Kura

Baku

1805

AZERBAIJAN

1813

ceded temporarily by Persia 1723-32

Colonial America 1519-1783

The daring conquest of Mexico by Hernán Cortés in 1519-20 and of Peru by Francisco Pizarro in 1531-3 (page 69) laid the foundations of a huge Spanish colonial empire in the Americas. By 1535, when the crown established viceregal government in Mexico and Lima became the capital of Peru, all the major centres of indigenous population in the former Aztec and Inca empires lay in Spanish hands: an area four times the size, and containing eight times the population, of the country from which the conquerors had come. Although the frontiers of colonial settlement continued to advance – with new viceroyalties in New Granada (1739) and Rio de la Plata (1776) and new military governments in Texas (1718) and California (1767) – none of these later, sparsely inhabited conquests compared with Mexico and Peru in wealth and importance. Potosí in Peru and Zacatecas in Mexico became the largest producers of silver in the world, and by 1560 silver formed America's principal export to Europe.

Elsewhere on the continent colonization proved slower. The Portuguese only settled the Atlantic coast of South America after 1549 for fear that the French might do so. By 1600, although coastal Brazil had become studded with profitable sugar plantations and mills, worked by slaves from Africa, the Brazilian interior remained the domain of native Indian tribes until the 1690s, when the discovery of enormous gold deposits in the interior provoked a new wave of colonization. In the northwest, Russian explorers and traders pressed on; but by 1819 only 19 settlements existed between the Aleutian islands and California (map 1).

The Atlantic seaboard of North America, with its harsher climate and poor soil, also at first attracted few Europeans (who came mostly for fish and furs). Settlement only began with the foundation of Acadia (Nova Scotia) by the French in 1604, of Virginia (1607) and Massachusetts Bay (1620) by the English, and of New Amsterdam (later New York) by the Dutch (1624). Gradually, however, the Europeans pressed inland: the French advanced down the St Lawrence and (after 1682) the Mississippi, creating a chain of fortified posts all the way to the Gulf of Mexico and founding New Orleans in 1718; the English spread out around the rich fur-hunting grounds of Hudson Bay. Wars between the European states now regularly involved the Americas, with England gaining first the Dutch colonies along the Hudson (1664) and then French Canada (1763). By 1700, perhaps 250,000 Europeans lived in North America, but by 1820 that number had soared to 9 million (compared with just over 3 million in Spanish America).

The Spaniards in America relied from the first on Indian labour, both in ranching and mining, and readily intermarried; hence an extensive mestizo population developed, especially in Mexico and Peru.

The British, however, who wanted land for farms and plantations, expelled or exterminated the native population: by 1820, only 600,000 lived in the English speaking areas (compared with 7.5 million in Spanish America). Instead, in Virginia, and then later in the Carolinas, where tobacco was introduced as a cash-crop, African slaves were imported to work on the plantations (like those of the sugar producers of Brazil and the Caribbean islands). By 1820, almost 2 million Africans lived in North America (compared with 800,000 in Spanish America).

Throughout the period, each mother country maintained a tight grip on its colonies. The colonists tolerated this as long as they felt insecure – whether from the threat of native uprisings or through the series of wars between the mother countries. Britain's resounding victory over France in 1763, however, brought total security to her American colonies, whose elites soon came to resent the continuing tax demands of the government in London. In 1776 they demanded their independence (page 98) and the colonies of Latin America followed suit in 1808. (page 106).

RUPERT'S LAND
Fort Albany (Hudson's Bay Company's trading post) 1679
Rupert's House (Hudson's Bay Company's trading post) 1668
Fort Tadoussac (1600)
Quebec (1608) *capital of New France*
Trois Rivières (1634)
NEW FRANCE
L. Superior
Sablt Ste. Marie (1639)
Fort Frontenac (1673)
Albany 1664 NEW YORK
L. Huron
Fort Niagara (1679)
L. Michigan
Fort Pontchartrain (1701)
L. Erie
PENNSYLVANIA
Philadelphia 1682
Chester 1682 NEW JERSEY
Fort St. Joseph (1680)
Fort St. Louis (1682)
Fort Crèvecoeur (1680)
DELAWARE
Annapolis 1708
Ohio R.
VIRGINIA
MARYLAND
Missouri R.
Cahokia (1698)
Kaskaskia (1703)
Tennessee R.
NORTH CAROLINA
Fort Prudhomme (1682)
SOUTH CAROLINA
Mississippi R.
LOUISIANA
Pensacola (1696) *founded to counter French claims*
Fort Maurepas (1699)
Gulf of Mexico

1 The development of colonial America

- French territory
- Spanish territory
- Portuguese territory
- Dutch territory
- Russian territory
- British territory by 1763
- ceded by France to Britain 1763
- ceded by France to Spain 1763
- United States 1783
- international boundary
- provincial boundary
- major exports

colonisation route
- Spanish
- Portuguese
- British
- Russian
- French

Arctic Ocean

GREENLAND

unexplored

RUPERT'S LAND
(Hudson's Bay Company)

Hudson Bay

disputed by Russia and Spain

QUEBEC
St. Lawrence River
NEWFOUNDLAND
furs
ceded to Britain 1763
Quebec
Montréal
NOVA SCOTIA
whale products, fish

UNITED STATES OF AMERICA 1783

San Francisco

INTERIOR PROVINCES

LOUISIANA

Ohio R.

Mississippi R.

Los Angeles (1780)

THE THIRTEEN COLONIES

o Boston
New York
Philadelphia
Jamestown

naval stores, furs, fish, grain

North

tobacco, grain

Atlantic

WEST FLORIDA
New Orleans

skins

EAST FLORIDA
(Br. 1763-83)

Gulf of Mexico

Zacatecas

silver
Mexico

BAHAMA ISLANDS
(Br. 1783)

sugar, tobacco

CUBA

WEST INDIES

JAMAICA
(Br. 1655)

SANTO DOMINGO
SAINT-DOMINGUE
GUADELOUPE (Fr.)

silver

Belize
(Br. 1683)

CENTRAL AMERICA

Caribbean Sea

MARTINIQUE (Fr.)

CURAÇAO (Dutch 1634)

cochineal, gold

gold

Caracas

VENEZUELA

tobacco, cocoa beans, hides

Panama

Paramaribo

GUIANA

Cayenne

Santa Fé de Bogotá

drugs, rare plants

Pacific Ocean

Quito

gold, naval stores

R. Amazon

BRAZIL

Treaty of Tordesillas 1494/1506

R. São Francisco

dyewoods, sugar, tobacco, cotton

Bahía

PERU

silver, drugs

Lima

Potosí
Cuzco

UPPER PERU

R. Paraná

R. Paraguay

gold, diamonds

Rio de Janeiro

copper, grain

beef

CHILE

RIO DE LA PLATA 1776

Indian frontier

hides, silver

Buenos Aires

South Atlantic Ocean

FALKLAND IS.

---

2 European settlement in North America

- English settlements
- French settlements
- Spanish settlements

St. Lawrence R.

ILE ROYALE
ILE ST. JEAN

NOVA SCOTIA

NEW ENGLAND

MAINE

Penobscot 1628

Portsmouth 1653
Boston 1630
Plymouth 1620
Providence 1636

New Haven 1640
New York (New Amsterdam 1624-1664)

Atlantic Ocean

South-East Asia and Japan 1511-1830

In 1603 the Japanese emperor conferred the title of Shogun (military leader) on Tokugawa Ieyasu, who had established control over the state re-unified in the 1590s (page 64). The Tokugawa dynasty exercised power until 1868, giving Japan a much-needed period of political stability. A complex system of government emerged in which the shoguns in Edo (modern Tokyo) dominated or regulated the 250 or so fiefs of the feudal lords, organized society in a hierarchy of classes, and enacted a comprehensive legal code. From 1612 they banned the Christian missionaries (active in many areas since the mid-16th century) and persecuted their adherents. They also forbade all Japanese to travel abroad; limited foreign contacts to the Dutch (who maintained a trading post at Nagasaki), the Chinese and the Koreans; and until 1853 successfully repulsed various attempts by the Russians, British, French and Americans to open trade (map 1). Yet despite this isolation, Tokugawa Japan prospered: trade and cities grew rapidly; the population rose from 20 to 30 million; high literacy rates prevailed; industry and credit spread widely. By the mid-19th century, Japan was far better prepared than any other part of Asia to meet the challenge of Western expansion (page 116).

Initially, however, Western traders showed far more interest in the spices of South-East Asia. The disintegration of the empires of Srivijaya and Majapahit (page 60) left behind scores of petty states, with little cohesion, opening the way to Portuguese acquisition of Malacca (1511) and footholds in the Moluccas (page 74). Their presence at first changed little: in Asia they came to dominate the spice trade through a chain of fortified stations, linked by naval power, not to acquire territory. The arrival of the Dutch and then the English after 1595 (page 74) did not initially change this, for they too sought primarily to monopolize the spice trade, and even after the establishment of a fortress at Batavia (1619) the Dutch directed most of their territorial ambitions towards acquiring Portuguese and English bases, rather than to conquering native states. The only substantial European colony in the area remained the Philippines, where the Spanish authorities began to foster the cultivation of tobacco, sugar, hemp and other commercial products from the later 18th century (map 2).

The mainland monarchies of South-East Asia – Arakan, Burma, Siam, Cambodia, Luang Prabang and Annam – had little direct involvement in European trade, and concentrated instead on extending their power at the expense of their neighbours. Over the period as a whole, Annam (Vietnam) and Siam expanded at the expense of Luang Prabang (Laos) and Cambodia. Burma almost disintegrated after the Mons rebelled in 1740, set up a king of their own at Pegu, and in 1752 captured the Burmese capital

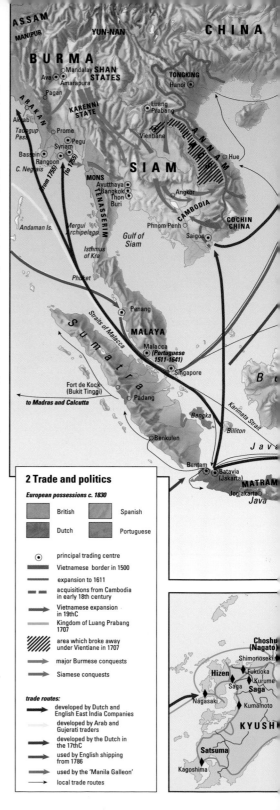

2 Trade and politics

European possessions c. 1830

	British		Spanish
	Dutch		Portuguese

⊙ principal trading centre

▬ Vietnamese border in 1500

▬ expansion to 1611

▬ ▬ acquisitions from Cambodia in early 18th century

➤ Vietnamese expansion in 19thC

▬ Kingdom of Luang Prabang 1707

▨ area which broke away under Vientiane in 1707

➤ major Burmese conquests

➤ Siamese conquests

trade routes:

➤ developed by Dutch and English East India Companies

➤ developed by Arab and Gujerati traders

➤ developed by the Dutch in the 17thC

➤ used by English shipping from 1786

➤ used by the 'Manila Galleon'

➤ local trade routes

of Ava. However a charismatic leader, Alaungpaya (1735-60), defeated the Mons and established Rangoon as the southern port of a reunited Burma (1755), while his successors invaded Siam (1767) and conquered Arakan (1785).

Two factors complicated state-building in the area: the constant pressure of the hill peoples of the interior (like the Mons), always eager to assert their independence, and the steadily increasing interference of the Europeans. A group of Iberian adventurers temporarily seized power in Cambodia in the 1590s; the French briefly garrisoned some Siamese strongholds in the 1680s; both the French and English East India Companies intervened in Burma in the 1750s. Meanwhile, the Dutch began to extend their control over Java and the Spice Islands, and at the same time the British established their base at Penang (1786) and a free trade port at Singapore (1819) on the Malayan peninsula.

These acquisitions led to tension between the two colonial powers, which only abated after a treaty in 1824 obliged the British to withdraw from Sumatra and the Dutch from Malacca. Secure in the east, the British now turned on Burma and, after a short war (1824-6), annexed Arakan, Assam and Tenasserim. The future Dutch and British colonial empires in South-East Asia were taking shape, but their control remained loose and indirect. Only after the industrial revolution, and the expanding demand for raw materials and markets, did the Europeans seriously impinge upon the lives and fortunes of the peoples of the region.

1 Japan in isolation

——	provincial borders
——	Five Highways
- - -	extensions to the Five Highways
——	secondary roads
——	sea routes
◆	important castle towns

feudal territories:

■ major Tokugawa domains

American, Russian, British and other naval visits

The Reformation 1517-1660

The decades around 1500 saw a great revival of popular religion in Latin Christendom, which the established church could not control. The fall of Constantinople (page 44) allowed the Roman church to ignore the Orthodox areas; and, except in Bohemia and Moravia, heresy scarcely existed in the West. Complacent, the Papacy failed to deploy its immense wealth adequately, producing widespread pluralism and absenteeism; this, coupled with the materialism of the hierarchy, discredited the Western church in the eyes of many Christians. Some, like Erasmus of Rotterdam (1466-1536) and Thomas More (1478-1535), hoped for spiritual renewal within the church; but in Saxony Martin Luther (1483-1546) criticized clerical abuse and in 1520 called upon the German nobility to reform the church. Meanwhile, inspired by Huldreych Zwingli (1484-1531), the magistrates of the Swiss canton of Zürich renounced allegiance to Rome.

These successful protests sparked others. By 1560, seven out of every ten inhabitants of the Holy Roman Empire no longer accepted papal authority, and Protestantism (as the dissident creeds became known) also prevailed in Scandinavia, the Baltic lands, and England. Further defections from Rome came through the teaching of John Calvin (1509-64) in Geneva. Calvinism made rapid progress in France, Poland, Hungary and Scotland (where it became the official creed after 1560).

In addition, a number of more radical sects sprang up, called 'Anabaptists' by their enemies because of their belief that only adult baptism was valid. They rejected ritual, spiritual and temporal authority, and many social conventions in favour of Biblical simplicity. Many combined evangelism with social protest, and participated both in the major rising of the German peasantry in 1524-5 and in the radical government of the city of Münster in 1534-5. Both movements were brutally repressed and Anabaptism, where it survived, became a secret, separate creed.

Eventually the Catholic church reformed itself. The Council of Trent (three sessions 1545-63) condemned abuses, defined doctrine, and created a more effective and educated clergy; at the same time new religious orders (most notably the Jesuits, incorporated in 1540) targeted key areas for reconversion. By 1650 the Protestants had been expelled from Bavaria (1579), Austria (1597) and France (1685), and the number of Protestant churches in Poland had declined from 560 in 1572 to 240 in 1650. Spain eradicated its small Protestant minorities, and in 1609 expelled its substantial Moorish population. In the Holy Roman Empire, however, the Protestants fought back, provoking the savage religious conflict known as the Thirty Years' War (page 86).

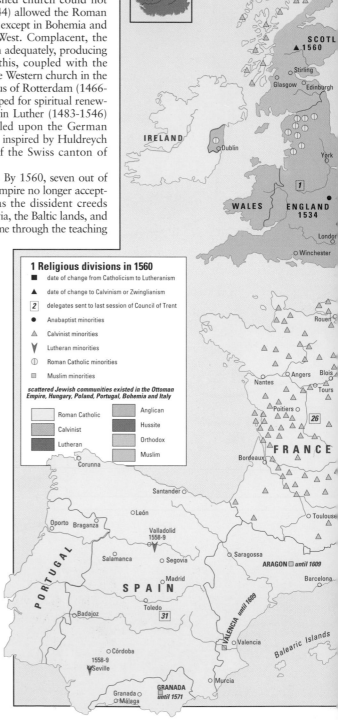

1 Religious divisions in 1560

■ date of change from Catholicism to Lutheranism

▲ date of change to Calvinism or Zwinglianism

2 delegates sent to last session of Council of Trent

● Anabaptist minorities

△ Calvinist minorities

Ⅴ Lutheran minorities

◑ Roman Catholic minorities

▢ Muslim minorities

scattered Jewish communities existed in the Ottoman Empire, Hungary, Poland, Portugal, Bohemia and Italy

- Roman Catholic
- Calvinist
- Lutheran
- Anglican
- Hussite
- Orthodox
- Muslim

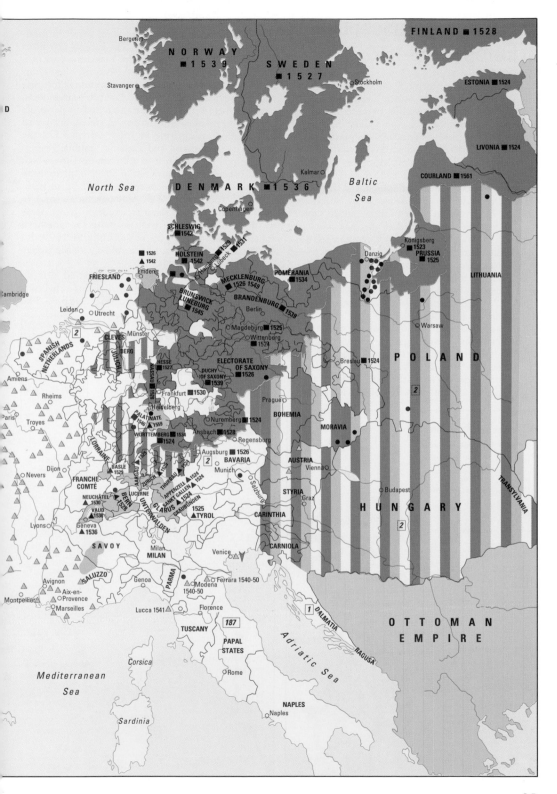

The Habsburg ascendancy in Europe 1519-1659

Charles V's election as Holy Roman Emperor in 1519 created a Habsburg hegemony in Europe. He already ruled lands in Austria, South Germany and the Netherlands, and the realms bequeathed by his maternal grandparents in Spain, Italy and North Africa. Each of these inheritances soon increased. In 1526 his brother Ferdinand succeeded to the crowns of Bohemia (which included Moravia, Silesia and Lusatia) and Hungary. In 1535 Charles himself acquired both Lombardy and Tunisia, and throughout his reign he added to his holdings in the Netherlands (map 1). Moreover, in America, his Castilian subjects toppled first the Aztec and then the Inca states (see page 80). Although at Charles V's death in 1558 the central European lands (and the Imperial title) passed to Ferdinand and his successors, Charles's son Philip II also ruled a formidable inheritance. He, too, managed to extend it – adding the Philippines by conquest after 1571, and Portugal with her overseas possessions by inheritance after 1580.

Such centralization did not prove popular, however. Apart from provoking the enmity of France, which felt encircled, Charles V faced rebellions from his subjects in Spain (1520-2) and Germany (1552-5), the former provoked by taxation, the latter arising from religious dissent provoked by the Reformation (page 84). Philip II (1556-98) contended, in the Netherlands, with the longest-lasting revolt in modern European history (map 2). The various provinces inherited or acquired by Charles V became part of a single state only in 1548. Local customs, often guaranteed by charter against central government interference, nevertheless survived and Philip II's attempts to override them – both to raise taxes and to persecute heretics – provoked insurrection. A timely display of force stifled an uprising in 1566; but in 1572 the provinces of Holland and Zealand sustained rebellion, helped by the threat of a French invasion which made difficult a concentration of Spanish forces, until the cost of opposing them compelled Philip to withdraw his troops in 1576-7. Although forces loyal to (and maintained by) Spain reconquered many areas in the 1580s, fighting went on with the northern rebels for more than 20 years. Only in 1609 did Spain finally conclude a 12-year truce with the largely Calvinist Dutch Republic.

The Netherlands' struggle resumed during Emperor Ferdinand II's war against his rebellious subjects in Bohemia and Austria (map 3). The

2 Dutch Revolt, 1572–1648

- Netherlands boundary 1548
- rebel areas December 1572
- furthest extent of Dutch revolt (July 1577)
- rebel areas December 1606
- Dutch conquests 1621–48
- Dutch Republic 1648

3 The Thirty Years' War in Germany 1618–48

- route of the Spanish Army 1634
- route of Gustavus Adolphus 1631–32
- ✗ Imperial (Catholic) victory
- ✗ Imperial (Catholic) defeat
- boundary of the Holy Roman Empire
- areas affected by Edict of Restitution 1629
- ■ date region became Lutheran
- ▲ date region became Calvinist

the religious position in 1640:

- Lutheran
- Catholic
- Calvinist
- regained by Roman Catholics

1 The Habsburg Empire in Europe

- Aragonese inheritance of Charles V
- acquisitions by Charles V with date
- Austrian inheritance of Charles V
- acquisitions by Charles V with date
- Castilian inheritance of Charles V
- Burgundian inheritance of Charles V
- acquisitions by Charles V with date
- states favourable to Charles V
- 'The Spanish Road' connecting Habsburg dominions

ENGLAND

NETHERLANDS 1523–43

Brussels

LUSATIA 1526

SILESIA 1526

BOHEMIA 1526

MORAVIA 1526

HUNGARY 1526

BAVARIA

Vienna

LORRAINE

FRANCHE-COMTÉ

ALSACE

TYROL 1363

AUSTRIA

STYRIA

CARINTHIA AND CARNIOLA 1335

SAVOY

Genoa

LOMBARDY 1535

CROATIA 1526

NAVARRE 1512

PORTUGAL

CASTILE (including New World possessions 1492)

ARAGON

CORSICA (GENOESE)

SARDINIA

NAPLES

GRANADA 1492

Algiers 1510–25

Bugia 1510–55

Bona 1535–74

Bizerta 1535–74

SICILY

Melilla 1497

Oran 1509

TUNIS 1535–74

SWEDEN

Baltic Sea

from Stockholm

MECKLEN-BURG

Peenemünde

Wittstock 4 October 1636

BRANDENBURG
Berlin ▲1613

POLAND

Breitenfeld 17 September 1631

Liegnitz ○ ▲1611

Brieg ○ ▲1611

Prague ○

White Mountain 8 November 1620

BOHEMIA

Jankau 5 March 1645

MORAVIA

AUSTRIA

HUNGARY

STYRIA

Protestants were expelled from Austria (1597) and from Styria (1600). Encouraged by his success, with Spanish and Papal support Ferdinand turned in 1621 against the German Protestant states, especially the Calvinists. Despite aid from Britain, Denmark and the Dutch, they lost and in 1629 Ferdinand issued an 'Edict of Restitution' by which he reclaimed Church lands acquired by Protestant rulers. Swedish military aid turned the tables against the emperor, and saved the German Protestants from collapse: an army led by King Gustavus Adolphus routed the Imperialists at Breitenfeld (1631) and drove them from much of Germany. A Spanish army intervened to restore Habsburg fortunes but, although victorious at Nördlingen (1634), their aid to the emperor also provoked France to declare war first on Spain (1635) and then on the emperor (1636). The war turned into a free-for-all with fighting spreading to almost the whole continent.

After many more years of largely unsuccessful campaigning, at the peace of Westphalia (1648) the emperor was forced to abandon virtually all his powers in Germany, to agree to toleration for Protestants and Catholics, and to promise not to assist his Spanish cousins in their war against the Dutch rebels; by the peace of Münster (1648) Spain formally recognized the independence of the Dutch Republic (and their possession of all territories conquered since 1621); and by the peace of the Pyrenees (1659), Spain ceded all areas gained by France on the frontiers of both Spain and the Netherlands. The religious and political frontiers of central Europe which were agreed by these treaties lasted unchanged for 100 years. The Habsburg bid for European hegemony had failed.

China under the Ch'ing dynasty 1644-1911

A new era in Chinese history opened in 1644 when the Ming dynasty, beset for a century by Japanese raids, civil wars, and northern invaders (see page 64), fell to the forces of a Manchurian dynasty which ruled the country until 1911. The Manchu, or Ch'ing, rulers met with resistance in southern China for half a century, but quickly established a working relationship with the gentry who staffed the Chinese bureaucracy and, with its support, began a successful policy of territorial expansion which continued until the mid-18th century (map 1).

At the same time population trebled from about 100 million in 1650 to 300 million in 1800 and reached 420 million by 1850, while vast quantities of tea, silk, cotton, lacquer and porcelain were exported (mostly to Europe). But the financial strain of the wars of expansion and the pressure of the growing population on land and food caused hardships that led to recurrent unrest and revolt, not only among the ethnic minorities who were harshly exploited by Chinese and Manchus alike, but also in the heartland itself, beginning with the 'White Lotus' rebellion, 1795-1804. China remained the world's largest and most populous state, but its economic difficulties and inadequate bureaucracy prevented effective resistance to the pressures of the Western powers who sought to open the Chinese market for the goods produced by their empires.

China's defeat in the Opium War (1839-42) resulted in the cession of Hong Kong to Britain and the opening of the first five Treaty Ports (their number steadily increased) in which foreigners enjoyed extra-territorial rights. More seriously, it served to weaken imperial authority and encouraged the Taiping rebellion

1 Imperial expansion, 1644-1760

Manchu expansion
Phase 1: China

- Manchu homeland
- expansion before 1644
- expansion 1644-59
- 1644 date of incorporation

tributary states:
- before 1644
- after 1644

- sectarian risings of Chinese
- official centre of foreign commerce
- risings of non-Chinese people

Phase 2: New Territories
- 1724 date of incorporation
- border of China under the Ch'ing dynasty, at its greatest extent

2 The dismemberment of the Chinese Empire, 1842-1911

RUSSIAN EMPIRE

TANNU TUVA
Russian protectorate 1912

MONGOLIA
autonomous 1912

to Russia 1858
MARITIME PROVINCE

Manchouli
Aigun
Harbin
Suifen
Vladivostok
Hunchun

occupied by Russia 1897-1905
Japanese influence after 1905

ILI
to Russia 1864
to Russia 1871-81

Changchun
Mukden
Newchwang
KOREA
Japanese 1910

Yellow River (Huang Ho)
Kalgan
Peking
Tientsin
Taiyuan
Dairen
Port Arthur
Antung
to Russia 1898
to Japan 1905
Weihaiwei *British 1898*
Chefoo
Tsingtao *German 1898*

SINKIANG

CHINA

TIBET
autonomous after 1912
under British influence

R. Yangtze
Ichang
Chungking
Changsha
Yochow
Hankow
Wuhu
Kiukiang
Nanking
Chinkiang
Wusung
Shanghai
Soochow
Hangchow
Ningpo
Pukow

NEPAL
SIKKIM
BHUTAN
British protectorate 1817

ASSAM
British 1826

Wenchow
Santuao
Foochow
Tamsui
Taiwan to Japan 1895
Amoy

Ryukyu Is.
to Japan 1872

JAPAN

Tengyueh
Kunming
Mengtze
Manhao
Szemao
Lungchow
Nanning
Canton
Swatow
Kowloon *British 1898*
Hong Kong *British 1842*
Macao *Portuguese 1557*
New territories British 1898

BURMA
British 1886

FRENCH INDO-CHINA *1884*
Pakhoi
Haiphong
Kwangchowan *French 1898*
Kiungchow

LAOS
French 1893

SIAM

Hainan

to China under treaty of Nerchinsk 1689
R. Amur
MANCHURIA

1629-30
KHORCHIN

Mukden
(capital 1625-44)

KOREA
Manchu invasions
1627, 1636-37
vassal status
1637

Eight Trigrams sect
1786-88

1645
KIANGSU

1645
NHWEI

1646
CHEKIANG

1646
FUKIEN

TAIWAN
Dutch 1624-83;
Ming loyalists 1662-83;
incorporated into
China 1683

*rising of
aboriginal
peoples
1787-88*

Legend:

colonial possessions:

spheres of influence:

railways:
- – – – – Russian
- - - - - British
- –·–·– Japanese
- ·········· French
- ⊢⊢⊢⊢ German
- ⊢⊣⊢⊣ Chinese

boundary of Ch'ing Empire in 1850

Taiping rebel control 1853-7
Taiping rebel control 1857-63
states formerly tributary to China

Treaty ports and towns:
- ● 1842 Treaty of Nanking
- ◖ 1858 Treaty of Tientsin
- ◉ 1860 Peking Convention
- ◐ 1876 Chefoo Convention
- ◑ 1897 Sino-French Trade Convention
- ⊗ additional ports opened by 1911

(1850-64), the most serious of the many revolts that shook Manchu power. The Taiping and Nien uprisings alone left 25 million dead. These grave disorders also convinced the Western powers that Ch'ing China stood on the verge of collapse and encouraged them to secure a share: Russia gained the Amur basin, the Maritime Province (1858-60) and, temporarily, the Ili valley in Turkestan (1871-81); France occupied Indo-China (1884-5); Britain took Burma (1886); Japan annexed Taiwan (1895) and Korea (1910) (map 2). These losses convinced many Chinese that radical changes were inevitable, and when in 1911 a small mutiny broke out among the Manchu army, disaffection spread rapidly throughout the whole country and the imperial government collapsed (page 122).

India 1707-1947

Shortly after Aurangzeb's death in 1707 (page 58), Mughal power declined. In the north, Oudh and Bengal became effectively independently, owing only nominal allegiance to Delhi; in the centre, the power of the Maratha confederacy increased; in the south the Muslim state of Mysore expanded rapidly. Meanwhile European influence in India continued to increase, with both the French and English East India Companies acquiring new territory in the southeast. Robert Clive's victory at Plassey in 1757 gave the English control over the lands and resources of Bengal, Orissa and Bihar, allowing the Company to maintain an army of over 100,000 men – most of them Indian soldiers (sepoys) trained to fight in European fashion – with which they not only destroyed France's Indian ambitions but also extended their control over the entire eastern coast of the subcontinent (map 1). Mysore went down to defeat in 1799, the Marathas in 1805, both delivering extensive new territories to British control, and most other major Indian rulers soon recognized British suzerainty.

Over the next half-century the conquest of Sind (1843) and the Punjab (1849), brought the dominions of the Company up to the country's natural frontier in the northwest, while a war with Nepal (1814-16) extended them to the Himalayas. To the east the British clashed with the Burmese empire and in 1824-6 annexed Assam and Arakan (page 83). Within India, the 'Doctrine of Lapse' introduced by Governor-General Dalhousie (1847-56) resulted in the absorption of autonomous but dependent states, such as Oudh and several Maratha kingdoms, into the directly administered territories (map 2). Not surprisingly, this policy provoked disaffection which found violent outlet in 1857. Beginning as a mutiny of the Company's native soldiers, the revolt soon involved princes, landlords and peasants throughout northern India; but the loyalty of the Sikhs and the passivity of southern India enabled the British to restore control after 14 months of bitter fighting.

The mutiny proved a watershed in the history of British India. It thoroughly discredited the Company and in 1858 the London government assumed direct control. The subcontinent now acquired a pivotal position in Britain's Imperial system, leading to intervention in Afghanistan

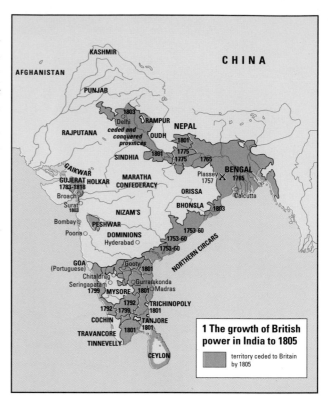

1 The growth of British power in India to 1805

☐ territory ceded to Britain by 1805

2 India, 1805–57

☐ territory under British rule in 1805

☐ territory under British rule at close of Lord Dalhousies's administration, 1856

– – – main area affected by Indian mutiny, 1857

to block Russian expansion into central Asia (page 108), and in Burma to counter French influence in Southeast Asia. From East Africa to China, the Indian army regularly acted to advance British interests. Within India, the autonomy of the princes was henceforth respected and active steps were taken to develop the economy: the construction of first-class roads and a major rail network, together with the opening of the Suez Canal in 1869, made possible the exploitation of raw materials and the introduction of export crops, such as tea. Between 1869 and 1929 India's foreign trade increased sevenfold. However, although some modern industries developed under Indian entrepreneurs, most of the trade involved importing British manufactures and exporting raw materials; and in most areas neither the character of the economy nor traditional agriculture experienced any basic change (map 3). The gross national product increased only slowly, while from 1921 (thanks to sustained population growth) per capita income declined.

The rise of a new middle class, partly through industry but more through the recruitment of educated Indians into the colonial administration, coupled with overt British racism, awakened a new political consciousness. The Indian National Congress (established with official blessing in 1885) at first accepted British rule, but soon developed an extremist wing which questioned the foreigners' right to rule India. The decision to partition the province of Bengal in 1905 provoked mass agitation and terrorist attacks; and from 1919, under the leadership of Mohendas K. Gandhi (1869-1948), Congress fought actively for home rule and, after 1929, for independence. Profiting from the unrest caused by unemployment and the world economic depression, Gandhi launched a civil disobedience campaign (1930-4) that galvanized the Indian masses, and forced Britain to pass the Government of India Act (1935) which provided a framework for participation in central and provincial government.

By 1937 Congress controlled 11 of the 14 provincial administrations, but failed to represent adequately the interests of the large Muslim minority whose leaders in 1940 passed a resolution calling for an autonomous Islamic state in the subcontinent: Pakistan. In 1942 Gandhi launched a 'Quit India' campaign and in 1946-7, faced by massive disaffection, a naval mutiny, and strong pressure from the United States, the British drew up hasty plans for partition along sectarian lines. India and Pakistan became independent in 1947, Burma and Ceylon in 1948 (page 152).

3 The Indian Empire in 1931

territory under British rule

territories permanently administered by Government of India (mostly tribal)

states and territories under Indian administration

Portuguese enclave

French enclave

Hindu majority provinces

Muslim majority provinces

area of Buddhist predominance

area of large Sikh population

— railways

cotton textiles

woollens

tea

chemicals

tobacco

sugar

rice mills

iron and steel (large scale)

metals

machinery and transport material

shipping

mills (various grains)

The age of revolution
1755-1815

The later 18th century saw unprecedented uprisings throughout the western hemisphere (map 1). Many reflected a long-standing desire for independence, as in Corsica (1755, 1793), Haiti (1791), Sardinia (1793),

1 Revolts and revolutions in Europe and America

—— borders in 1789

■ areas affected by revolution 1773-1814

Ireland (1798), Serbia (1804) and Spain (1808). Most, however, owed something to the Enlightenment, a European intellectual movement which emphasized certain fundamental rights of human beings and rejected traditional authority. Paradoxically, this could lead to rebellions by conservative elements against reforming rulers – such as the Austrian Netherlands (1787)

2 The Empire of Napoleon

- French territories ruled directly from Paris c.1810
- states ruled by members of Napoleon's family c.1810
- other dependent states c.1810
- British or British occupied territory

- ☒ French victory
- ☒ French defeat
- ☒ battles of the Italian campaign
- ☒ battles of the War of the Second Coalition
- ☒ battles of the War of the Third Coalition
- ☒ battles of the Austrian War of 1809
- ☒ battles of the Peninsular War
- ☒ battles of the Russian campaign
- ☒ battles of the War of Liberation from French Rule
- ☒ battles in the defence of France
- ☒ battles of the War of 100 Days

and Hungary (1790) against the 'Enlightened' policies of Emperor Joseph II – or the resistance of colonial societies to the centralizing policies of the home government – as in North America after 1775 (page 98) and in South America after 1808 (page 106). More commonly, however, opposition came from the middle classes: against a closed patriarchate in the Dutch Republic (1785-7); against the absolute monarchy and its aristocratic supporters in France.

In France, between 1789 and 1791 a representative assembly, summoned to solve a financial crisis, abolished feudalism, and created a constitutional monarchy and equality before the law. The king, however, refused to cooperate and was deposed in 1792, provoking Austrian, Prussian and (from 1793) British attempts to overthrow the Republic by force. They failed: instead, the revolutionary government in Paris purged its opponents at home and, by mobilizing unprecedented numbers of its citizens, conquered the Low Countries, Switzerland and Italy, imposing satellite republics.

In 1799 a successful general, Napoleon Bonaparte, took power as military dictator. He secured peace

abroad (1802), and reorganized French local government, laws and education. But Britain declared war again in 1803 and, although her command of the seas (confirmed at Trafalgar, 1805) provided immunity from invasion, Napoleon defeated her continental allies – Austria, Prussia and Russia – in a brilliant series of battles (1805-7). Next, in order to create a continental blockade against British trade, Napoleon overran Spain (1808) and extended France's frontiers to Catalonia, the Baltic and Rome (1809-10). However Britain supported his opponents in the Iberian peninsula, expelling French forces by 1814. Meanwhile Russia's refusal to cooperate in the continental blockade led to a French invasion in 1812 which, although it reached Moscow, exhausted Napoleon's resources and led to his defeat and abdication in 1813-14 and again in 1815 (the 'Hundred Days').

Nevertheless, despite his failure, Napoleon's success inspired even his enemies: throughout the 19th century, Spanish, German and Italian reformers envisaged the state in essentially Napoleonic mode (page 110), while his administrative, legal and educational reforms in France survived the restoration of royal power.

93

The Industrial Revolution in Europe *c.*1750-1914

The Industrial Revolution, which began in England in the later 18th century, became the catalyst of the modern world. Nevertheless the speed of change can be exaggerated. Even in continental Europe its impact remained limited before 1850 to a few enclaves; and not until the last quarter of the century did the great surge forward occur. Outside Europe, except for the United States, industrialization took place even later (page 120). In 1895, even in Germany, one-third of the population still worked on the land, and most of eastern and southern Europe remained virtually untouched by industry.

Until 1900, when its lead began to be challenged by Germany and the United States, Great Britain remained the workshop of the world and its industrial strength, which enabled it to dominate world markets, explains its pre-eminence in the age of imperialism (page 112). Britain's precedence rested upon many factors. On the one hand, unlike much of the rest of Europe, it possessed abundant coal, iron and other basic materials, and it enjoyed an advantageous position in the Atlantic trade which generated much capital. On the other hand, it possessed several unique advantages. First, it escaped direct damage from the various wars that ravaged Europe between 1688 and 1815; second, unlike most continental states which bristled with customs barriers and internal frontiers, after the union of England and Scotland in 1707 Great Britain formed a single economic unit; third, again in contrast to continental Europe, the early disappearance of serfdom in England meant that the surplus labour released by rising agricultural productivity could move, without legal obstacles, to the growing industrial centres. Finally, England possessed a unique network of navigable rivers and canals (map 1), which proved of immense importance before the railway age for moving both raw materials and finished goods.

In its earliest phase, English manufacturers had also relied on water as a source of energy; but in the century to 1870 industrial power depended on steam, generated by the combustion of coal. At first, except in Britain and (from 1820) Belgium, steam

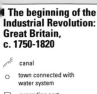

The beginning of the Industrial Revolution: Great Britain, c. 1750-1820

〰 canal

◦ town connected with water system

▢ expanding port

◯ expanding town

∴ coalfields

▲ iron ore mining

C copper mining

■ lead mining

▨ tin mining

power came only slowly, held back by political fragmentation, lack of capital and, above all, poor communications which severely limited markets. The steel firm of Krupps, founded in 1810 and later to be a giant of German industry, still employed only 7 men in 1826 and 122 in 1846. The pace of industrialization only accelerated with railway development. Between 1830 and 1870 the rail networks of Britain, Belgium and Germany became virtually complete, and construction began elsewhere. At much the same time, barriers to trade came down: France demolished her internal tariffs in 1790, Prussia followed suit in 1818 and in 1834 joined the German Customs Union, which included 17 states and some 26 million people.

A new period, sometimes called the Second Industrial Revolution, opened in the 1870s (see map 2). The new German empire (page 111) led the way, increasing its coal output from 38 million tons in 1871 to 279 million tons in 1913, and its iron output from 1.5 million tons to 15 million tons. But it also led in new areas of industrial enterprise, especially chemicals, electricity and steel. By 1910, Krupps employed 70,000 men. At a time of growing international tension (page 118), such rapid economic growth was bound to produce a reaction among Germany's neighbours and Russia began a campaign of rapid industrialization in 1890 (page 108), France in 1895 and Italy in 1905. In all these states, much heavy industry was keyed to armaments. Although the bulk of the population of Europe remained largely untouched, industrialization had both changed the face of the continent and rendered its future uncertain.

2 The Industrial Revolution in Europe, 1850-1914

areas of industrial concentration

▨ developed by 1850

▨ developed by 1914

■ centres of textile industry

∴ coalfields

▲ iron ore fields

▢ centres of engineering, armaments and metal industries

◖ lignite fields

◗ potash fields

❙ centres of petroleum and chemical industries

The emerging global economy *c.* 1775

In 1775, the areas of Spanish conquest and settlement in central and south America still ranked as the most valuable European overseas possession, thanks to the silver production of Mexico and Peru and the gold exports of Brazil, most of which went to Europe in return for manufactured goods. Along the Atlantic coast from Brazil to the Chesapeake, but above all in the Caribbean islands, plantation societies had developed to meet the rising demand both in Europe and in British North America (where over 2 million whites now dwelt) for tropical agricultural produce: cacao, tobacco, cotton and (especially) sugar. Since most plantations depended on the labour of African slaves, increased consumption in Europe meant increased shipments of slaves from Africa.

A closely integrated Atlantic economy had thus emerged. By 1775 the mainland colonies throughout the Americas were generally self-sufficient in food and some supported limited manufacturing. But their white populations consumed prodigious quantities of imported European manufactured goods, and prosperity almost everywhere depended on the ability to export to Europe. Transatlantic commerce, in turn, contributed substantially to the economic development of Spain, France and Britain (almost 40 per cent of whose total exports in 1775 went to America).

In Asia, although the volume of European trade also greatly increased in the 18th century, it remained largely confined to ports or small coastal enclaves to which Asian merchants delivered goods. The Dutch and English East India Companies, founded in 1600-2 (page 74), still dominated trade with maritime Asia, but the shipment of spices to Europe had by the 18th century been overtaken by a boom in textiles (above all silks and cottons) and new drinks (tea and coffee). Since, however, in contrast to the Americas, few European manufactures proved competitive in Asia (except in the Mediterranean ports of the Ottoman empire), increased imports of Asian goods generally depended on shipments of American silver, either re-exported from Europe or carried across the Pacific to the Philippines and thence to China.

1 The Atlantic economy

exports of goods in £ millions (x25 for approximate modern equivalent)

movement of migrants and slaves

sugar New World export commodities

GUIANA areas linked economically with Europe

European trade also stimulated the demand for export commodities from, and injected large quantities of silver into, India and China; but most of Asia's economic life remained relatively unaffected by contact with the West, and much of its long-distance trade continued to be conducted by Asian merchants using their own caravans of pack-animals or ships. However, conditions were changing rapidly in two areas of great economic importance: the British had gained control of Bengal, a major centre of textile manufacture, in the 1760s and now used its huge tax revenues to maintain a substantial army ready to annexe other areas of the subcontinent; and the Dutch in Java could impose commercial controls and receive commodities (above all coffee) as tribute.

Only Africa remained almost totally resistant to European penetration. Although the slave trade reached its apogee in the 18th century, with some 2.3 million slaves shipped out between 1770 and 1800, the prices paid by the Europeans for each slave steadily rose – suggesting that the African rulers who dealt in slaves more than held their own, despite the disruption arising from wars and slave-raiding, and the sustained loss of population.

In short, Europe's rapid commercial expansion overseas (for better or worse) hastened the economic integration of the world. The Americas outside the plantations enjoyed a degree of self-sufficiency, but Europe still determined the economic development of much of the continent. Although, except in Bengal, Java and the Philippines, the West could not yet shape the economies of Asia and Africa, with Britain now poised to conquer India (page 90) and with the Industrial Revolution underway in Europe (page 94), the stage was set for the creation of an integrated global economy.

2 Trade in Africa and Asia

	routes of European trade
	routes of trade primarily of African and Asian merchants
coffee	African and Asian export commodities
•	centres of European trade in Africa and Asia

East India Company trade: value of imports to Europe		
	British	Dutch
Bengal	£800,000	£200,000
China	£300,000	£250,000
Madras	£200,000	-
Bombay	£100,000	-
Batavia	-	£200,000
Ceylon and Coromandel	-	£150,000
Total	**£1,400,000**	**£800,000**

Levant trade: value of imports to Europe	
French £2,200,000	Dutch £1,100,000
British £600,000	Venetian £600,000

The United States 1775-1865

The disputes and difficulties leading to the American War of Independence and the foundation of the United States began almost immediately after the English victory over France. In the Seven Years' War (page 80) Britain began to reorganize her vastly expanded North American possessions, establishing a huge Indian reserve west of the Alleghenies (1763) and extending the boundaries of Quebec (formerly French Canada) to the Mississippi and Ohio rivers (1774). The 'thirteen colonies' bitterly resented both this check to their westward expansion and the simultaneous insistence by Britain that its colonies should henceforth bear a greater share of the costs of their defence. Armed opposition began at Lexington and Concord in Massachusetts in 1775 (map 1). The colonies' representatives declared Independence in 1776, compelled the main British field army to surrender at Yorktown (1781), and fought on until the Treaty of Versailles (1783) recognized their sovereignty and extended the frontiers of the 'United States of America' to the Great Lakes and the Mississippi.

Expansion now proceeded rapidly. In 1783 the new republic comprised some 800,000 square miles (2,072,000 km²) of territory, but the purchase of Louisiana from France (1803) more than doubled its size. West Florida was taken by force in 1812 and East Florida (60,000 square miles, 155,400 km²) during the presidency of James Monroe. Thereafter extensive territories in the south and west were added, largely at the expense of Mexico (map 2), and in 1846 a compromise with Britain was reached over Oregon, increasing the number of states from 13 to 34. The population expanded from 3 million in 1783 to 31 million in 1860, fuelled by the arrival of a new wave of European immigrants, predominantly German and Irish.

2 Territorial expansion, 1803–1853

expansion of white settlements by

1750	1850	largely unsettled by 1890
1790	1890	

HUDSON'S BAY COMPANY

QUEBEC OHIO

Allegheny Mountains

LOUISIANA
to Spain, 1763

INDIAN RESERVE

NORTH CAROLINA

Camden ✕
August 1780

SOUTH CAROLINA

GEORGIA

WEST FLORIDA
to Britain, 1763-83

EAST FLORIDA

Gulf of Mexico

Oregon Country 1846

1818

Louisiana Purchase from France 1803

USA 1783

Mexican Cession 1848

Gadsden Purchase 1853

MEXICO

Texas annexed 1845

West Florida annexed 1812

East Florida annexed 1819

These developments had important political consequences. The ruling elites of the southern states, with their plantation economy and large black slave population, felt increasingly threatened by the industrializing north and the growing Midwest. This, rather than the issue of slavery, underlay the American Civil War (1861-5); but the issues in fact proved inseparable because, with over 90 percent of the black population living in the South, the moral question was also a regional question. Abraham Lincoln, elected President in 1860 by the votes of the Northern states, was right to claim that the nation could not permanently remain 'half slave and half free'.

Soon after Lincoln's election, South Carolina seceded from the Union and was quickly joined by ten other states which came together as the Confederate States of America with their capital at Richmond, Virginia (map 3). For Lincoln the fundamental issue was whether a constitutional republic could preserve its territorial integrity; he recognized no constitutional right of secession. By 1863, however, pressure from radical Republicans added the aim of freeing the slaves in the rebel states to the commitment to restore the Union. Thanks to the superior military skill of their commanders, and to their shorter lines of communications, the confederacy fought on for four years (1861-5). The Northern strategy was to deny the South vital resources by a naval blockade, to gain control of key river routes and forts in the west and to capture Richmond. Eventually the superior demographic and economic resources of the North prevailed – albeit at the cost of 635,000 Union and 383,000 Confederate military casualties – and created the 'second American Revolution' which, by crippling the southern ruling class and liberating its labour force, determined that the thrusting, urban, industrialized North, with its creed of competitive capitalism, would stamp its pattern (for good or ill) on the entire United States.

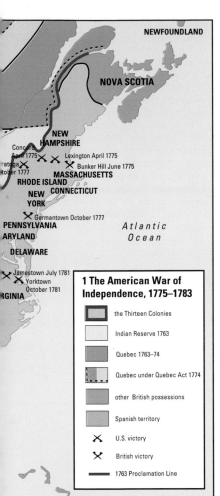

1 The American War of Independence, 1775–1783

- the Thirteen Colonies
- Indian Reserve 1763
- Quebec 1763–74
- Quebec under Quebec Act 1774
- other British possessions
- Spanish territory
- ✗ U.S. victory
- ✗ British victory
- — 1763 Proclamation Line

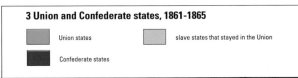

3 Union and Confederate states, 1861-1865

- Union states
- Confederate states
- slave states that stayed in the Union

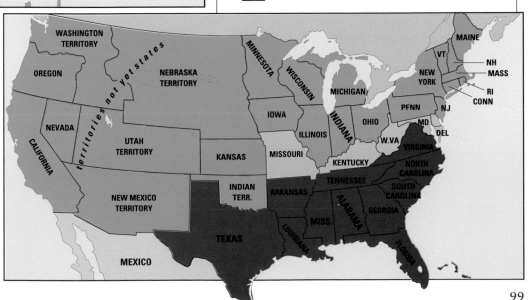

Australia and New Zealand from 1788

Although Australia and New Zealand were reconnoitred by the Dutch explorer Abel Tasman in 1642, colonization only began in 1770 when James Cook raised the British flag at Botany Bay. New South Wales served as a penal colony from 1788 to 1839, as did van Diemen's land (later Tasmania) from 1804 to 1853, but in 1829 the British government, in order to forestall the French, claimed the whole Australian continent. Fear of France also led to the annexation of New Zealand in 1840. However, the geographical obstacles, the lack of exportable goods (at first chiefly seal products and sandalwood), and (especially in the case of New Zealand) the opposition of the indigenous population complicated the colonization process in both territories. In 1850, the total white population of Australia still numbered only 350,000, and that of New Zealand was less than 100,000.

The discovery of gold in New South Wales and Victoria in 1851 initiated a new phase, and encouraged the growth of the inland population. Even more important was the rapid growth of sheep-farming: in 1850 Australia sent 17,000 tons of wool to Great Britain, but 134,000 tons in 1879. Nevertheless, as centralizing systems of communications and transportation developed, the dominance of the coastal cities – especially Sydney and Melbourne – increased. By the 1890s, two-thirds of Australia's population lived in urban areas along the coast (a pattern that steadily intensified throughout the 20th century.) In New Zealand, where wool

1 The settlement and development of Australia

areas occupied by 1850

areas occupied by 1890

more than 2 persons per square mile 1961 (by statistical division)

no significant use c. 1960

■ penal settlements

○ settlements

railways:

before 1881

---- 1881-1900

— 1901-1920

after 1920

Melville Island 1824-9

Raffles Bay 1827-9

all Torres Strait and Barrier Reef Islands included in Queensland 1879

Darwin

Port Essington 1838-49

Groote Eylandt

Gulf of Carpentaria

Cooktow

overland Telegraph Line

Yampi Sound

Kimberley Plateau

Derby

Broome

NORTHERN

TERRITORY

Normanton

Croydon

part of NSW to 1863 part of SA 1863-1911 to Commonwealth of Australia 1911

Mount Isa

Cloncurry

Port Headland

Great Sandy Desert

Winton

Dampier

Pilbara

Barrow I.

Tropic of Capricorn

Alice Springs

Longre

Gibson Desert

Simpson Desert

WESTERN AUSTRALIA

Great Victorian Desert

26°S

Oodnadatta

SOUTH AUSTRALIA

29°S

Charle

Wiluna

Big Bell

Geraldton

R. Darli

Broken Hill

Kalgoorlie

Nullarbor Plain

Great Australian Bight

130°

Port Augusta

Whyalla

NEW SOUT

Perth 1829

Fremantle 1829

Esperance

Port Lincoln

Port Pi

Adelaide 1836

Augusta

Albany 1826

Launceston

Macquarie Harbour 1821-34 Maria Island 1825-32

Hobart 1803-53 Port Arthur 1830-77

VAN DIEMEN'S LAND (renamed Tasmania 1856)

Mildura

R. Muck

VICTORIA

separated from NSW 1

Ballarat

Melbou

Portland 1834

140°

Bas

20°

30°

120°

remained largely a South Island product, exports rose in value from £67,000 in 1853 to £2.7 million twenty years later. The development of the North Island, which was held back by the bitter Maori Wars (1860-71), only came after the introduction of refrigeration, which made possible the export of frozen lamb, butter and cheese. Dairy farming developed rapidly, and the North Island now drew ahead of the South in population.

Political development kept pace with economic growth. In 1855 New South Wales, Victoria, South Australia and Tasmania became self-governing colonies, followed by Queensland in 1859; in 1901 they joined together to form the Commonwealth of Australia. New Zealand, which had been divided in 1852 into six provinces, each with an elected council, became a united Dominion (after measures had been taken to safeguard the rights of the Maori population) in 1876. Both countries achieved sovereign status under the Statute of Westminster in 1931. The economy of both dominions remained heavily dependent on primary exports – wool, meat, grain and dairy products – which enjoyed preferential treatment in the British market. Even the spectacular discoveries of minerals, coal, oil and gas in and about Australia after 1950 went largely into exports. However Britain's decision to join the European Economic Community and dismantle 'imperial preference' in 1973 (page 156), coupled with the conviction that the countries of the Pacific Rim will become the economic hub of the world in the 21st century, drove both Australia and New Zealand to develop new economic activities and to foster trade with countries outside the British Commonwealth.

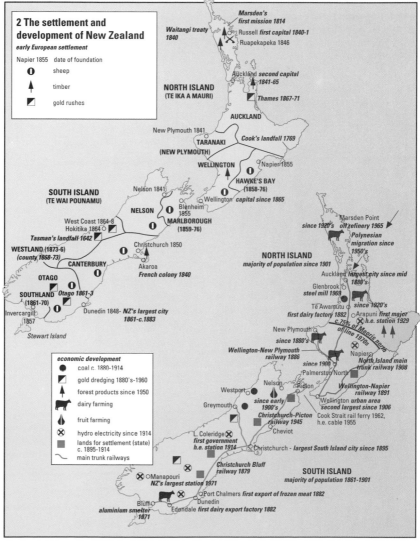

The decline of the Ottoman Empire 1798-1923

The period between 1798 and 1923 saw the disintegration and final collapse of the Ottoman Empire, the major power in the Near East since the 16th century (see page 66). Plagued by foreign invasions, wars, and the revolts of subject peoples demanding national independence, the empire steadily lost territory.

In 1798 a French army led by Napoleon Bonaparte invaded Egypt and Syria, only to be defeated by the British. Peace was arranged in 1802 and three years later the sultan appointed Mohammed Ali governor of Egypt. Under his rule, however, the province gained *de facto* independence and in 1841 Mohammed was recognized as hereditary viceroy. Meanwhile, between 1830 and 1847 the French conquered Algeria, and in 1881 they annexed Tunis; the following year the British occupied Egypt. There were also wars with Russia, rebellions in the Arab provinces and almost con-

stant revolts in the Balkans – starting with the Greek War of Independence in 1821, which resulted (following the pressure of foreign powers) in the recognition of a sovereign Greek state in 1830. Foreign intervention also precipitated the Crimean War (1853-6) and the Lebanese crisis of 1860-1, while Russian and Austrian demands helped secure the independence of Bulgaria, Montenegro, Serbia and Romania by 1878. By 1882, the Ottomans had lost 40 per cent of their empire.

Their finances also deteriorated rapidly until in 1875 the state became virtually bankrupt and Sultan Abdul-Aziz suspended payment of the interest due on the Ottoman debt. In 1881, he agreed to supervision of his treasury by European bankers: the empire's survival became dependent on foreign governments who preferred the preservation of a weakened Ottoman state   to   the

The decline of the Ottoman empire, 1798-1923

Ottoman empire by 1800	Turkey in 1920
Ottoman empire by 1914	

Areas of rule or control after the First World War

British	Spanish
French	Russian
Italian	frontiers after the First World War

dangerous power vacuum that would follow Turkish collapse. Nevertheless, further territorial losses followed: Italy annexed Libya in 1911 and, at the end of the Balkan wars in 1913 (page 118), the Ottomans surrendered Crete, most of the Aegean islands, Thrace, Macedonia and Albania. In all, between 1908 and 1911, the Turks lost 30 per cent of their remaining possessions.

Throughout the 19th century the sultans made various attempts to modernize their empire, but not always successfully: Selim III, who aimed to create a modern army, was deposed in 1807 when his troops mutinied against the proposed reforms. The Janissaries rebelled in 1826 against reforms decreed by Mahmud II, but this provoked their abolition. After a decade of agitation, in 1876 Sultan Abdul Hamid II introduced a constitution, and a Parliament met the following year; but it was dissolved almost immediately and only pressure by the Ottoman Society for Union and Progress

(the 'Young Turks') forced its restoration in 1908. The following year Abdul Hamid abdicated, and the Young Turks came to dominate the administration. However, their nationalist policies and opposition to any further surrender of territory contributed substantially to the Arabs' willingness to seek accommodation with the Turks' enemies, once the Ottoman empire entered World War I on the side of Germany and Austro-Hungary (page 124).

Despite tenacious resistance, the Turks were eventually defeated and the Middle East (despite earlier promises to the Arabs) came under the control of the victorious French and British governments. The Sultan collaborated with Great Britain after his defeat, and in 1920 agreed to the treaty of Sèvres which envisaged the dismemberment of the empire. However, the arrival of Greek troops at Izmir provoked a nationalist uprising which crystallized around the Turks' only undefeated general, Mustafa Kemal. The sultanate was abolished and, after some reverses, Turkish forces drove the Greeks back and secured recognition of the sovereignty of the Turkish Republic at the treaty of Lausanne in 1923.

Africa in the 19th century

By 1870 the Western powers had finally ended the slave trade, responsible for the forced migration of at least 10 million Africans to the Americas since 1500. Otherwise, however, Europe's impact on the African interior remained limited to two areas: Algeria, conquered by France between 1830 and 1847, and Cape Colony, where Dutch settlers (subjected to British rule after 1806) moved north-east in the Great Trek (1835) in search of land and freedom, and founded settlements which eventually became the Orange Free State and Transvaal. In West Africa, the followers of a Muslim religious leader from Hausaland, Uthman dan Fodio, conquered much of Upper Nigeria after 1804, and Uthman's son became sultan of Sokoto. Somewhat later, two other charismatic Islamic leaders also carved out new states: al-Hajj Umar north of the Niger in the 1850s, and Samory south of it in the 1870s and '80s. In the north-east, Mohammed Ali of Egypt conquered northern Sudan in 1820, and his grandson Ismail consolidated Egyptian control over much of the littoral of the Red Sea. Finally, in the south, the formation of the Zulu kingdom by Shaka in 1818 led to widespread disruption as neighbouring peoples moved away from the aggressive new state.

Meanwhile, the progress of industrialization in Europe (page 94) created a demand for new sources of raw materials and new markets, while the mass-production of quinine (which offered protection against the malaria endemic in Africa) and machine-guns gave the Europeans the ability to satisfy these demands by force. In the 1870s the French advanced inland from Senegal while the British began the conquest of Nigeria. In 1882 the British invaded and occupied Egypt, and the Belgians advanced up the Congo river. Next, Germany laid claim to Togoland, the Cameroons, South-west Africa and East Africa, each move provoking parallel actions by other powers. Portugal revived her effort to colonize the interior of Angola and Mozambique, while Britain claimed parts of East Africa (later Kenya and Uganda) and, on the initiative of the Cape politician and industrialist Cecil Rhodes, central Africa (later Zimbabwe, Zambia and Malawi).

Even larger gains accrued to the French, who swept into sub-Saharan Africa from three directions and gained control over almost one-third of the continent (map 1). With the conquest of Libya and Cyrenaica by Italy in 1911 and the partition of Morocco between France and Spain in 1912, of the 40 political units into which Africa had been arbitrarily divided, only two could claim any real independence: Ethiopia, which had defeated an Italian attempt at annexation in 1896, and Liberia, which enjoyed financial support from the United States. In little more than a generation, the Europeans had gained control over an additional 12 million square miles of territory.

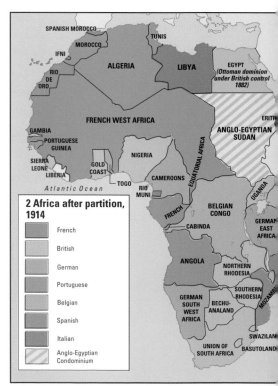

2 Africa after partition, 1914

- French
- British
- German
- Portuguese
- Belgian
- Spanish
- Italian
- Anglo-Egyptian Condominium

Algiers 1830 (French occupation)
ALGERIA 1870
TUNIS
○ Tunis
TRIPOLITANIA
○ Tripoli 1911
LIBYA
○ Ghadames
○ Benghazi 1912
CYRENAICA
Alexandria ○
Cairo ○
ARABIA
Mediterranean Sea
10°
30°
20°

○ In Salah 1901 (French)
FEZZAN
S a h a r a   D e s e r t
EGYPT
Red Sea

○ Tamanrasset 1902 (French)
S u d a n
○ Bilma
Agadès ○
NIGER
Gao ○
Zinder 1899 ○
Sokoto 1903 (British) ○
○ Say 1896
NIGERIA
Zaria ○
Kano 1902 ○
Lake Chad
○ Port Lamy
RABIH'S DOMAIN
SUDAN
Sudan – Anglo-Egyptian Condominium established 1899
○ Omdurman
○ Khartoum
○ Massawa
Adowa 1896 ✕ Italian invasion defeated
ETHIOPIA
Djibouti ○
Berbera ○
10°
50°
30°

Mahdist State in the Sudan 1881–98
○ R. Nile

SOKOTO
NIGERIA
Northern Nigeria occupied by Royal Niger Company
○ Nikki 1894
ILORIN
NUPE
○ Lokoja 1885
○ Ibadan
YORUBA
○ Lagos
TOGO
DAHOMEY
CAMEROONS
○ Douala 1884
○ Fashoda 1898 (British)
SHOA
○ Addis Ababa
Ethiopian expansion under Emperor Menelik
ITALIAN SOMALIA 1889–1892
○ Gondokoro
SIDAMA KINGDOMS
○ Mogadishu

Principe and São Tomé (Portuguese)
RIO MUNI
GABON
0°
FRENCH CONGO
○ Cabinda
○ R. Congo
CONGO FREE STATE
King Leopold's Congo Free State (became Belgian Congo in 1908)
TIPPU TIB'S DOMAIN
UGANDA 1893
○ Kampala 1890
BRITISH EAST AFRICA (KENYA)
Imperial British East African Company
○ Nairobi
Lake Victoria
GERMAN EAST AFRICA
○ Mombasa
○ Zanzibar *(British 1890)*
Dar es Salaam 1885 (German occupation)
Lake Tanganyika
Indian Ocean
0°

○ Luanda
10°
○ Benguela
ANGOLA
○ Moçâmedes
KATANGA
Lake Nyasa
British Central Africa (Nyasaland) Protectorate 1891
○ Zomba
○ Mozambique
NORTHERN RHODESIA
○ R. Zambezi
○ Quelimane
10°

○ Swakopmund
Walvis Bay 1878 (British)
GERMAN SOUTH WEST AFRICA
○ Salisbury
SOUTHERN RHODESIA
Rhodes's British South Africa Company
Pioneer Column 1890
○ Beira
MOZAMBIQUE
MADAGASCAR
○ Tananarive
○ Tamatave
20°

○ Lüderitz
BRITISH BECHUANALAND
TRANSVAAL
○ Pretoria
○ Johannesburg
Delagoa Bay
Merina Kingdom
20°
40°

○ Kimberley
Orange R.
ORANGE FREE STATE
○ R. Vaal
NATAL
○ Durban
CAPE COLONY
○ East London
30°

○ Cape Town
○ Port Elizabeth
20°

FRENCH SOMALILAND
BRITISH SOMALILAND
ETHIOPIA
ITALIAN SOMALILAND
BRITISH EAST AFRICA (KENYA)
MADAGASCAR
Indian Ocean

Legend:
1 European penetration after 1880
→ French colonies or settlements 1880
→ French penetration
→ British colonies or settlements 1880
→ British penetration
→ Portuguese colonies or settlements 1880
→ Portuguese penetration
→ German penetration
→ Italian penetration
→ Spanish penetration
→ Belgian penetration
★ anti-colonial resistance

105

Latin America 1808-1929

Napoleon's invasion of Spain and Portugal in 1808 (page 93) enabled these countries' American colonies to gain independence. The revolt began in Argentina in 1810 and in Venezuela in 1811, helped by the decision of Great Britain and the United States to oppose intervention by the Iberian powers. The fall of Lima (1821) and Simón Bolívar's victory at Ayacucho (1824), deprived Spain of control over South America. I·· the North, early rebellions in Mexico were suppressed, but in 1823 a republic was proclaimed, and a last Spanish attempt at reconquest in 1829 met with defeat. Only Brazil made the transition to independence peacefully, as Portugal agreed to provide a constitution and in 1822 the Portuguese king's eldest son became Emperor Pedro I of Brazil. Only in 1889 when, following the abolition of slavery (1888), disgruntled plantation owners rose in revolt, did a federal republic replace the empire.

Independence remained in essence a political movement confined to the colonial aristocracy, who desired a transfer of authority without social change. The next half-century was dominated by military dictators who ruled in the interests of the privileged classes and squandered their assets on repeated territorial disputes. Mexico lost most, forfeiting vast territories to the United States (see page 98); but it was also the first state to introduce limited social reforms after the election of the Indian Benito Juarez as President in 1858.

A subsistence economy still prevailed in most areas. Although Brazil with its slave-operated coffee plantations offered an exception, elsewhere the great rural estates showed little interest in producing for the market. After 1880, overseas investment increased rapidly, but selectively, concentrated mainly in Argentina, Brazil, Mexico and Chile. Moreover, even there, the foreign stimulus shifted those economies sharply towards the export of primary products: grain and meat from Argentina, nitrate from Chile, coffee and rubber from Brazil, oil from Mexico, and fruit from the so-called 'Banana Republics' of the central isthmus.

Most of these countries modernized and commercialized their production, and built docks and railways to expedite the export of food and raw materials. This attracted a new wave of immigrants and created a new urban and industrial proletariat as well as a middle class prospering from the export trade; but it left the majority of the rural population in abject poverty. Mexico under the repressive regime of Porfirio Díaz (1876-1911) exemplified these trends until in 1910 the country erupted in revolution: eventually, in 1917, a constitution incorporating major social and political reforms was adopted. Elsewhere, as long as prosperity continued – that is, until the Great Crash of 1929 (see page 130) – political and social pressures remained under control (albeit sometimes only thanks to armed intervention by the United States); but rapid and unbalanced economic expansion steadily undermined the regimes that promoted it.

1 Political development in Latin America

see map below left

Páez 1830–48

Guzmán Blanco 1870–88

Cartagena
Panama
Maracaibo
Caracas
Mompós
R. Orinoco
Angostura
Georgetown
PANAMA 1903
Antióquia
NEW GRANADA 1831
VENEZUELA 1830
BRITISH
Bogotá
DUTCH FRENCH
Cayenne
violent constitutionalism
COLOMBIA 1886
GUIANA
Balaiada 1839
Confederation of Equator 1824
García Moreno 1860–75
Quito
to Ecuador 1880
R. Amazon
RIO GRANDE DO NORTE
Guayaquil
ECUADOR 1830
Oriente
Iquitos
Tabatinga
Manaus
PARÁ
MARANHÃO
CEARA
to Ecuador 1880
RIO NEGRO (later Amazonas)
PARAIBA
Cabanagem 1835–40
PIAUI
PERNAMBUCO
ALAGOAS
Castilla 1845–62
PERU 1821
to Bolivia 1867
to Peru 1909
EMPIRE OF BRAZIL
kingdom 1815
empire 1822
republic 1889
GOIÁS
BAHIA
Lima
Callao
Cuzco
Ayacucho
Melgarejo 1864–71
Tacna
to Peru 1929
La Paz
BOLIVIA 1825
MATO GROSSO
Santa Cruz
MINAS GERAIS
Minas Novas
Arica
Potosi
Corumbá
Diamantina
ESPIRITO SANTO
Chilean gains
GRAN CHACO
SÃO PAULO
RIO DE JANEIRO
Rio de Janeiro
Jujuy
Conceptión
PARAGUAY 1811
Asunción
Ciudad Real
São Paulo
Sabinada 1837
Praieira 1848–49
Liberal Revolution 1842
SANTA CATERINA
Córdoba
RIO GRANDE DO SUL
Farroupilha Revolution 1835–45
Valparaíso
Mendoza
San Luis
Rosario
URUGUAY 1828 part of Brazil 1816-28
Santiago
Buenos Aires
Montevideo
Rio de la Plata
Battle 1903–15
Constitución
Rosas 1829–52
Valdivia
ARGENTINA 1810
conservative republic 1862–1910
aristocratic presidentialism
War of the Desert 1880–81
Patagonia
FALKLAND IS. (ISLAS MALVINAS)
1770–1820 Spanish
1820–33 Argentine
1833 British

Legend:

northern boundary of Mexico, 1824

Mexico, 1867

1821 date of independent statehood

Republic of Colombia, 1819–30

United Provinces of Central America, 1823–38

later Brazilian acquisitions

areas affected by Mexican revolution from 1910

disputed between Ecuador and Peru

disputed area between Bolivia and Paraguay

▽ caudillismo (military dictatorship)

○ revolutionary movements

◇ constitutionalism

□ radical reformism

French territory   Dutch territory
British territory   Spanish territory

GUADELOUPE *French*
MARIE GALANTE *French*
DOMINICA *British*
MARTINIQUE *French*

ST LUCIA *British*
BARBADOS *British*
GRENADA *British*
TRINIDAD *British*

The expansion of the Russian Empire 1815-1917

For 40 years after the Congress of Vienna (1815) Russia remained the strongest military power in Europe, focusing her interests on the Balkans and on the straits leading from the Black Sea. Since most Balkan subjects of the Ottoman empire were Orthodox Slavs, Russia considered herself their natural protector; and because Turkey lay in the way of Russia's access to the Mediterranean, it desired Constantinople to remain amenable to Russian influence alone. However, France and Austria also had imperial ambitions in these areas, while Britain opposed any further Russian expansion. In 1854, therefore, following Russia's invasion of Turkey's Danubian provinces and destruction of the Ottoman fleet, France and Britain (supported by Austria) declared war and invaded the Crimea, eventually forcing Russia to evacuate the Balkans and to dismantle its Black Sea fleet. A further Russian attempt to liberate the Balkan Slavs from Turkish rule in 1877-8 also failed (page 102).

Russia proved far more successful in Asia (map 1). Her forces subdued the Kazakhs (1816-54), completed Russian control of the Caucasus (1857-64) and annexed the khanates of central Asia (1865-76). The imperial frontier now reached – and sometimes penetrated – the great mountain chains that separated it from Persia, Afghanistan, India and China. The colonization of North America also continued into the early 19th century, and forts were built as far south as California; but most were soon abandoned and Alaska was sold to the United States in 1867. On the other hand, China ceded to the Tsar the Amur basin and parts of the Pacific coast (where Vladivostok was founded in 1860), and leased Port Arthur (1898). This warm-water harbour, unimpeded by winter ice, was soon linked to the main Trans-Siberian railway (completed in 1903). But Russian expansion conflicted with Japanese designs. The two powers had already clashed over their interests in Korea and south Manchuria, following Japan's victory over China in 1894-5 (page 116), and in 1904-5 Japan attacked Russia, forcing her to return most of her gains in the Far East.

This humiliating defeat fanned the flames of domestic unrest. Shaken by the backwardness exposed in the Crimean War, Tsar Alexander II (1855-81) had initiated a number of reforms in the 1860s: new local government organizations; educational improvements; and radical changes to the legal system. The emancipation of the serfs in 1861 was the cornerstone of the reforms. However, still confined to their villages, many peasants felt aggrieved that they often had to acquire by purchase less land than they had previously worked. At the same time, from 1890 the government embarked on an industrialization programme with railways at its centre. Many of the lines aimed to facilitate the movement of troops to frontier areas in case of war, but it allowed not only migration from overcrowded central Russia to western Siberia, but also the movement of peasants to urban areas to man a growing number of factories. Between 1863 and 1914 Russia's urban population increased from 6 to 18.6 million.

In 1905, in the wake of Japan's victory, revolutionary parties proved quick to exploit the low incomes and general hardships created by these rapid changes, while the new professional classes pressed for political

1 Russia in Asia, 1815-1900

the Russian Empire, 1815

acquisitions 1816-56

acquisitions 1856-76

acquisitions 1877-1900

vassal khanates

railway

Arctic Ocean

Yukon R.

ALASKA

Bering Strait

Bering Sea

Kamchatka

Port Alexander

sold to USA 1867

Aleutian Is.

Kurile Islands
to Japan 1875

2 The first Russian revolution, 1905

● major strikes and armed workers' uprisings

▬ peasant unrest and land seizures

▲ workers' soviets

■ army mutinies

⬆ naval mutinies

– – – voyage of the battleship Potemkin

reform (map 2). Unrest in the towns spread to the countryside and even to the Black Sea fleet, led by the battleship Potemkin, forcing Tsar Nicholas II (1894-1917) to grant a constitution, including a *duma*, or parliament; but by 1907 the government had regained full control. Nevertheless the 1905 revolution irreparably weakened the old order, and after 1912 another wave of social unrest swept the empire. Internally, Russia was in no position to meet the challenge of the First World War in 1914.

109

Nationalism in Europe 1815-1914

Nationalism flourished in Europe in the wake of the French Revolution (page 93), but it remained confined largely to the middle classes and proved relatively short-lived. The Great Powers at the Congress of Vienna in 1815 aimed to restore Europe (as far as possible) to its pre-war condition by combating both liberalism and nationalism and by creating a barrier around France. To that end Holland received the Austrian Netherlands (later Belgium); Prussia took over Westphalia and much of the Rhineland; Sardinia-Piedmont annexed Genoa; Russia retained Finland and most of Poland; and Austria gained Venetia and Lombardy.

By 1830, however, when a new wave of liberal and national agitation arose, the Great Powers no longer worked in unison, enabling Greece (page 102) and Belgium to obtain independence. In 1848-9, when an outburst of nationalism erupted into full-scale revolution, the solidarity of the conservative powers – coupled with divisions among the nationalists themselves – still sufficed to maintain

1 The unification of Italy, 1859-70

- Kingdom of Sardinia in 1815
- territory annexed 1859
- territory annexed May 1860
- territory annexed November 1860
- territory annexed 1866
- territory lost to France 1860
- French from 1768, formerly Genoese
- ----- Italian border 1914

2 The unification of Germany, 1815-71

- Prussia in 1815
- acquired by Prussia 1815-66
- —— boundary of German Confederation of 1815
- --- boundary of North German Confederation 1866
- Imperial territory of Alsace-Lorraine 1871
- • free city
- —— boundary of German Empire 1871
- ◀--- Austro-Prussian forces attack Denmark 1864
- ◀—— Prussian armies in the war with Austria 1866
- ◀--- German armies in the Franco-Prussian war 1870-71

the status quo. Shortly afterwards, a new generation of statesmen began to use nationalism for their own ends. Cavour sought a unification of Italy along conservative lines, in the interests of Piedmont-Sardinia, and was hostile to the more revolutionary nationalism of Garibaldi and Mazzini. Bismarck in Prussia, too, wanted unification to achieve his aim of a conservative, Prussian-dominated German state. Both used diplomacy and war to achieve their objectives: Cavour allied with France before attacking Austria in 1859, securing the unification of Italy (except for Venetia and the Papal States) by 1861 (see map 1). Bismarck allied with Austria in order to defeat Denmark (1864), then in concert with Italy attacked Austria (1866), and finally defeated France (1870-1),

achieving in the process the unification of Germany (map 2).

Liberal nationalists later endorsed both achievements, but neither satisfied the nationalism they had aroused. Italy still laid claim to the Alto Adige and Istria; Bismarck's 'Small German' solution, which excluded Austria, disappointed those who hankered after a Greater Germany. Nevertheless, the four short wars fought between 1859 and 1871 solved the Italian and German questions, and re-drew the map of Central Europe. Moreover, the Great Powers now remained at peace for over four decades, and although nationalist grievances continued to fester, territorial disputes within Europe ceased to divide most governments.

Imperialism 1830-1914

Until 1830, the search for oriental luxuries remained the driving force behind European imperialism, and (with the important exception of India: page 90) the European stake in Asia and Africa remained confined to trading stations and the strategic outposts necessary to protect trade. Thereafter two new factors transformed the situation. First came the enforced 'opening' of the key markets – Turkey and Egypt (1838), Persia (1841), China (1842), Japan (1858) – to European, particularly British, commerce. Then, from the 1870s, a new phase of the Industrial Revolution (page 94) provoked a search for raw materials to feed the new industries. In the scramble for these resources between 1880 and 1914, Europe added almost 9 million square miles (23.4 million km²) – one-fifth of the land area of the globe – to its overseas colonial possessions.

France and Britain took the lead. The former conquered Algeria after 1830, annexed Tahiti and the Marquesas in the 1840s, expanded its colony in Senegal in the 1850s and began the conquest of Indo-China in 1859. Britain, both to forestall the French and to safeguard its position in India, claimed sovereignty over Australia and New Zealand (page 100),

and acquired Singapore (1819), Malacca (1824), Hong Kong (1842), Burma (1852), and Lagos (1861) (map 1).

The same imperatives underlay British expansion after 1880, except that the number of competitors to forestall increased. Thus the French empire grew between 1871 and 1914 by nearly 4 million square miles (10.4 million km²) and 47 million people (mainly in north and west Africa and Indo-China, where Laos and Tongking were added to Cambodia and Cochin-China, but she also secured Madagascar and some Pacific islands); Germany also acquired an empire of 1 million square miles (2.6 million km²) and 14 million colonial subjects (in South-West Africa, Togoland, the Cameroons, Tanganyika and the Pacific islands); Italy obtained several outposts in Africa; the United States annexed the Philippines, Guam, Hawaii and some Caribbean islands; and Russia began to expand in central Asia. Britain too managed to acquire extensive new territories in Africa which almost linked Cape Town with Cairo, more Pacific islands (including Fiji), and parts of the Indonesian archipelago (map 2). She added 88 million subjects to her empire and, by 1914, exercized authority over a fifth of the world's landmass and a quarter of its peoples.

2 The colonial empires in 1914

(for 1815-70 see inset maps above)
colonial powers:

■ British	■ Dutch	**1883** date of European control
■ French	■ Italian	1822 date of independence
■ German	■ Spanish	Princely states of India
■ Portuguese	■ Belgian	—— spheres of influence
■ Ottoman	■ Russian	≡≡≡ proposed spheres of influence
		—— major sea routes

African colonies:

B. Basutoland
BE. Bechuanaland
D. Dahomey
G. Gambia
G.C. Gold Coast
I.C. Ivory Coast
N. Nyasaland
N.R. North Rhodesia
S. Swaziland
S.R. South Rhodesia
T. Togoland

In retrospect, the fragility of these European empires, so hastily assembled, is obvious. None of the imperial powers possessed the resources to govern them effectively and European imperialism proved more ephemeral than anyone at the time imagined; yet it left an indelible mark on the peoples of Africa and Asia, propelling them willingly or unwillingly into the 20th century.

1 Colonial expansion, 1815-70

(TO USA 1867)
CANADIAN CONFEDERATION
B.C. 1871
M. 1870
O. 1867
Q. 1867
N.B. 1867
N.S. 1867
1846
1848
1853
1845
USA

provinces of Canadian Confederation:
Q. Quebec
N.B. New Brunswick
N.S. Nova Scotia
B.C. British Colombia
M. Manitoba
O. Ontario

MEXICO 1821
CUBA (Spanish)
CENT. AMERICAN REPUBLICS 1821
COLOMBIA 1830
VENEZUELA 1830
ECUADOR 1830
PERU 1821
BRAZIL 1822
B. 1825
P. 1811

abbreviations:
P. Paraguay
B. Bolivia

Tahiti 1842
CHILE 1818
URUGUAY 1828
ARGENTINA 1816
Falklands Is (Islas Malvinas) British 1833

RUSSIAN EMPIRE
OTTOMAN EMPIRE
ALGERIA 1830
1846
CHINA
SENEGAL 1854-65
Suez Canal opened 1869
INDIA 1852
treaty ports:
S Shanghai
N Ningpo
F Foochow
A Amoy
C Canton
S. N. ON. OF. A. C
Macao
Hong Kong 1842
GAMBIA
PORTUGUESE GUINEA
SIERRA LEONE
Lagos 1861
OBOCK
ADEN 1839
CEYLON 1815
Malacca 1924
Singapore 1819
COCHIN CHINA
PHILIPPINES (Spanish)
GOLD COAST
SPANISH GUINEA
GABON
Seychelles 1815
SUMATRA
BORNEO
LABUAN 1846
NEW GUINEA
Ascension I.
St. Helena
ANGOLA
MOZAMBIQUE
Mauritius 1815
Réunion
JAVA
TIMOR
Indian Ocean
AUSTRALIA
NEW 185
CAPE COLONY
NATAL
WESTERN AUSTRALIA
S. AUST.
N.S.W.
VICTORIA
NEW ZEALAND 1840
TASMANIA

GERMANY
RUSSIAN EMPIRE
MONGOLIA
MANCHURIA
AUSTRO-HUNGARIAN EMPIRE
ITALY
1895
1873
TURKESTAN
1884-5
KOREA (to Japan 1910)
JAPAN
Samoa 1888-99 (to Germany)
Fiji 1874 (to UK)
Tonga 1900 (to USA)
MALTA
TUNISIA
CYPRUS (leased by UK 1878)
OTTOMAN EMPIRE
PERSIA
KUWAIT
CHINA
TIBET
LIBYA 1912
Suez Canal opened 1869
EGYPT 1882 (Ottoman Dominions under British control)
AFRICA
ARABIA
OMAN
Diu (Portuguese)
INDIA
Goa (Portuguese)
BURMA 1886
TONKIN
ANNAM
SIAM
FORMOSA (to Japan 1895)
Hong Kong (UK)
Macao (Portuguese)
PHILIPPINES (to USA 1898)
Guam (to USA 1898)
Marianas (Ladrones) 1899
Marshall Is. 1888
ANGLO-EGYPTIAN SUDAN 1898
ERITREA 1889
OBOCK 1884-8
Socotra 1876
Karikal (French)
Pondicherry (French)
Nicobar Is.
INDO-CHINA 1859-93
CAMBODIA
Caroline Is. 1899 (to Germany)
CAMEROON 1884
ABYSSINIA
BRITISH SOMALILAND 1884
ITALIAN SOMALILAND 1893
CEYLON
Maldives
MALAYA 1874-95
SARAWAK 1888
BRUNEI 1881
Pacific Islands
Gilbert 1892
Nauru
CONGO FREE STATE 1885
Uganda
BRITISH EAST AFRICA (KENYA)
GERMAN EAST AFRICA (TANGANYIKA) 1886
Zanzibar 1890
Singapore
SUMATRA
DUTCH BORNEO
NEW GUINEA
BISMARCK ARCHIPELAGO 1885
Ocean I.
Solomon Is. 1893
FRENCH CONGO 1875-92
(BELGIAN CONGO) 1908
Seychelles
Chagos Archipelago
JAVA
TIMOR
PAPUA (to Australia 1906)
Elli 188
ANGOLA
Comoro Is.
N.R. 1891
S.R. 1890
MADAGASCAR 1895-96
Mauritius
Réunion
Cocos Is.
Indian Ocean
New Hebrides 1906
NEW CALEDONIA
GERMAN SOUTH WEST AFRICA 1884
B.E. 1894-8
PORTUGUESE EAST AFRICA
1902
O.F.S. 1871
UNION OF SOUTH AFRICA 1910
COMMONWEALTH OF AUSTRALIA
Norfolk Islan
TASMANIA
NEW ZEALAND

North America 1865-1929

Although the United States made a remarkably rapid recovery after the Civil War (page 99), development remained very uneven. In the defeated South, the period of Reconstruction (1865-77) proved a bitter experience. South Carolina, which in 1860 had ranked third in the nation in per capita wealth, ranked 40th ten years later; and other once-prosperous states did scarcely better. The 4 million liberated black slaves fared worst, being left (as Frederick Douglass wrote) without money, property or friends. Although the population of the Union surged from 31 million in 1861 to 92 million in 1910, most of the increase by-passed the South and concentrated wealth and power in the north-east and the upper Mid-West. Only around 1920 did cheap labour attract textile industry to the South (map 1).

The settlement of the Great Plains, made possible by the railway boom after 1870, constituted perhaps the most striking achievement of the post-war period. The track in operation increased from 30,000 miles (48,000 km) in 1860 to 163,000 (262,000 km) in 1890 (at which point it exceeded the size of the entire European rail system); the number of farms rose from 2 million in 1860 to 6 million in 1910; and the population living west of

the Mississippi grew from 6 million to 26 million. Yet the bulk of the population remained concentrated in the north-east (map 3), and most of the 25 million immigrants arriving between 1870 and 1914 stayed there, providing cheap labour for American industry.

Railways played an even more prominent role in the development of Canada. The United States made no secret of its hope to absorb the provinces and thus create a continent-wide empire. After the acquisition of Alaska by the United States, this pressure grew, but the Canadians frustrated their neighbours' intentions by forming the Canadian Federation in 1867, completed by the purchase of Rupert's Land from the Hudson's Bay Company (1869) and the adhesion of

1 Urban and industrial growth, 1860-1929

main industrial areas:

- 1860
- 1900
- 1920

urban population 1920:

- 100,000–500,000
- 500,000–1,000,000
- over 1 million

industry:

- textiles
- iron and steel
- motor manufacturing
- strikes and industrial unrest

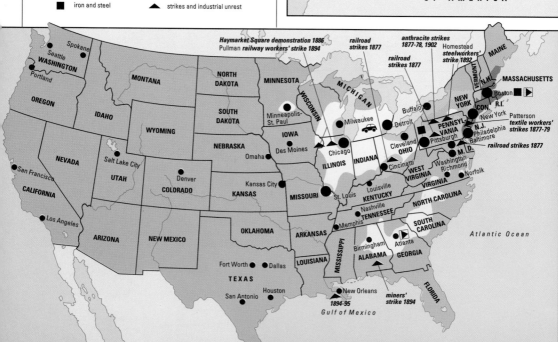

Manitoba (1870) and British Columbia (1871). The great transcontinental railways – the Canadian Pacific (completed 1885) followed by the Canadian Northern and the National Transcontinental – became the lifeblood of the new Dominion, opening Manitoba and Saskatchewan, and turning Canada into one of the world's leading wheat producers. It also facilitated the exploitation of rich wheat deposits, particularly copper and nickel (map 2). Overall, Canada's industrial output increased from $190 million in 1890 to over $500 million in 1914.

This achievement was dwarfed, however, by the economic and territorial growth of the United States. Output of iron and steel increased 20-fold between 1870 and 1913, by which time steel production exceeded that of Britain and Germany combined, and the United States remained the world's leading agricultural producer. Meanwhile, in 1867 Alaska was purchased from Russia; in 1898 (following a successful war with Spain) the Philippines, Guam, Puerto Rico and Hawaii were annexed, the latter after many years of American encroachment in the islands' affairs; and in 1903 Cuba and the Panama Canal Zone became protectorates. The United States now possessed the political and economic might to intervene almost anywhere on the world stage: in Mexico in 1914 and again in 1916, and – on a far greater scale – in Europe in 1917-18 (page 124).

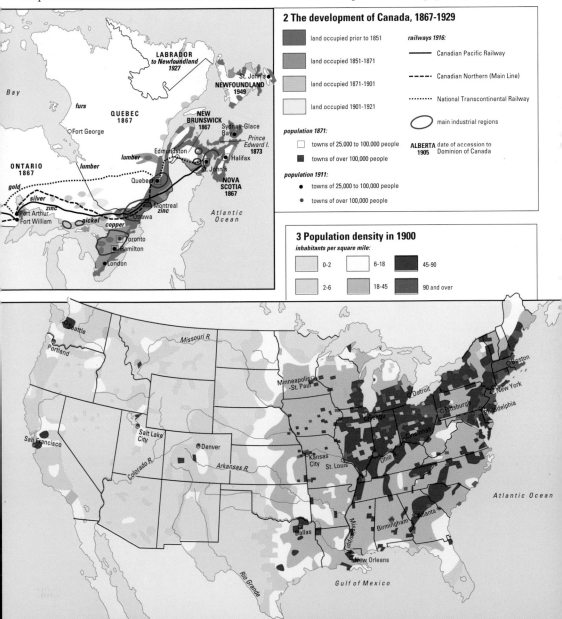

2 The development of Canada, 1867-1929

- land occupied prior to 1851
- land occupied 1851-1871
- land occupied 1871-1901
- land occupied 1901-1921

railways 1916:
- —— Canadian Pacific Railway
- – – – Canadian Northern (Main Line)
- ········· National Transcontinental Railway
- ⬭ main industrial regions

population 1871:
- ☐ towns of 25,000 to 100,000 people
- ■ towns of over 100,000 people

population 1911:
- • towns of 25,000 to 100,000 people
- ● towns of over 100,000 people

ALBERTA date of accession to
1905 Dominion of Canada

3 Population density in 1900

inhabitants per square mile:
- 0-2
- 2-6
- 6-18
- 18-45
- 45-90
- 90 and over

Japan 1868-1941

The Tokugawa shoguns (page 82) gave Japan over two centuries of peace and prosperity. In 1868, however, internal tensions, combined with the pressure of Western powers to open Japan to foreign trade, resulted in a revolution (known as the Meiji Restoration) which replaced the shogun and the feudal structure with a modern system of government. The new Japanese leaders implemented widespread reforms in the belief that a modern economy and military would ensure Japan's international independence and equality. They instituted a national education system (which by 1900 provided teaching for 90 per cent of children), a conscript army, and a navy with modern ships. Legal codes, largely based on French and German models, were introduced from 1882. The economic reforms were wide-reaching; the first railway opened in 1872 and by 1906 the system linked most parts of the country; up to one-third of state expenditure went on developing commerce and industry (map 1); and a land tax reform in 1873 provided a secure source of revenue for the government. The shifting structure of Japanese foreign trade (see inset table) illustrates the dramatic impact of these changes. Whereas in 1878-82, manufactured goods represented half of all imports but only 7 per cent of exports, in 1918-22 the ratio had reversed: finished manufactures now accounted for over 40 per cent of sales and only 15 per cent of purchases. Moreover the total value of Japan's exports rose in this period from 30 million to 1.8 billion yen.

International recognition of Japan's new status was nevertheless slow in coming: consular jurisdiction survived until 1894, and the unequal treaties negotiated in the 1850s with the Western powers remained in force until 1911. As Japan's strength and confidence grew, however, so did nationalist and imperialist ambitions. In 1894-5 a victorious war against China, arising from disputes in Korea, ended in a treaty granting Taiwan to Japan. Russo-Japanese rivalry over Manchuria led to clashes in Manchuria and culminated in Japanese victory in the war of 1904-5. The Treaty of Portsmouth (1905) which ended that war gave Japan a lease of territory in China and extensive rights in South Manchuria. In 1910 she acquired Korea. Japanese support for the victorious Western powers in World War I brought few further rewards, however, and the country's military leaders became frustrated. After 1931, under the impact of the Great Depression (page 130), Japan overran first Manchuria and then – despite strong opposition from the United States – northern China in an attempt to achieve economic self-sufficiency (map 2). Germany's victory over France and the Netherlands in 1940 offered an opportunity to expand southwards – thereby gaining control over valuable oil fields in Borneo and Burma – precipitating full-scale war with the Western powers (page 134). Paradoxically, Japan's total defeat and the ensuing American occupation propelled her even more decisively into the modern world than the Meiji restoration had done.

2 Japanese expansion, 1931-41

- Japan 1928
- expansion to 1933
- expansion to 1941
- ● Chinese capitals
- ✸ Japanese conflict with USSR
- ← Japanese attacks
- ◉ Japanese support for independence movements
- ■ Allied bases

The changing pattern of Japanese trade

food, drink · raw materials · semi manufactured goods · finished goods · other

export 1878-82
import

export 1918-22
import

1 Industrialization and economic growth, c.1880-1922

town population 1918:
- ○ less than 50,000
- ◉ 50,000-100,000
- ⊕ 100,000-500,000
- ⊞ 500,000-1 million
- ■ over 1 million
- KYOTO prefecture

— railways in 1906
--- additions to railways 1906-1918
main manufacturing areas

minerals:
- ● coal
- C copper
- ▲ iron
- ▲ oil

industry:
- ceramics
- chemicals
- food
- ⊞ machinery
- manufacturing industry
- ■ metal
- shipbuilding
- + textiles
- ▲ wood
- ◀ silk

The European powers 1878-1914

The unification of Germany and Italy (page 110) seemed for a time to have resolved the major questions which had disturbed the peace of Europe since 1848. Bismarck, the architect of German unification, concentrated after 1871 on building a system of alliances that would ensure the future of the new empire, mainly by isolating France, which proved unable to reconcile itself to the rise of the new German empire, and for almost 20 years he succeeded in convincing the rest of Europe of Germany's conservative and pacific intentions. In time, however, the alliances that had seemed defensive became aggressive and destabilizing. Meanwhile, although the achievements of Bismarck and Cavour reduced nationalist fervour in central Europe, they stirred up a hornet's nest in the Balkans, where the struggles of various national groups for independence from the Turks inevitably involved the neighbouring powers, Russia and Austria (which, after its exclusion from Germany in 1866 became far more interested in the Balkans: map 1).

Revolts in the Balkans between 1875 and 1878, culminating in Russian intervention and war with the Turks, resulted in the treaty of Berlin (brokered by Bismarck) which either confirmed or established the independence of Serbia, Montenegro, Romania and Bulgaria and granted Austria a mandate to govern Bosnia and Herzegovina. In 1879 Germany and Austria signed a defensive alliance, expanded to include Italy in 1882 (map 2a). Russia, satisfied that Slav interest had been met in the Balkans, turned increasingly to her interests in Central Asia and the Far East. The main European rivalries were now between Britain and Russia in Asia, and Britain and France in Africa. Britain remained isolated in Europe, while France and Russia signed an alliance in 1894 as a counterweight to the strength of the alliance bloc based around Germany.

The situation changed after 1897, however, when Germany began to seek a 'place in the sun'. This was not unreasonable; but by then most places in the sun had been occupied by others, and German policy – which involved building a High Seas Fleet to rival that of Britain – therefore seemed a constitute a threat to the established imperial powers. As a result, Britain resolved its differences with France in 1904, and with Russia in 1907, and France settled its long-standing dispute with Italy in 1902. Thereafter, the Triple Entente with France and Russia became the lynch-pin of British foreign policy, the only firm assurance against the German 'threat'. Germany, on the other became concerned with the danger of 'encirclement' by a hostile ring constructed by Great Britain (map 2b).

As a result, a dangerous simplification of alignments occurred into a bi-polar system: the Triple Alliance and the Triple Entente drew tighter, and Germany in particular grew closer to its only dependable ally, Austria. When Austria annexed Bosnia and Herzegovina in 1908, Germany gave her qualified support, though enough to rekindle Austro-Russian antagonism in the Balkans. During the Balkan wars (1912-13), in which a Russian-sponsored Balkan League consisting of Serbia, Greece and Bulgaria attempted to drive the Turks out of Europe, the two diplomatic systems still cooperated; but Austria stood aghast at the consequent enlargement of Serbia – which almost doubled its size – and feared Serb agitation for an independent south Slav state (map 2c).

The assassination of the heir to the Austrian throne at Sarajevo (Bosnia) in June 1914 provided what seemed to the Austrian government like its last chance to deal with Serbia before it grew too powerful, and Germany threw its entire weight behind its ally. Russia, however, could not afford to leave Serbia in the lurch and began to mobilize against Austria. Germany regarded this as a direct threat, and also began to mobilize. However, fearing attack from Russia's allies in the West, German Grand Strategy called for an immediate attack on France – in the hope that it could be knocked out of the war before Russia advanced in force. On 28 July, Austria declared war on Serbia; on 1 August 1914 Germany declared war on Russia, and two days later on France. The diplomatic system created by Bismarck, coupled with the volatile situation in the Balkans, had produced a world war (page 124).

2 European alliances

╬	Austro-German alliance (the Dual Alliance) 1879-1918
⁙	Three Emperors' Alliance 1881-87
◩	Austro-Serbian Alliance 1881-95
▲	Triple Alliance 1882-1915
■	Austro-German-Romanian Alliance 1883-1916
○	Franco-Russian Alliance 1894-1917
✦	Russo-Bulgarian military convention 1902-13

stripes, similar and identical colours indicate an entente or community of interests

1883
2a

abbreviations:
R. ROMANIA   E.R. EASTERN RUMELIA
B. BULGARIA   B.H. BOSNIA HERZEGOVINA
              M. MONTENEGRO

RUSSIAN EMPIRE

Carpathian Mountains

Vienna

R. Danube

Lake Balaton

Budapest

AUSTRO-HUNGARIAN EMPIRE

Banja Luka

R. Sava

BOSNIA-HERZEGOVINA
administered by Austria-Hungary 1878; annexed 1908

Sarajevo

Belgrade

S E R B I A

principality 1817; independent 1878

Nish

MONTENEGRO

Kotor (Cattaro)

Cetinje

Scutari

Tirana

ALBANIA

principality 1913

Koritsa

Monastir

Usküb (Skoplje)

to Serbia 1913

WALLACHIA
semi-independent 1829

Vidin

R O M A N I A

Bucharest

MOLDAVIA
semi-independent 1829

united 1859; independent 1878; kingdom 1881

Jassy

Galatz

Sofia

B U L G A R I A

principality 1878 independent 1908

R. Danube

to Bulgaria 1885

Balchik

Varna

Burgas

EASTERN RUMELIA

R. Maritsa

Black Sea

Adriatic Sea

EPIRUS

Yannina

Preveza

Arta

to Greece 1864

Corfu

Ionian Islands

Ionian Sea

to Greece 1864

THESSALY

Larissa

to Greece 1881

KINGDOM OF GREECE

independent 1830

Patras

Tripolis

Athens

Piraeus

Macedonia

Salonica

Kavalla

to Bulgaria 1913

to Greece 1913

Thasos

Lemnos

to Greece 1913

Mytilene

Aegean Sea

Chios

Nikaria

to Greece 1913

T h r a c e

Adrianople

Constantinople

Smyrna

OTTOMAN EMPIRE

Dodecanese

Rhodes

occupied by Italy 1912

to Greece 1864

CRETE

Candia

independent 1898 to Greece 1913

1 The Balkans, 1878-1913

- – – frontier of Ottoman empire, 1800
- ——— frontier of Ottoman empire, 1885
- ——— national frontiers after the Balkan wars 1912-13

48°

46°

40°

22°

36°

24°

28°

1904
2b

1914
2c

The world economy on the eve of the Great War

The integration of the world's economy into a single interdependent whole formed one of the principal developments of the period 1870-1914. Europe (and to a lesser extent the United States) stood at the heart of this process, emitting the impulses that opened up the remaining areas of the globe to Western exploration and exploitation.

Three interrelated aspects deserve special attention. First came the development of better means of communication. In 1870, railways remained largely confined to Europe (60,400 miles, 97,250 km of track) and North America (56,300 miles, 90,600 km): the rest of the world could boast only 9100 miles (14,650 km). By 1911, however, the total network of tracks had increased to 657,000 miles (1.06 million km) – 175,000 miles (280,000 km) of them outside Europe and North America – and included some spectacular transcontinental links: across the United States (four between 1869 and 1893), Canada (1885), Russia (1904) and the Andes (1910). The expansion of world shipping was equally striking, with not only a spectacular rise in the total tonnage, but a shift from sail to steam which increased the speed and regularity of shipments. However, the main shipping traffic, both passenger and freight, took place among the advanced countries and the white dominions, or between them and the producers of the raw materials they required. Canal construction also continued apace – above all the Suez Canal, completed in 1869, which carried 437,000 tons in 1870 and over 20 million in 1913; and the Panama Canal, completed in 1914, which carried 5 million tons of cargo in its first year. These spectacular totals reflected the enormous savings in distance – 41 per cent for vessels sailing from Liverpool to Bombay, 60 per cent for vessels sailing from New York to San Francisco.

Finally, messages travelled around the world with increasing speed. Cables laid beneath the oceans linked the continents – between Britain and North America (1858); from Vancouver to Brisbane (1902) – followed by telephones (with international lines from 1887) and wireless stations (from 1897).These developments parallelled a boom in commerce.

Foreign trade tripled in volume between 1870 and 1914, although (again) most of the activity occurred among the industrialized countries, or between them and their suppliers of primary goods or their new markets. In 1913, only 11 per cent of the world's trade took place between the primary producers themselves. Britain ranked as the world's largest trading nation in 1860, but by 1913 it had lost ground to both the United States and Germany: British and German exports in that year each totalled $2.3 billion, and those of the United States exceeded $2.4 billion.

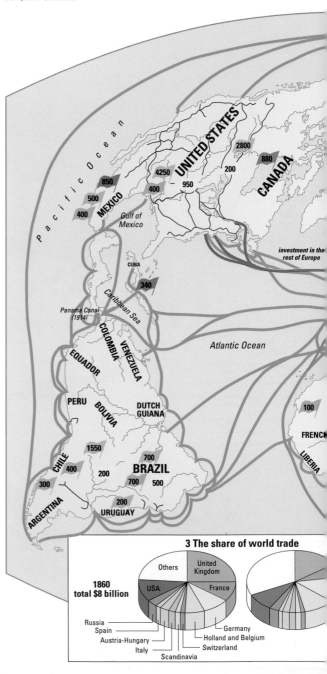

3 The share of world trade

1860 total $8 billion

Britain remained the world's financial capital, however, as well as its largest lender, with almost $20 billion in foreign investments by 1914 – slightly more than those of France, Germany, Holland and Belgium combined. The United States and Russia were in fact net borrowers of foreign capital. Investments within Europe and North America on the whole assisted and accelerated economic advancement, helping to create the costly infrastructure (such as railways and other public works) for developing nations that would in time repay these debts. By contrast, investments in non-industrial regions (such as the Russian and Ottoman empires) and overseas territories that lacked both the knowledge and the power to direct the capital flow, served to colonize rather than develop them, destroying native industries and creating dangerous political and economic pressures which would, in time, produce conflict between rich nations and poor nations and demands for a new economic order (page 160).

1 The development of the world economy

—— major railways

▬▬ busiest shipping routes

—— other major shipping routes c. 1900

—— international telegraph cables

concentration of investment 1914 (in $ million):

UK German

French USA

GREENLAND

JAPAN

Pacific Ocean

500

550

2400 400

R U S S I A

C H I N A

600

200

180 535

(NORWAY AFTER 1904)

SWEDEN

1050 UNITED KINGDOM

420

GERMAN EMPIRE

AUSTRIA HUNGARY

750

FRANCE

SPAIN

ITALY

650 450

GREECE

OTTOMAN EMPIRE

PERSIA

AFGHANISTAN

1850

INDIA

BURMA SIAM

200

CELEBES

BORNEO

MALAYA

SUMATRA JAVA

1700

AUSTRALIA

300

NEW ZEALAND

Persian Gulf

Suez Canal (1869)

ALGERIA EGYPT

LIBYA

200

500

Red Sea

SUDAN

600

Indian Ocean

WEST AFRICA

TOGO

NIGERIA

GOLD COAST

FRENCH EQUATORIAL AFRICA

UGANDA

BRITISH EAST AFRICA

BELGIAN CONGO

GERMAN EAST AFRICA

500 (all of Africa)

ANGOLA

GERMAN SOUTHWEST AFRICA

MOZAMBIQUE

1550

UNION OF SOUTH AFRICA

Madagascar

1913 total $39 billion

2 Foreign investment in 1914 (in $ million)

Russia 500
Belgium 900
USA 3510
Holland 4100
Germany 5650
France 9280
United Kingdom 19935

121

The Chinese republic 1911-1949

By 1911 the imperial government of China was thoroughly discredited (page 89) and an army mutiny led to the emperor's abdication. But the Republic proclaimed in 1912, with Sun Yat-sen as its first president, was overwhelmed by its inherited problems, and Sun was soon deposed by Yuan Shih-k'ai, the most powerful general of the old regime. After Yuan's death in 1916 power passed to provincial warlords, whose armies caused untold damage and millions of casualties. Compounding this misery were the expansionist policies of Japan and the foreign powers, based in the Treaty Ports (page 88), who interfered in the Chinese economy and in Chinese politics.

In 1919, the refusal of the Paris Peace Conference to abrogate foreign privileges provoked spontaneous urban uprisings. These provided a new constituency for Sun Yat-sen, who in 1923 reorganized his Nationalist (Kuomintang; KMT) Party, allied with the Chinese Communist Party (founded 1921), and prepared to reunite the country. But Sun died in 1925 and it was Chiang Kai-shek, the Moscow-trained general of the KMT army, who in 1926 marched northwards to eliminate the warlords. Helped by peasant and workers' uprisings along his route, Chiang proved remarkably successful, but in 1927 he turned on his allies, massacring the Communists in Shanghai. However KMT direct rule remained limited to the lower Yangtze (map 1). Nevertheless, the Japanese, fearing the potential challenge from a reunited China, decided to reinforce their hold in the north and overran Manchuria (1931) and Jehol (1933).

Although KMT purges had virtually eliminated Communism from the cities, peasant disaffection – arising from the absence of land reform – offered an alternative constituency. From his base at Chingkang Shan, Mao Tse-Tung and others created a new centre of revitalized communism, developing a peasant-based party rather than an urban, proletarian party on the Russian model. In 1929 KMT pressure compelled Mao and his followers to move first to Kiangsi, and then in 1934 to the north-west (the 'Long March': map 2).

In 1937 Japanese forces invaded northern and central China and the KMT retreated to the interior, where they remained until the Japanese surrender in 1945. A race to occupy the liberated areas now ensued, with the Communists gaining much of the north and most of Manchuria, and the KMT re-occupying the south. In 1947 hostilities between the two sides erupted into civil war from which the Communists emerged victorious. The People's Republic of China was proclaimed in October 1949, and soon afterwards the KMT fled to Taiwan. For the first time since 1911, a strong regime controlled all of mainland China – albeit most of the country had been devastated by the warlords, the Japanese occupation and the civil war.

1 China under the Kuomintang, 1928-37

occupied by Japan 1933
Japanese sponsored puppet state 1935
under executive control of Nationalist government at Nanking 1928
Nanking control 1929-34
Nanking control 1935-37
Nanking influence 1935-37

MANCHURIA (nominally subordinate to Nanking, 1928; invaded by Japan, 1931; Japanese puppet state of Manchukuo from 1933)

SINKIANG (under autonomous warlords; 1933-44 under strong Soviet influence under Sheng Shih-ts'ai)

OUTER MONGOLIA

CHAHAR (independent of Nanking)

JEHOL 1933

SUIYUAN (independent of Nanking)

SHANSI (Yen Hsi-shan (warlord); virtually independent)

SHANTUNG

KANSU

(Nationalist control 1930)

Nanking (capital of China, 1927-38)

SZECHWAN (no central control until 1934; Nationalist control, 1937; seat of government, 1938-45)

Chungking (capital of China, 1938-45)

(Nationalist control 1929)

HUNAN (under Ho Chien (warlord))

KIANGSI

FUKIEN

(under Lung Yun (warlord) until 1945)

KWEICHOW

YUNNAN (under independent regime; reached accommodation with Nanking, 1936)

KWANGSI

KWANGTUNG

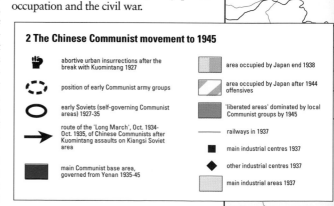

2 The Chinese Communist movement to 1945

abortive urban insurrections after the break with Kuomintang 1927
position of early Communist army groups
early Soviets (self-governing Communist areas) 1927-35
route of the 'Long March', Oct. 1934-Oct. 1935, of Chinese Communists after Kuomintang assaults on Kiangsi Soviet area
main Communist base area, governed from Yenan 1935-45

area occupied by Japan end 1938
area occupied by Japan after 1944 offensives
'liberated areas' dominated by local Communist groups by 1945
railways in 1937
main industrial centres 1937
other industrial centres 1937
main industrial areas 1937

BURMA

5

U S S R

MANCHURIA

Hailar

Manchouli

Tsitsihar

Kiamusze

Harbin

OUTER MONGOLIA

(independent 1924)

Kirin

Changchun

Mukden   Fushun

Anshan

Chinchow   Yingkow   Antung

KOREA

Kalgan

Paotow

Peking   Tangshan   Dairen

Tatung   Tientsin   Port Arthur (Lushun)

(Japanese 1910-45)

Taiyuan   Tsingtao

Tsinan

*Yellow R.
(Huang Ho)*   *Yellow Sea*

SHEN-KAN-NING

Pao-an; Soviet 1930-35

Yenan

Kaifeng   Lienyunkang

Lanchow   Loyang   Chengchow   Suchow

Sian

Nanking   Soochow

*4th army group; Chang Kuo-tao
Hsü Hsiang-ch'ien*   Shanghai

C H I N A

Hangchow   Ningpo

Chengtu

Wuhan

10th army group, Fang Chih-min

Chungking

Kiukiang

W. Hunan

Nanchang
Aug. 1927

Changsha

*Chingkang Shan,
Mao Tse-tung
and Chu Te
1927-29*

Tsunyi Jan. 1935   Hengyang

*Kiangsi Soviet under Mao Tse-tung
and Chu Te, 1929-34*

Foochow

Kweiyang

Juikin

Kunming   Amoy

TAIWAN

Canton *(Dec. 1927)*   Swatow

Hailufeng Soviet under P'eng P'ai, 1927-28

Hong Kong *(British)*

**FRENCH
INDO-CHINA**   *South China Sea*

Hainan

THAILAND

The First World War
1914-1918

All the war-plans of the Great Powers in 1914 envisaged a short war. The German Schlieffen Plan called for an attack on northern France through Belgium, leading to the rapid collapse of the French government before Russia had time to mobilize (page 118). It almost succeeded: the Germans came within 40 miles of Paris, but not before Russian armies had invaded East Prussia. Although their advance was halted at Tannenberg (August), important German reserves were diverted from the Western front just as a spirited counter-attack by French and British troops began at the Marne (September). The two sides now spread their forces out and dug in, until their trenches stretched from the Channel coast to Switzerland.

The war in the west (map 2) turned into a war of attrition. Each side launched repeated offensives, with appalling casualties but little gain, for railways were able to bring up reinforcements before the slow-moving front-line troops could make good any advantage. In 1916 the British, under Field Marshal Douglas Haig, made a major frontal assault on German lines at the river Somme. On the first day of the battle there were 60,000 British casualties, mowed down as they advanced through the barbed wire. Haig threw his forces into an unwinnable conflict for another four months. Both sides experienced terrible losses and little was achieved. Neither side could break the trench stalemate by pursuing alternative strategies. The British and French attempted a series of attacks from the rear: in the Dardanelles and Mesopotamia against the Ottoman empire, which entered the war in November 1914 on the side of the Central Powers (Germany and Austria); on Austria's southern frontier after Italy declared war in May 1915; at Salonika in Greece in support of Serbia. All failed. The Germans countered by building a fleet of submarines with the express intention of bringing Britain to its knees by attacking vulnerable food imports on which Britain relied. In 1917 unrestricted submarine warfare failed to reduce Britain's food supply by more than a fraction, but provoked the United States into war with Germany.

On the eastern front, which stretched for twice the distance of that in the west, warfare remained more mobile and both Germany and Austria scored major successes. In 1915 the former overran a huge area of Poland, whose resources it ruthlessly exploited, while the latter occupied most of Serbia. In 1917 the combination of huge losses and economic chaos broke the fighting spirit of the Russian forces and provoked revolution and military collapse (page 126). At the peace of Brest-Litovsk in March 1918 Germany gained the Ukraine, Poland, Finland and the Baltic provinces.

1 The Great War in Europe, 1914-8

- Entente Powers
- Central Powers
- → major Entente Power offensives
- → major Central Power offensives
- — farthest advance by Entente Powers: (east 1914, west 1918)
- — farthest advance by Central Powers: (west 1914, east 1918)
- ★ battle
- ★ battle costing over 250,000 lives
- ⚓ naval base

2 The Western Front, 1914-18
- → Entente offensives
- → German offensives
- — farthest German advance, 5 September 1914
- — Armistice line, 11 November 1918
- ★ battle
- ★ battle costing over 250,000 lives

Instead of moving its forces across to the West, however, Germany sent its troops to occupy these new territories – even Finland – and at the same time launched a final, all-out offensive in the West, in an attempt to break the deadlock. Once again it came close to success but the Allied line held and in July, aided by tanks and reinforced by American forces and money, a counter-attack began that not only pushed the German army back towards the German frontier, but that won the war. The German line began to fall back and morale collapsed: by October 1918, with Austria close to disintegration and with Germany facing a grave political crisis at home, the Berlin government sued for an armistice, granted on 11 November 1918.

At the peace conferences held in and around Paris in 1919, the victors imposed upon Germany, Austria, Hungary, and Bulgaria notable losses of territory, huge reparations and stringent reductions in their armed forces. The draconian nature of the settlement made it inevitable that, although over 8 million men had perished in the fighting, and the financial cost of the war totalled over $186 worldwide, it would not be (as so many had hoped) 'the war to end all wars'.

125

The Russian Revolution
1917-1945

By 1917 the strain of war had fatally weakened the Tsarist government: liberals, businessmen, generals and aristocrats all plotted its overthrow. In the end sheer hunger turned a general strike and bread queues into a revolutionary movement which in February forced the Tsar to abdicate, and power passed to a provisional government of prominent *duma* (parliament) politicians. The revolutionary committees (soviets) did not disband, however, and gradually the 'peace, bread and land' programme of the Bolshevik group, led by V. I. Lenin, gained support. In October, the Bolsheviks seized control of strategic points in Petrograd (formerly St Petersburg), arrested the Provisional Government, and assumed power in the name of the soviets. The same soon happened in other cities (map 1).

No one thought they would retain power for long. The overriding need was for peace, and Lenin insisted, on accepting the onerous terms imposed by Germany in the treaty of Brest-Litovsk (March 1918: page 124); but almost immediately the Bolsheviks (who now took the name 'Communists') faced massive invasions by forces loyal to the Tsar and assisted by troops from Britain, France, Czechoslovakia, Poland and other 'Entente' (anti-Bolshevik) powers. Nevertheless, by 1920 the civil war had been won, albeit at the cost of 13 million lives and immense damage to property. Lenin now introduced his 'New Economic Policy', which by 1925 allowed the Russian economy to regain its pre-war industrial level. In 1928 Lenin's successor, Joseph Stalin, introduced a Five Year Plan of industrialization, and the following year embarked on the forced collectivization of agriculture, which transformed small, individual peasant holdings into huge state and collective farms. The results of the policy proved disastrous, however. It was implemented without adequate machinery, and poorly organized. Crop yields fell, and a great famine in 1932-3 claimed millions of victims. This rural catastrophe caused some 40 million people to move into the cities, where their fresh labour was used mainly for construction, making the industrial growth rates of the Soviet economy under the first and second Five Year Plans (1928-37) look both startling and unique.

But this industrialization took place against a background of state-directed terror as Stalin consolidated the Communist dictatorship. The security forces (the NKVD) executed perhaps 12 million people, while a further 10 million suffered imprisonment in forced labour camps (see map 2). Economic growth enabled Russia to survive the German invasion in 1941 (page 132) partly because over 1500 factories were moved to safety further east. Nevertheless the setback remained undeniable: a further 20 million Soviet citizens died in the conflict and, although the USSR mobilized more fully than any other state in World War II, its industrial output in 1946 stood at only 70 per cent of the 1940 level.

2 Collectivization and population movements, 1923-39

principal areas of collectivization

- 2-10% of all farms collectivized by 1928
- 25-50% of all farms collectivized by 1933
- 50-70% of all farms collectivized by 1933
- 70-85% of all farms collectivized by 1933
- principal famine areas, 1932
- **Kraslag** labour camp administration zone
- ☠ corrective labour camps, 1932

city populations by census of Jan. 1939 (in thousands)

over 1 million | 500-1,000 | 250-500 | 100-250 | 50-100

population by census of Dec. 1926 — growth of population Dec. 1926 to Jan. 1939

—— frontiers, 1930

1 Russia in war and revolution

— Russian empire, 1914
- - - front between Russia and Central Powers, 12 Mar. 1917
👤 serious Russian mutinies in Aug. 1917
★ principal towns where Bolsheviks took power, Nov. 1917-Feb. 1918 (dates in new calendar)
━━ boundary of Russian territory occupied by Central Powers following the Treaty of Brest-Litovsk, Mar. 1918
∙∙∙∙ area controlled by the Bolsheviks, Aug. 1918
▲ towns occupied Entente forces Aug. 1918-19
- - - eastern boundary of area controlled by Bolsheviks, Apr. 1919
▨ area controlled by Bolsheviks, Oct. 1919
areas controlled by anti-Bolshevik forces, May 1920
➤ White Russian armies
➤ non-Russian anti-Bolshevik forces (Entente Powers)
━━ boundary of Soviet territory, Mar. 1921
— frontiers, 1923

Norwegian Sea

Barents Sea

Narvik
Murmansk
Entente fleet

NORWAY
SWEDEN

FINLAND
independence of Finland recognized Dec. 1917

White Sea

British French Canadians Italians Serbs

Canadians Americans

Archangel 17 Feb. 1918

British French

Finns

Lake Onega
Petrozavodsk 17 Jan. 1918

Mezen

Onega

Sukhona

Trondhjern

Stockholm

Åbo
Helsingfors

British/French naval assistance

Revel 8 Nov. 1917
ESTONIA
Yudenich

Riga Letts
LATVIA Baltic Germans
Dvinsk

Vologda 8 Feb. 1918

Vyatka 8 Dec. 1917

Perm 14 Nov. 1917

Nicholas II and family shot by Bolsheviks July 1918

Baltic Sea

Königsberg
Danzig
GERMANY (E. PRUSSIA)
Vilna
LITHUANIA

Minsk 17 Nov. 1917

Pskov 10 Nov. 1917

Petrograd 7 Nov. 1917
Novgorod 27 Nov. 1917
Kornilov's attack on Petrograd Sep.1917
Tver 10 Nov. 1917
Government moved from Petrograd Mar. 1918

Yaroslavl 9 Nov. 1917
Kostroma 15 Dec. 1917

Ivahovo 7 Nov. 1917
Nizhniy Novgorod 10 Nov. 1917

Izhevsk 9 Nov. 1917
Kazan 10 Nov. 1917

RUSSIA

Yekaterinburg 9 Nov. 1917

Ufa 8 Nov. 1917

Kolchak 1918-19

POLAND
Warsaw
Brest-Litovsk
Poles

Vitebsk 9 Nov. 1917
Smolensk 12 Nov. 1917
Mogilev 1 Dec. 1917

BOLSHEVIK

Moscow 15 Nov. 1917
Kaluga 11 Dec. 1917

Tula 20 Dec. 1917
Orel 14 Nov. 1917

Trans-Siberian Railway

Czechs

Samara 9 Nov. 1917

Lodz
Cracow
Lemberg
CZECHOSLOVAKIA
HUNGARY
Debrecen

Gomel 12 Nov.1917

Kursk

Don

Tambov 13 Nov. 1917

Penza 4 Jan. 1918

Saratov 9 Nov. 1917

Orenburg 31 Jan. 1918

Ural

Zhitomir 22 Jan. 1918
Vinnitsa
Kiev 8 Feb. 1918
Denikin 1919
Poltava 19 Jan. 1918

Kharkov 24 Dec. 1917

Voronezh 12 Nov. 1917

Don Cossacks 1917-19

Volga

Ural Cossack Army 1918-20

Kolozsvár
Temesvár

Kishinev 10 Dec. 1917
BESSARABIA

Dniester

Yekaterinoslav 11 Jan. 1918
Nikolayev 27 Jan .1918

Dnieper

Don

Tsaritsyn 27 Nov. 1917

Romanians
Jassy
Brassó

Odessa 31 Jan. 1918

Novocherkaessk 25 Feb. 1918
Rostov 10 Nov. 1917

Cossacks

Astrakhan 7 Feb. 1918

Kuma

Caspian Sea

SERBIA
Belgrade
ROMANIA
Bucharest

Wrangel 1920
French

Simferopol 26 Jan. 1918

Sea of Azov

Cossacks

Volga

Danube Ruse

French
Sebastopol 29 Dec. 1917
Novorossiysk 14 Dec. 1917

BULGARIA
Sofia
Varna
Burgas

Plovdiv
Adrianople
Salonica
Constantinople

Black Sea

French

British

British

Georgians 1919-20
Batum
Mensheviks

Baku 15 Nov. 1917

GREECE
Athens
Smyrna

Angora

Trebizond

Caucasus

Tiflis
Erivan

TURKEY

PERSIA

British 1918-19

European political problems 1919-1939

The collapse of the Central Powers in the autumn of 1918, and the subsequent peace treaties (page 124), brought about major frontier changes, the emergence of several new states, and the enlargement of others on the winning side (see map 1). The dismemberment of the Austro-Hungarian empire, the disarmament and the imposition of reparation payments on Germany and her allies, and the effects of the Russian Revolution and civil war (page 126) completely altered the balance of political power in Europe (map 1). In terms of population and industrial strength, however, Germany, although weakened, still had no rival in central Europe. The only hope of those who stood to lose by a revision of the peace treaties was the maintenance of overwhelming collective military strength against any revival of German strength. France tried to restrain Germany by signing alliances with the new states of Poland and

Czechoslovakia, but Britain proved reluctant to enter into new continental commitments, and the United States withdrew into isolationism. However, Germany's formal recognition of the post-war frontier settlements with France and Belgium by the Locarno treaties (1925) inaugurated a new spirit of cooperation. Germany was welcomed back into the community of nations and after 1928 many nations signed the 'Kellogg-Briand Pact', which outlawed aggressive war.

But indications of stability proved illusory. Many states, especially in eastern Europe, displayed alarming political instability; and all European participants emerged economically weakened from the World War. Italy – which had run up huge debts and lost 600,000 men in the war, but gained only 9000 square miles (14,400 km²) of new territory at the peace – soon became ungovernable, with civil war between left- and right-wing extremists prevailing in many cities until in

1 National conflicts and frontier disputes, 1919-34

— frontier of German Empire in 1914
— frontier of Austro-Hungarian Empire in 1914
— frontier of Russian Empire in 1914
— post settlement frontiers
◼ new states
■ conferences
▲ plebiscites held
◼ areas of dispute
◻ areas temporarily autonomous or independent
◼ areas under armed occupation
◼ areas under League of Nations High Commissioners

1922 the Fascist party, led by Benito Mussolini, took power. In other parts of Europe, the cost of the war and the defects of the peace settlements, coupled with the strains of economic readjustment and disastrous inflation, strengthened anti-parliamentary and revolutionary movements of both left and right. And with the onset of the Great Depression in 1929 (page 130), financial and economic chaos returned to the entire continent. Unemployment rose drastically, especially in Germany where after 1930 the anti-parliamentary movements of both right and left, the Nazis (National Socialists) and the Communists, increased their strength enormously until in 1933 the Nazi leader, Adolf Hitler, became Chancellor and proceeded to absorb or abolish all the other parties.

Hitler's victory, combined with the economic weakness of Britain and the political instability of France, irretrievably damaged the precarious balance of peace in Europe. The League of Nations, created in 1920 to regulate international disputes and protect member states from aggression, remained only as strong as its members; and its failure to prevent Italy's annexation of Ethiopia in 1935-6, or Germany's remilitarization of the Rhineland in 1936 encouraged further aggression (map 2 and insert). Hitler, who rapidly increased and modernized Germany's armed forces, annexed Austria and parts of Czechoslovakia in 1938, then Bohemia and Memel in spring 1939, while Italy invaded and occupied Albania (1939). Whether an early alliance between the western democracies and the Soviet Union would have halted the aggressors is a matter of dispute. However, fearing that he might be next in line, and already engaged in hostilities with Hitler's ally, Japan, in August 1939 Stalin signed a non-aggression pact with Germany. The collapse of the unstable system created after World War I was now unavoidable.

1 plebiscite Feb. 1920 divided between Denmark and Germany
2 occupied by France 1923-5
3 to Belgium 1919
4 to Belgium 1919
5 evacuated 1930, remilitarized 1936
6 League of Nations Mandate, by plebiscite to Germany 1935
7 to France 1919
8 divided between Germany and Poland, plebiscite March 1921
9 allied occupation 1920-3, annexed Lithuania 1923, autonomous 1924
10 Marienwerder and Allenstein plebiscite for Germany July 1920
11 to Poland Dec. 1918
12 partitioned between Czechoslovakia and Poland 1920
13 to Hungary 1921
14 annexed by Poland 1920, plebiscite for Poland, 1922
15 to Greece from Bulgaria 1919
16 demilitarized 1924, remilitarised 1936
17 Greek-Bulgarian conflict 1925
18 independent, Personal Union with Denmark 1918

2 German and Italian expansion, 1935-39

1 Czech territory given to Germany by Munich agreement Sept. 1938
2 Czech territory given to Hungary Nov. 1938
3 occupied by Hungary March 1939
4 Czech territory taken by Poland Sept. 1938
5 annexed by Germany 1938
6 plebiscite to join Germany 1935
7 Italian expansion
8 annexation of Memel March 1939
9 annexation of Bohemia March 1939
10 Slovakia (client state of Nazi Germany), nominally independent from Mar. 1939

North Sea
Baltic Sea
Memel
LITHUANIA
Danzig
NETHER-LANDS
R. Elbe
Berlin
R. Vistula
Warsaw
USSR
(reoccupied by Germany 1936)
Rhineland
GERMANY
POLAND
Saar 6
Prague 9
CZECHOSLOVAKIA 10
Teschen 4
FRANCE
Munich
Vienna
Ruthenia 3
R. Rhine
AUSTRIA 5
HUNGARY
SWITZERLAND
ROMANIA
Caspian Sea
Caucasus Mts
GEORGIA independent 1918-21
AZERBAIJAN independent 1918-20
ARMENIA independent 1918-21
YUGOSLAVIA
R. Danube
Corsica
Rome
ITALY
Adriatic Sea
ALBANIA (annexed by Italy 1939)
Sardinia
Mediterranean Sea
ERITREA
7
Addis Ababa
ETHIOPIA (conquered by Italy 1935-36)
KENYA
ITALIAN SOMALILAND
Mogadishu
Alexandretta to Syria 1920, to Turkey 1939
Sicily
Italian campaigns 1935-36
Indian Ocean

The Great Depression 1929-39

The New York Stock Market crash in October 1929 reflected deep weaknesses in the world economy. Commodity prices world-wide had been falling since 1926, reducing the capacity of exporters such as Australia and Latin America to buy products from Europe and the United States. Within the latter, wages lagged behind profits, impairing the development of domestic markets and limiting the potential of new industries, such as automobiles, to replace old ones, such as textiles. International finance never recovered from the strains of World War I, which caused a dramatic increase in productive capacity, particularly outside Europe, without a corresponding increase in sustained demand. Fixed exchange rates and free convertibility gave way to a compromise – the Gold Exchange Standard – that lacked the stability necessary to rebuild world trade.

In the scramble for liquidity that followed the Great Crash, funds flowed back from Europe to America and Europe's fragile prosperity crumbled. In many industrial countries one-quarter of the labour force was thrown out of work. Prices and wages plummeted, industrial production fell to 53 per cent of its 1929 level in Germany and the United States, and world trade sank to 35 per cent of its 1929 value (see diagrams and map 1). Early attempts to solve the problem did more harm than good. In 1930 the United States imposed the highest tariff in its history; in 1932 Britain responded with the Ottawa agreements, a

2 The Depression in the United States

population decrease or increase:

decrease	10-15%
0-5%	15-20%
5-10%	20% and over

1 The world economy, 1929-39

major currency blocs:

- gold bloc
- yen bloc
- German-dominated exchange control area
- dollar area
- sterling area
- areas of shifting or dubious allegiance due to German-American rivalry
- areas of loose currency bloc allegiance

production indices:

- 1929=100
- 1930
- 1932
- 1934
- 1936
- 1938

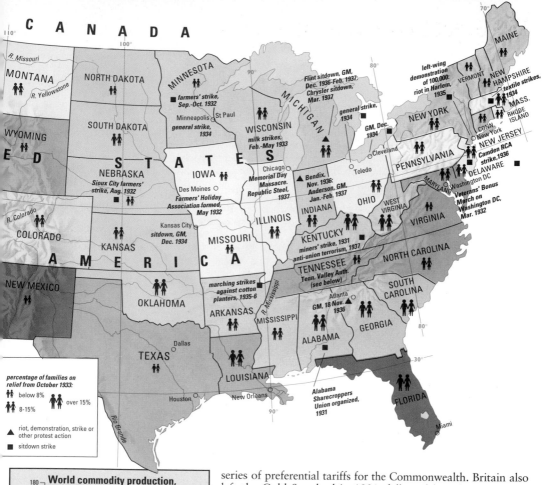

C A N A D A

R. Missouri
MONTANA
R. Yellowstone

WYOMING

NORTH DAKOTA

SOUTH DAKOTA

NEBRASKA
Sioux City farmers' strike, Aug. 1932

COLORADO
R. Colorado

KANSAS

NEW MEXICO

OKLAHOMA

TEXAS
Dallas
Houston

Rio Grande

MINNESOTA
farmers' strike, Sep.-Oct. 1932
Minneapolis   St Paul
general strike, 1934

IOWA
Des Moines
Farmers' Holiday Association formed, May 1932

Kansas City
sitdown, GM, Dec. 1934

MISSOURI

ILLINOIS
Chicago
Memorial Day Massacre. Republic Steel, 1937

ARKANSAS

LOUISIANA
New Orleans

WISCONSIN
milk strikes, Feb.-May 1933

MICHIGAN
Flint sitdown, GM, Dec. 1936-Feb. 1937, Chrysler sitdown, Mar. 1937

Cleveland
Toledo
Bendix, Nov. 1936: Anderson, GM, Jan.-Feb. 1937

INDIANA   OHIO   WEST VIRGINIA

KENTUCKY
miners' strike, 1931 anti-union terrorism, 1937

TENNESSEE
Tenn. Valley Auth. (see below)

marching strikes against cotton planters, 1935-6

MISSISSIPPI
R. Mississippi
ALABAMA
GM, 18 Nov. 1936

Atlanta
GEORGIA

Alabama Sharecroppers Union organized, 1931

FLORIDA
Miami

NEW YORK
general strike, 1934
GM, Dec. 1934

left-wing demonstration of 100,000: riot in Harlem, 1935

MAINE
VERMONT   NEW HAMPSHIRE
textile strikes, 1934
MASS.
RHODE ISLAND
CONN.
New York
NEW JERSEY
Camden RCA strike, 1936
DELAWARE
PENNSYLVANIA
MARYLAND   Washington DC
Veterans' Bonus March on Washington DC, Mar. 1932

VIRGINIA

NORTH CAROLINA

SOUTH CAROLINA

U N I T E D   S T A T E S   O F   A M E R I C A

percentage of families on relief from October 1933:
below 8%
8-15%
over 15%

▲ riot, demonstration, strike or other protest action
■ sitdown strike

World commodity production, 1926-38
180
160
140
120
*100
80
60
40
30
stocks
production
prices
1926 28 30 32 34 36 38
*base inox 1929 = 100

World unemployment in the 1930's
30
20
10
0
1930 1932 1934 1936 1938
%

series of preferential tariffs for the Commonwealth. Britain also left the Gold Standard in 1931, followed by other countries, dividing virtually the entire world into closed currency blocs which inhibited trade still further. Only Soviet Russia, largely isolated from the world economy, continued to increase its industrial production (page 126).

Economic nationalism fostered political nationalism, just as mass unemployment and the erosion of middle-class living standards fostered political extremism. In Japan, the fall of the Hamaguchi government in 1931 marked the end of constitutional democracy and the beginning of aggression in Manchuria (page 117). In Europe, Hitler rose to power in 1933 partly in response to the deflationary policies of his predecessors that raised unemployment from 3 million in 1930 to 6 million in 1932 (page 129). Even in Britain and the United States, fascist movements exercised considerable pressure. In the former, a right-wing National Government, formed in 1931, preserved democratic rule; in the latter, President Franklin Roosevelt, elected in 1932, implemented a 'New Deal' that laid the foundations for recovery. Nevertheless in 1934 some 20 billion days were lost in the US through industrial action and in 1938 over 10 million Americans remained out of work (map 2). Only World War II, and the boost it gave to production, pulled the United States out of the Depression.

131

The Second World War: the West 1939-45

Hitler's accession to power in 1933 added a new dimension to international politics. At first his expansionist designs had to await economic recovery, but his virtually unopposed annexation of Austria and Czechoslovakia (1938-9) and the Nazi-Soviet Pact of August 1939 (page 129) led him to expect similar acquiescence when, the following month, he invaded Poland. This time he miscalculated: the western democracies declared war (though this did nothing to aid the Poles).

Over the next two years, Germany rapidly secured first Denmark and Norway, then France and the Low Countries, and finally Yugoslavia and Greece, while Italy annexed Albania and invaded Egypt (map 1). Despite the Nazi-Soviet pact, however, Hitler's ultimate

goal was the conquest of Russia: his operations in the West, like the Schlieffen Plan in 1914 (page 124), merely aimed to eliminate Germany's western enemies before the main struggle began in the east. In this Hitler failed because Britain – though defeated on the continent and subjected to sustained aerial bombing – refused to concede defeat. Nevertheless, in June 1941 Hitler launched his forces on Russia and, thanks to the combination of strategic surprise and tactical superiority, made rapid progress, taking over 3 million Russian prisoners-of-war. But the winter killed many Germans, who had far outrun their logistical support and lay stranded outside Moscow, Leningrad and Rostov. At precisely this point, on 7 December 1941, Japan attacked the United States (page 134), and Hitler – in an act of egregious folly – also declared war.

Although Germany launched another major thrust in Russia in 1942, reaching the Volga at Stalingrad, that too failed, with the loss of a major army, and her

1 The German advance, 1939-43

- Axis territory 1 September 1939
- Axis satellites
- Axis occupied
- neutral powers
- British Empire
- airborne landings
- German advances 1939-41
- Italian advances
- Axis attack on USSR 1941
- Axis advances in USSR 1942
- Allied forces
- Allied withdrawals
- cities severely damaged by bombing
- Soviet occupied territory 1939-40

troops fell back in the face of superior Soviet forces, supplied both by the industrial complex built up beyond the Urals (page 126) and by the United States. Meanwhile, Anglo-American troops cleared Axis forces first from Africa and then from Sicily in 1942-3, leading Italy to make peace (though German forces there fought on); partisans gradually took over Yugoslavia; and from June

1944 allied armies liberated France and Belgium before moving into Germany. They met the Soviets on the Elbe in May 1945.

The costs of the war were appalling: 15 million military personnel and 35 million civilians had perished, 20 million of them Soviet citizens. The Germans had murdered prisoners of war (Canadians, Americans and Britons in the West as well as Russians in the east); they had murdered all captured partisans and members of the communist party; and they murdered all Jews they could find, many in mass shootings and at least 6 million in special extermination camps. However, they also lost heavily: the Anglo-American strategic bombing offensive reduced most of their major cities to rubble, and the Soviet troops carried out a systematic campaign of destruction as they advanced in 1944-5. By war's end, almost all Europe lay in ruins, yet already the differences between the victors had appeared which would darken the post-war years (page 154).

2 The defeat of Germany, 1942-45

— "Grossdeutches Reich" 1942

— maximum extent of Axis control, 1942

← Axis attacks

←- - Axis withdrawals

← Allied attacks

♠ cities under heavy air attack

♦ airborne landings

✊ partisan/resistance movements

✳ major battle with date

╱ V1 launching sites

⌐ V2 launching sites

The Second World War: Asia and the Pacific 1941-45

Japanese expansion in Asia after 1931 (page 117) stemmed from a desire for economic self-sufficiency, military security and a self-imposed leadership of East Asia. By 1940, however, with no end in sight to the Chinese war, Japan widened its ambitions to include the empires of the colonial powers – those of France and the Netherlands, recently defeated by her ally Germany, and those of Britain, at war with Germany (page 132) – as an alternative source of raw materials and markets that would free Japan from economic dependence on an increasingly unfriendly United States.

In September 1940 Japan occupied French Indo-China and the United States promptly placed an embargo on sending all iron and steel scrap to Japan. Next, following a sharp defeat at Nomonhan (Kalkhin Gol), Japan concluded a neutrality pact with Russia – which had been seen as the empire's principal potential enemy since the Russo-Japanese war (page 116) – and prepared to occupy the rest of the European colonies in South-East Asia. But first she felt it necessary to forestall a counterstrike by the United States: at dawn on 7 December 1941 her aircraft attacked and partially destroyed the US Pacific fleet at Pearl Harbor, Hawaii.

Japan hoped to fight the world's greatest industrialised power to a stalemate that would result in a negotiated peace recognizing Japanese hegemony in east Asia. Within six months, her forces had conquered

1 The Japanese advance 1941-2

- - - - Japanese empire, 1941

⟶ Japanese advance or strike

● Japanese base

■ Allied base

✗ battle

the American outposts of Guam and the Philippines, and occupied the British and Dutch colonies throughout South-East Asia. Their forces also overran the Bismarck archipelago and much of New Guinea, and captured most of the island redoubts necessary to create a defensive perimeter in the mid-Pacific (map 1). In June 1942, however, at Midway Island, aggressive tactics shaped by superb intelligence allowed the aircraft carriers of the US Pacific fleet (which had not been in Pearl the previous December) to destroy a major Japanese carrier force. The United States, although following a 'Europe first' policy in the world war, still possessed abundant resources to advance on two distinct axes against Japan: in the south Pacific, an island-hopping strategy (by-passing the major centres of Japanese resistance and executed by amphibious forces) aimed for the Philippines; in the central Pacific, carrier-borne forces advanced towards the Marianas, from whose airbases bombing raids could be launched on Japan itself. At the same time, Allied forces moved into Burma; and in August 1945 Russia finally broke her neutrality pact and invaded Manchuria (map 2).

But Japan, though utterly exhausted, succumbed to none of these conventional threats: rather two atomic bombs, dropped on Hiroshima and Nagasaki in August 1945, precipitated the unconditional surrender of the millions of her troops still in arms. The brief Japanese colonial adventure had caused almost as much destruction as Hitler's war in Europe; but it also unleashed forces of revolutionary nationalism that would shape events throughout Asia over the next five decades (page 142).

2 The Allied counter-offensive against Japan, 1942-5

- ◉ Japanese base bypassed or neutralized
- ✳ atomic bomb target
- —✚— Allied air attack
- ➡ Allied advance
- ● Japanese base
- ■ Allied base
- ✕ battle

135

The United States since 1945

The requirements of wartime production solved the unemployment problem (page 130) of the United States at last, and the gigantic output achieved to meet the needs of army, navy, air force and allies demonstrated the economic potential which, when realized, would create an era of unprecedented prosperity for the United States. Gross national product almost trebled in real terms between 1950 and 1990, while real income per head nearly doubled.

A number of factors brought about the economic surge: rapid population increase (from 132 million in 1940 to 250 million in 1990); technological advances coupled with the emergence of new consumer goods; the sudden spending of wartime savings between 1945 and 1948; and the rearmament programmes connected with the Cold War and the Korean War (page 154 and 142). Affluence came to seem entirely normal and business confidence was seldom less than buoyant: on this basis of wealth and hope most American people began to transform their entire way of life. The expansion of the suburbs constituted perhaps the most obvious change. Easy credit, cheap fuel (both for homes and cars), mass production of housing and automobiles, and giant road-building programmes (40,000 miles of interstate highways by 1980), all helped encourage Americans in their millions to move off the farms and out of the cities into endless miles of suburbs. So although the population of the central cities grew from 48 million to 79 million between 1950 and 1990, that of their urban fringes also rose from 21 million also to 79 million (map 1).

By 1990, less than one-third of the US population lived in non-metropolitan areas, but the flight from the farms did not reduce productivity: on the contrary, the number of people fed by one farm worker doubled from 15 in 1950 to 30 in 1970. Thanks to mechanization (by 1990 almost 100 per cent of the cotton crop was harvested by machine, as against only 10 per cent in 1949), improved seeds and fertilisers and government subsidies, the United States provided a significant proportion of the world's staple foods, such as wheat, maize and soya beans. The economy at large grew steadily, with the service sector (as in western Europe: page 156) expanding far more rapidly than manufacturing.

But beneath the prosperity lurked tensions. American capitalists tended to spend their profits rather than re-invest them, and industrial workers claimed higher wages and easier conditions of work without regard to the effect such claims (if successful) might have on prices and on the international competitiveness of American industry. The Vietnam War (1965-73: page 152) created high inflation and bitter internal divisions. Explicit discrimination against Blacks and Asians exploded in urban riots during the 1960s and gave rise to a widespread movement for civil rights led by Dr Martin Luther King (map 2). Then came the policies of Presidents Ronald Reagan (1981-9) and George Bush (1989-93), who cut taxes by a third (releasing a flood of spending power on the markets), slashed welfare programmes (turning the inner cities into ghettoes), vastly increased expenditure on armaments (so creating the biggest deficit in history), and failed to remedy the structural defects of American industry (so that the new purchasing power went overwhelmingly into imports, creating an equally unprecedented trade deficit).

On the other hand, winning World War II, engineering the reconstruction of western Europe through the Marshall Plan (page 138), the space exploration programme, major advances in the rights, education, income and social acceptance of minorities, and the successful resistance to Soviet expansionism without war were all achievements of which Americans could feel proud.

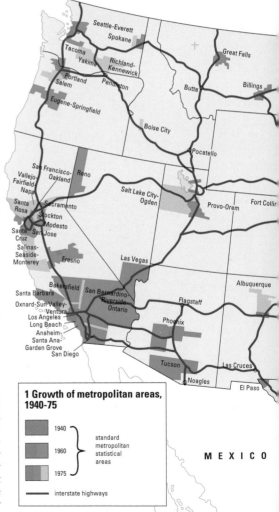

1 Growth of metropolitan areas, 1940-75

- 1940 ⎫
- 1960 ⎬ standard metropolitan statistical areas
- 1975 ⎭

— interstate highways

MEXICO

2 Civil rights and urban unrest, 1960-8

- civil rights demonstrations
- riots and urban unrest
- civil rights marches

San Francisco 1963,1966

Los Angeles (Watts)
Aug. 1965: rioting, 34 dead, $175 m. damage, 14,000 National Guards called in

Apr. 1968: rioting as a result of King's assassination

4 Apr. 1968: Martin Luther King assassinated; riots in over 100 cities; 350,000 troops and National Guards alerted

1957-9: police protection for black students

1962: University of Mississippi, 5,000 National Guards used to control rioting whites
Jun. 1966: James Meredith shot and wounded on way to 15,000-strong demonstration

7-25 Mar. 1965: Freedom Ride

Jan.-Mar. 1965: black suffrage movement organized by Dr Martin Luther King

Milwaukee 1966

Detroit 1963, 1968

1967: rioting, 43 dead, 4,700 State troopers called in

Chicago 1964, 1966, 1967, 1968

Kansas City 1968

Memphis

Little Rock

Birmingham

Jackson   **Selma**

Montgomery

Dec. 1955: beginning of desegregation movement

Cleveland 1966,1967

Dayton 1966¹

Cincinnati 1967

Nashville 1967

Atlanta 1967

Tampa 1967

1965: rioting against integration

Rochester 1967

New York

Philadelphia 1964, 1968

Pittsburgh 1968

Washington DC
Apr. 1968: rioting after King's assassination; June 1968 black and white Solidarity March

1964: rioting, 1000 National Guards called in

1967,1968, 1964: racial rioting

Boston 1967

Newark 1967, 1968: rioting 26 dead

Baltimore 1968

New Jersey 1964

Greensboro 1960: anti-segregation protests

4, 19-25 May 1961: Freedom Rides; first major racial confrontation

Aug. 1955: University of Alabama riots caused after admission of first black student; May 1963: anti-black riots

CANADA

Duluth-Superior
Fargo-Moorhead
St. Cloud
Minneapolis-St. Paul
Eau Claire
Green Bay
Appleton-Oshkosh
Muskegon-Muskegon Heights
Bay City
Sioux Falls
Rochester
La Crosse
Madison
Milwaukee
Grand Rapids
Gary-Hammond
Flint
Detroit
Buffalo
Rochester
Lewiston-Auburn
Portland
Syracuse
Utica-Rome
Albany
Boston
New Bedford
New Haven
Sioux City
Waterloo
Cedar Falls
Dubuque
Cedar Rapids
Chicago
Fort Wayne
Lima
Akron
Erie
Binghamton
Scranton
New York
Jersey City
Cheyenne
Omaha
Des Moines
Peoria
Springfield
Jackson
Cleveland
Altoona
Harrisburg
Newark
Philadelphia
Atlantic City
Greeley
Lincoln
St. Joseph
Springfield
Decatur
Terre Haute
Dayton
Cincinnati
Columbus
York
Baltimore
Wilmington
Denver-Boulder
Columbia
Evansville
Louisville
Lexington-Fayette
Charleston
Washington
Richmond
Newport News-Hampton
Norfolk-Portsmouth
Colorado Springs
Pueblo
Topeka
Kansas City
Witchita
Owensboro
Clarksville-Hopkinson
Roanoke
Lynchburg
Petersburg-Colonial Heights
Greensboro
Winston-Salem-High Point
Springfield
Nashville-Davidson
Knoxville
Asheville
Raleigh-Durham
Amarillo
Tulsa
Oklahoma City
Fayetteville-Springdale
Little Rock-North Little Rock
Memphis
Chattanooga
Charlotte
Gastonia
Greenville-Spartanburg
Fayetteville
Wilmington
Lawton
Fort Smith
Huntsville
Atlanta
Columbia
Charleston
Lubbock
Wichita Falls
Sherman-Denison
Pine Bluff
Birmingham
Gadsden
Augusta
Fort Worth
Texarkana
Tuscaloosa
Macon
Savannah
Midland
Abilene
Longview
Monroe
Jackson
Montgomery
Columbus
Odessa
Dallas
Tyler
Shreveport
Albany
Jacksonville
San Angelo
Killeen-Temple
Waco
Alexandria
Biloxi-Gulfport
Mobile
Pensacola
Tallahassee
Gainsville
San Antonio
Bryan-College Station
Houston
Lake Charles
Baton Rouge
Lafayette
Pascagoola-Moss Point
Melbourne-Titusville-Cocoa
Laredo
Austin
Beaumont-Port Arthur-Orange
Galveston-Texas City
New Orleans
Orlando
Corpus Christi
Tampa-St. Petersburg
West Palm Beach-Boca Raton
McAllen-Pharr-Edinburg
Sarasota
Fort Myers
Fort Lauderdale-Hollywood
Brownsville-Harlingen-San Benito
Miami

Atlantic Ocean

Gulf of Mexico

Europe 1945-73

World War II left Europe politically disorganized and economically prostrate, a situation greatly exacerbated by large-scale population movements. The German collapse released millions of incarcerated prisoners-of-war and slave-workers, and a further 5 million Russian prisoners, refugees and servicemen were repatriated. Two more lasting shifts of population also occurred: some 12 million Germans abandoned (voluntarily or forcibly) their pre-war homes in the east, especially in lands annexed by the Nazis after 1938; and over 2 million Russians moved into the territories annexed by the Soviet Union during its westward advance (map 1).

The political frontiers of the new Europe were established at conferences between the victors (USA, USSR, Britain and France) held at Yalta and Potsdam in February and July 1945: the union of Germany and Austria decreed by Hitler in 1938 was dissolved and Germany lost territory to Poland and the Soviet Union; both countries were divided into occupation zones under four power control. In Austria the system worked relatively smoothly, and in 1955 the country achieved independence, albeit as a permanently neutralized state; but co-operation between the USSR and her allies in Germany broke down in 1948. Britain and the United States had already amalgamated their zones in 1947 and, in conjunction with France, they now prepared for the formation of a West German government (the Federal Republic: BRD). After an attempt to prevent this by means of a blockade on Berlin, the Soviets prepared their zone for quasi-independence as the German Democratic Republic (DDR): the two states came into existence in 1949 (map 2).

3 Military and economic blocs, 1947-73

military partitions:

- ● NATO 1949-55
- ● Warsaw Pact Organisation

- original members of EEC
- subsequent members of EEC (to 1973)
- Benelux Customs Union 1947 (and EEC)
- Council for Mutual Economic Assistance (Comecon) 1949
- subsequent members of Comecon
- members of European Free Trade Association (EFTA) 1960
- Countries joining or leaving EFTA

2 Post-war Germany 1945-90

- border of Germany in 1937
- border of German Democratic Republic 1949-90
- border of German post-war administrative regions
- ● administrative capital

They immediately took their place in the two political blocs into which Europe had become divided. The eastern republics had all come under communist rule by 1948 and economic growth, though continuous, remained slow thanks to Stalinist methods of production. In the western democracies, thanks largely to lavish American aid (the Marshall Plan from 1947), an economic miracle took place, with smooth and rapid growth year after year. The two blocs had their own military groups – NATO in the west (1949) and the Warsaw Pact in the east (1955) – and their own economic organizations – in the east Comecon (1949) and in the west the European Community (six members 1957; 12 by 1986) and the less successful European Free Trade Association (map 3). However the growth surge suffered a serious check in 1973 when the Arab-led Organization of Petroleum Exporting Countries (OPEC) increased the price of oil by 250 per cent.

FINLAND
associate member of EFTA 1961

NORWAY

SWEDEN

DENMARK
leaves EFTA Dec. 1972, joins EEC Jan 1973

SOVIET UNION

WEST GERMANY

EAST GERMANY

POLAND

GERMANY

CZECHOSLOVAKIA

SWITZ.

AUSTRIA   HUNGARY   ROMANIA

YUGOSLAVIA
limited involvement in COMECON from 1964

BULGARIA

ITALY

Corsica

Sardinia

ALBANIA
withdrew from Warsaw Pact 1968

TURKEY

GREECE

Sicily

1 Post-war population movements

- border of Germany in 1937
- Allied control zones of Germany and Austria
- cities divided into four occupation zones
- annexed by Russia 1940-45
- states which became Communist 1945-48
- Yugoslav gains from Italy in 1945

peoples resettled, evacuated or expelled (with numbers):
- Germans
- Baltic peoples
- Finns driven from area bordering Russia
- Soviet nationals
- Russians forcibly repatriated
- Poles
- Czechs
- peoples settled by International Refugee Organisation

FINLAND   Vyborg   410,000   Leningrad

ESTONIAN SSR   60,000   40,000   Pskov

SWEDEN   Riga   100,000

LATVIAN SSR   90,000   Klaipéda   50,000   LITHUANIAN SSR   SOVIET

Baltic Sea   1,950,000   Kaliningrad   80,000   Vilnius   Minsk   2,300,000

UNITED KINGDOM   North Sea

Hamburg   1,900,000   Gdansk   EAST PRUSSIA *(under Polish administration)*

NETHERLANDS   Bremen   Szczecin   Poznań   Minsk

BRITISH   RUSSIAN   Hanover   Berlin *(under Polish administration)*   Warsaw   UNION

BELGIUM   Cologne   1,850,000   Poznań   POLAND   3,000,000

LUX.   1,000,000   3,250,000   Leipzig   Wrocław   1,500,000

SAAR   Frankfurt   2,900,000   Prague   Cracow   Lvov

FRANCE   GERMANY   Stuttgart   1,950,000   5,500,000   NORTHERN BUKOVINA

FRENCH   Munich   AMERICAN   RUSSIAN   CZECHOSLOVAKIA   RUTHENIA   Chernovtsy

SWITZERLAND   FRENCH   Vienna   AUSTRIA   200,000   HUNGARY   Kishinev   Odessa

BRITISH   50,000   BESSARABIA (MOLDAVIA)

ITALY   Trieste   250,000   YUGOSLAVIA   ROMANIA

Belgrade   Bucharest   Black Sea

BULGARIA   Sofia

Istanbul

ALBANIA   GREECE   TURKEY

The Soviet Union 1945 to 1991

Despite the extensive loss of life and property inflicted on Russia during World War II (page 133 above), remarkable economic recovery began after 1945. The output of heavy industry rose steadily and light industry, neglected under Stalin (who died in 1953), also progressed under his successors. The agricultural problems created by collectivization (page 126) remained – grain production only increased in the late 1950s, and even then the USSR continued to depend on imports – but vast reserves of oil, gas and mineral ores were discovered and exploited in Siberia. Russia's east European satellites were obliged to supply high-quality engineering products and expert personnel (as well as more basic items), which immensely assisted the USSR's economic progress. The development of the atom bomb (1949), of the first satellite (the sputnik: 1957), and of the first manned space flight (1961) all indicated the ability of Russian science to innovate.

After 1945 the Soviet military became a central feature of the state (map 2). One-fifth of the budget was devoted to military spending while between 1952 and 1976 101 military leaders became full members of the Central Committee of the Communist Party. The Soviet Union, along with the United States, had become a 'superpower', with a comparable degree of military strength. Although its gross national product fell well short of its rival's, the USSR overtook the USA in the production of iron ore, cement, steel and oil. Nevertheless the Soviet economy entered a period of crisis in the 1970s. Increasingly, the USSR found the arms-race more costly than did the USA (not least because the latter enjoyed far better credit and so could finance much of its expenditure through loans: page 136), and the position became critical when the USA threatened to extend its defence system into outer space (the 'Strategic Defense Initiative'). In 1985 a new Soviet leader, Mikhail Gorbachev, came to power with a programme of reform designed to achieve a 'revolution within the revolution'.

From 1985 to 1990 Gorbachev successfully improved relations with both China and the west in order to provide peaceful external conditions for reconstruction. He introduced *glasnost* (openness) in the media to encourage criticism of deficiencies in the economy and society; but he could not assure an adequate supply of food, and unrest in the cities grew. In desperation, in 1989 he withdrew Soviet forces from eastern Europe, hoping to reduce costs and thus improve the situation at home; but the resurgence of nationalism in many constituent republics began to threaten the entire union. The Soviet Union comprised many different ethnic, religious, linguistic and cultural groups (map 1). The majority of the

1 The nationalities of the Soviet Union, 1989

Russians 53.19%	Moldavians 1.23%	Kazakhs 2.98%
Latvians 0.54%	Ukrainians 16.18%	Kirghiz 0.93%
Lithuanians 1.10%	Mordvins 0.42%	Chuvash 0.31%
Estonians 0.38%	Turkmen 1.00%	Tatars 2.44%
Belorussians 3.78%	Uzbeks 6.12%	Bashkirs 0.53%
Poles 0.41%	Tajiks 1.55%	Georgians 1.46%

2 Soviet armed forces deployment: military districts and bases

Leningrad · Baltic · Belorussian · Moscow · Carpathian · Odessa · Kiev · Nth. Caucasus · Transcaucasus · Volga · Ural · Turkestan · Central Asian · Siberian · Transbaykal · Far Eastern

HQ — naval fleet headquarters
▲ — principal Soviet military airfields
Soviet ICBM bases (7,000 mile range)
other Soviet missile sites
– – – ICBM belt
long-range ballistic missile submarine bases

Principal ethnic groups of the Soviet Union, 1989

Slav · Turkic · Caucasian · Finno-Ugric · Moldavian · Baltic · Iranian · others

ASSR — autonomous Soviet Socialist Republic
AO — autonomous Okrug
SSR — Soviet Socialist Republic
AD — autonomous district

Armenians 1.70%
Azerbaijanis 2.49%
Jews (scattered) 0.51%
Germans (scattered) 0.75%
others 3.73%

The Soviet economy 1950–85

year	steel (million tons)	coal (million tons)	exports (billion roubles)	cars (thousands)	televisions (thousands)
1950	27.3	261	1.6	65	12
1960	65.3	509	5.0	139	1726
1970	116.0	624	11.5	344	6682
1980	148.0	716	49.6	1327	7528
1985	155.0	726	72.7	1332	9371

population claimed Slavic origin, including the Russians (53 per cent) and Ukrainians (16 per cent) – by far the largest groups. But the minorities, especially those incorporated by force during the 19th century (page 108) and the Baltic states, violently annexed in 1945, eagerly anticipated the chance to assert their independence.

Their moment came in 1991, when the conservative opposition to Gorbachev attempted a coup. It failed, thanks to the intervention of Gorbachev's rival from the radical camp, Boris Yeltsin, and Yeltsin himself assumed power – but only in Russia. The former republics now became 15 independent states. The break-up of the USSR did not bring peace, however: a bitter civil war raged in Georgia; Armenian forces occupied most of Nagorno-Karabakh, claiming it from neighbouring Azerbaijan; and separatist movements arose in parts of the Russian federation itself, jeopardizing the prospects for Yeltsin's programme of economic reform, and with it the very existence of democratic forms of government.

141

East Asia since 1945

Japan, like Germany (page 138), was occupied by the victors following her surrender in 1945. The Far East Commission, which contained representatives of all the countries that had fought Japan but remained an American enterprise, sought to demilitarize Japan and create a peaceful, democratic state. It reformed the education system (removing from the syllabus all material which had encouraged military and authoritarian values), made the Diet (parliament) the highest political authority, established an independent judiciary, introduced a programme of land reform, and sought (with little success) to break up the great concentrations of corporate power. With the advance of communism in east Asia, however, the United States increasingly saw Japan as a potential ally, and worked to reconstruct the economic power destroyed by the war. The occupation formally ended in 1951.

Japan's defeat in 1945 also ended its harsh rule of Korea and led to its occupation by the victors: Japanese forces north of the 38th parallel surrendered to Soviet Russia, those in the south to the United States. The Soviets supported the establishment of a communist state in the north under Kim Il-sung, a guerrilla leader who had spent considerable time in the Soviet Union; and the Americans retaliated by sponsoring a representative regime under Syngman Rhee, a strong anti-communist. Both new governments entertained strong ambitions to unite the country under their own rule, and in June 1950 the North attacked, pushing the South Korean and remaining United States forces back toward Pusan (map 1). The US forces counterattacked in September with a daring amphibious landing at Inchon, leading to a further offensive that promised to unify Korea. In November, however, the Chinese committed substantial forces that regained most of the north. A stalemate ensued and an armistice was signed in 1953.

The establishment of the People's Republic of China in 1949 (page 122) marked a fundamental turning point in the modern history of China. After a century of severe internal conflict and disintegration, usually provoked or exacerbated by external aggressors, China was now reunified and strongly governed by leaders who had a decisive vision of the society they wished to create. Whatever the excesses and failures since 1949, that fundamental achievement must be recognized. For most of the 1950s, China closely followed the Soviet model of directed economic planning and achieved some modest progress in developing heavy industries. But in 1958 Mao Tse-Tung, the communist leader, became impatient and sought to mobilize the revolutionary energies of China's vast population, creating huge rural communes and urban associations for production in the 'Great Leap Forward'. It was abandoned in chaos three years later. In 1965 Mao once more became impatient and again tried to mobilize the energies of the masses in the 'Great Proletarian Cultural Revolution', intended to prevent the creation of vested interests and bureaucratic arrogance in the party and the state. Once again, however, ideology triumphed over expertise, producing chaos and misery. Nothing in China grew as fast as the population. After Mao's death in 1976, the new dominant figure Deng Xiao-ping authorized a major shift in economic policy. Material incentives were re-established and foreign trade and investment encouraged (map 2). Political dissent, however, remained prohibited, and pro-democracy protests in Peking in 1989 were brutally crushed.

With the end of occupation in 1951 Japan began a period of exceptionally high economic growth and within 20 years had become an economic super-power. The 1950s saw strong emphasis on the development of heavy industry: Japan soon became the world's principal ship-builder and third largest producer of iron and steel. But from the 1960s Japanese industry also produced high-technology consumer manufactures – cars, cameras and computers – largely directed towards export markets across the world. Many major Japanese companies established production or assembly plants overseas, notably in South-East Asia but also in Europe and North America. Hence Japan's foreign investment rose dramatically from the 1970s, much of it in other countries in East and South-East Asia (diagram 3), helping to make the Pacific Rim a lynchpin of the global economic system (page 160).

1 The Korean War

CHINA

Chosan

Antung
Chinese intervention Oct. 1950

UN maximum advance 24 Nov. 1950

Unsan
Hungnam

Wosan

US task force 77

Pyongyang

armistice line 27 July 1953

Panmunjon
Seoul
38th Parallel

Inchon
landing of US X Corps 15 Sept. 1950

Wonju
Chinese and North Korean maximum advance 25 Jan. 1951

SOUTH KOREA
Taejon

Pohang

North Korean advance 15 Sept. 1950
Taegu

Mokpo
Pusan

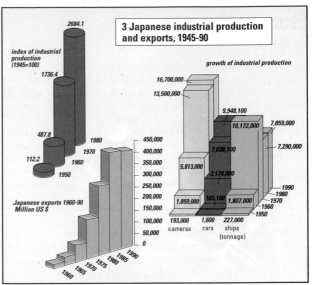

3 Japanese industrial production and exports, 1945-90

index of industrial production (1945=100)

2684.1

1736.4

487.8
1980

112.2
1960
1970

1950

growth of industrial production

16,700,000
13,500,000

9,948,100
10,172,000
7,859,000

7,038,100
7,290,000

5,813,000

3,178,000

1,859,000   165,100   1,807,000

1990
1980
1970
1960
1950

193,000   1,600   227,000
cameras   cars   ships
(tonnage)

Japanese exports 1960-90 Million US $

450,000
400,000
350,000
300,000
250,000
200,000
150,000
100,000
50,000
0

1960 1965 1970 1975 1980 1985 1990

MONGOLIA

HEILONGJIANG

Harbin 141 236

INNER MONGOLIA

Changchun

JILIN 120 123

Hohhot 1,417

63

513

848

LIAONING

Yinchuan

BEIJING 498 257 1,272

SHANXI

Peking

Tianjin Qinhuangdao

NINGXIA 91

TIANJIN

80

Shijiazhuang

Dalian

NORTH KOREA

Taiyuan

HEBEI Po-hai

Sea of Japan

84 60

Yantai

SHANDONG

SOUTH KOREA

SHAANXI

Zhengzhou

87 440

Qingdao

80 316

Xi'an

Yellow Sea

HENAN

Lianyungang

50 164

JIANGSU

Hefei 138 755

HUBEI

Nanjing

86 355

ANHUI Nantong

Chongqing

Wuhan 51 230

Shanghai

Hangzhou

SHANGHAI

Changsha Nanchang Ningbo

1106 2,523

HUNAN JIANGXI ZHEJIANG East China Sea

34 63 107 51 96 85 462

Wenzhou

GUANGXI FUJIAN 59

Nanning 8,133 Fuzhou

GUANGDONG 75 Xiamen

Beihai Canton Shantou

Zhuhai Shenzhen

Zhanjiang Hong Kong (Br.)

Macao (Port.) TAIWAN

HAINAN

2 The Chinese economy, 1979-92

51 — industrial production as % of national average, 1979

230 — foreign investment, 1979-88, by province, in million US$

Special Economic Zone (SEZ), 1984

GDP per capita <80% of national average, 1992

GDP per capita 80-120% of national average, 1992

GDP per capita >120% of national average, 1992

open coastal city

inland city with expanded authority

"golden triangle" development areas

▲ major oilfields

■ major coalfields

(pinyin name forms used)

Retreat from empire after 1947

The Western empires created in the 19th century (page 112) remained intact in 1939, though most German and Ottoman possessions had passed to Britain, France and Japan as League of Nations mandates. The United States planned to grant independence to the Philippines, acquired in 1898, and did so immediately after World War II; but none of the seven remaining European colonial powers – Britain, France, Spain, Portugal, Belgium, Italy and the Netherlands – surrendered their empires voluntarily. Only Britain even conceived of independence as the ultimate goal, albeit with continued membership of the Commonwealth, a goal already attained in 1939 by Canada, South Africa, Australia and New Zealand. The continental colonial powers thought more in terms of evolution towards a common citizenship, with their colonies as overseas parts of the metropolitan territory. Such plans were complicated, however, by the resistance of European settlers, with consequent inter-racial tensions, and by clashes between the European ideal of evolution along Western lines (in education and economic development) and the powerful Hindu, Muslim, Buddhist and Confucian cultures of the 'subject peoples'.

France fought stubbornly to maintain its control of Indochina (page 152), and the Netherlands struggled to contain the nationalists of Java, who had proclaimed the Indonesian Republic in 1945. Neither succeeded. Continual unrest forced Britain to grant independence to India and Pakistan (1947), followed in 1948 by Burma and Ceylon (page 152). Nevertheless Britain fought (and won) a long war against communist insurgents in Malaya, and resisted Indonesian attempts to annex Sarawak and Brunei. Only after the evacuation of Aden in 1967 did Britain abandon its presence east of Suez – save only for Hong Kong, to be retained until 1997, its economic success being of some benefit to Communist China.

In Africa resistance to independence was strongest in colonies with substantial white settler populations. In Algeria, with 1 million whites, a savage war of liberation occurred between 1954 and 1962; but conflict proved bitter, too, in Kenya and Rhodesia. However by 1974 all had achieved independence (page 150). By then, although Britain showed in the Falklands War (1982) her determination to fight on behalf of the few outposts still directly ruled from London, the formal structures of European imperialism had been dismantled and largely replaced by different forms of association such as the British Commonwealth or the French Community.

1 The post-colonial world

The Middle East since 1917

The Middle East has occupied world attention more consistently than any other region since 1945: Israel and its neighbours have engaged in four full-scale wars; Israel has invaded Lebanon twice; two Gulf wars have been fought; military coups have reinforced a regional pattern of internal repression; waves of refugees, from Cyprus to Afghanistan, have been forced to flee.

American support for the state of Israel (founded in 1948), sponsorship of the Baghdad Pact (1955), and intervention in Lebanon (1958) seemed to threaten the Soviet southern frontier, and so assistance was offered to Syria, Egypt and (after the revolution of 1958) Iraq. The Soviets also championed the Arab states during the Arab-Israeli war of 1967, despite which Israel occupied the west bank of the Jordan, Sinai and the Golan heights, provoking further large-scale Arab emigration (map 2). In 1973 an Egyptian and Syrian attack on Israel met with limited military success, and opened a new phase of negotiation. Egypt and Israel concluded the Camp David Accords (1978) which resulted in the return of Sinai in 1982; but the Israelis showed no intention of returning the other territories occupied since 1967, instead installing large numbers of new Jewish settlements. Moreover in 1982, to counter Palestinian guerrilla activity, they invaded and held south Lebanon. Nevertheless, in the wake of a prolonged period of resistance to Israeli rule in the West Bank and Gaza, which excited much outside sympathy, in 1991 the US succeeded in bringing Israel and its Arab neighbours into extended peace talks, which resulted in limited Palestinian self-rule in 1994-5.

As open conflict between Israel and her neighbours abated, it began in the Gulf. The replacement of the Shah of Iran by Ayatollah Khomeini in 1979 seemed to President Saddam Hussein of Iraq to offer the chance of territorial gain. He attacked in 1980.

2 Israel and Palestine, 1947–94

- Jewish state under UN partition plan for Palestine 1947
- Israel after Arab invasion and War of Independence 1948
- Israeli conquests 1967
- Egyptian re-conquests, and Israel conquests 1973

population movements:
- Jewish immigration 1948-64
- Arab emigration 1948 (total 726,000)
- Arab emigration 1967 (total 400,000)

3 The Gulf War, 1990-1

- states supporting Iraq
- members of anti-Iraqi UN Coalition
- Gulf Co-operation Council members
- maximum range of Iraqi Scud missiles
- Iraqi nuclear installations
- Iraqi chemical weapons plant
- Iraqi biological weapons plant
- Iraqi missile plant
- areas of post-war anti-Saddam uprisings
- northern limit of UN-imposed anti-Iraq air exclusion zone, Dec. 1992
- southern limit of UN-imposed anti-Iraq military exclusion zone, Apr. 1991

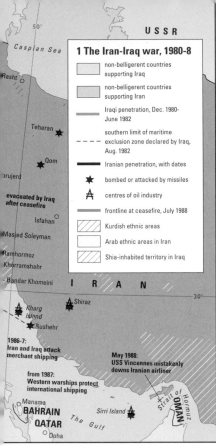

1 The Iran-Iraq war, 1980-8

- non-belligerent countries supporting Iraq
- non-belligerent countries supporting Iran
- Iraqi penetration, Dec. 1980-June 1982
- southern limit of maritime exclusion zone declared by Iraq, Aug. 1982
- Iranian penetration, with dates
- ★ bombed or attacked by missiles
- A centres of oil industry
- frontline at ceasefire, July 1988
- Kurdish ethnic areas
- Arab ethnic areas in Iran
- Shia-inhabited territory in Iraq

However, eight years of attritional warfare achieved virtually nothing and in 1990 (map 1), in an attempt to gain new resources with which to liquidate his war debts, Saddam invaded and annexed another neighbour, Kuwait. The United Nations, led by the US, put pressure on Saddam to withdraw and, when he refused, in 1991 used armed force to expel him (map 3). These events had a catastrophic effect on the oil production of the Persian Gulf, much of it located in the war zone. The area's share of global output fell from 41 per cent in 1979 to 26 per cent in 1991, with production in Iraq and Kuwait reduced almost to zero.

Nevertheless, oil remained the region's most valuable natural asset. Output and revenue both increased dramatically after the OPEC price-rise in 1973 (page 139), creating some of the highest per capita incomes in the world in the Arab Gulf states. Their prosperity also attracted massive immigration from Egypt, Jordan, Yemen and the Indian sub-continent, creating a potential problem. The rise of Islamic fundamentalism posed another. After 1979 it became a badge of hostility towards the West in Iran and towards Russia in Afghanistan, and elsewhere toward the regime in power – unless, as in Iran, that regime was an Islamic theocracy. In Algeria, the attraction proved so strong that the government in 1992 cancelled a second round of elections to prevent the fundamentalists gaining power.

Although the collapse of the Soviet Union (page 141) ended the superpower rivalry which once dominated the area, the Western powers continued to exert their influence, both to safeguard the oil supplies on which their economies still depended and to protect blatantly persecuted minorities like the Kurds of northern Iraq. Moreover, the enormous concentrations of conventional weapons – and the interest in developing chemical and biological weapons – in so many antagonistic states ensured that the Middle East continued to occupy world attention.

Latin America since 1930

The Great Depression (page 130) struck Latin America a shattering blow, cutting off supplies of foreign capital and lowering the price of its primary products in the world markets. Chile's exports fell by over 80 per cent between 1929 and 1933; those of Bolivia and Peru by 75 per cent. Only oil-exporting Venezuela more or less weathered the storm. The economic collapse led to widespread disillusion with middle-class liberal or radical parties: in 1930 and 1931, 11 of the 20 republics south of the Rio Grande experienced revolutionary changes in government. Mexico, where Lázaro Cárdenas (1934-40) revived the land distribution policies of 1911 (page 106), experienced a shift to the left; but elsewhere the swing was mainly to the right. The new dictators tended to be populists, appealing directly to the masses and cooperating with organised labour and the trade unions. They also introduced programmes of industrialization – following Soviet or, more often, Fascist models – to reduce dependence on overseas markets and hasten economic development.

Manufacturing industry received a further boost during World War II, which cut off imported consumer goods and stimulated the industrial sector. But industrialization made Latin America dependent upon imported capital goods, raw materials, technology and finance – especially from the United States – creating enormous foreign debts (map 2). Multinational corporations exploited the cheap labour of Latin America without stimulating economic development. Social tensions arose from income concentration, unemployment, lack of opportunities, and from the intrusion of foreign interests. Social revolutions were attempted but frustrated in Guatemala, Bolivia and Chile (map 1), underlining the obstacles to change in economies too narrowly based to sustain welfare programmes, where local elites were prepared to collaborate with the United States.

Cuba after 1959 attempted to achieve social change, economic growth and freedom from the United States simultaneously; but although its revolution led to greater social equality and some improvement in the lot of rural workers, it also brought a repressive regime and dependence on the Soviet Union. Moreover its attempts to spread revolution in Central and South America all failed.

In the face of revolutionary change, with some support from the upper and middle classes, the military seized power in many areas and combined political repression with economic liberalization. But by the late 1980s their policies too had largely failed and, in the face of economic recession and popular protest, their power gradually weakened. Instead, democratic government resumed in several states of the subcontinent, and in 1992 Mexico signed a free trade agreement (NAFTA) with Canada and the United States, creating the largest integrated trading bloc in the world.

148

Atlantic Ocean

Washington

Grenada 1983
Dominican Republic 1916-24, 1965-66
Haiti 1915-34, 1944, 1994

Miami

Bahama
Islands

Cuban revolution 1959

CUBA
Santiago

Cuban inspired
guerrilla movements 1959-68

HAITI

DOMINICAN
REPUBLIC

Grenada

NICARAGUA

Cartagena

COSTA RICA
San
José

Panama City

PANAMA

Caracas

VENEZUELA

Georgetown   Paramaribo

SURINAM

Cayenne

GUYANA

FRENCH GUIANA

Bogotá

COLOMBIA

Macapá

R. Amazon

Belém

Gurupá

Quito

ECUADOR
Guayaquil

Rio Negro

Manaus

R. Purus

Fortaleza

Piura

Recife

PERU

B R A Z I L

Salvador
(Bahia)

Trujillo
Huánco
Callao   Lima   Cuzco

Brasília

Belo Horizonte

Arequipa

La Paz

BOLIVIA

Sucre

São Paulo

Rio de Janeiro

Santos

PARAGUAY

Antofagasta

Asunción

Florianópolis

Copiapó

San Miguel de Tucumán

R. Uruguay

Porto Alegre

Rio Grande

Valparaíso
Santiago

Córdoba

Santa Fé

Rosario

Fray Bentos

URUGUAY

Montevideo

Mendoza

Buenos Aires

Concepción

A R G E N T I N A

Bahía Blanca

Valdivia

Osorno

Rawson

Comodoro Rivadavia

Santa Cruz

Falkland Islands
(Islas Malvinas)
occupied by Argentina 1982:
occupation ended by UK
Task Force June 1982

Tierra del
Fuego

1 Social and political movements, 1930-94

▢ Fundamental change (attempted or acheived) in economic
and social structure by nationalist or Marxist/Maoist movements

◯ Moderate socio-economic change or modernisation by democratic
or other process

☆ Revolutionary change by dictatorships appealing to popular forces,
especially urban labour

◇ Radical socio-economic change by Christian Democrat parties

▽ Military dictatorship of the right, with or without social or
modernising programme

⬡ Urban guerrillas from late 1960s following
failure of Cuban-inspired rural guerrillas

Rómulo Betancourt 1945-48, 1959-64; Carlos Andrés Pérez 1974-79 ◯

Rafael Caldera 1969-74; Luis Herrera Campins 1979; Jaime Lusinchi 1984 ◇

Getulio Vargas 1930-45; 1950-54 ☆
João Goulart 1961-64
Modernizing militarism 1964 ▽

Civilian rule 1985;
democratization 1986 ◯

☆ Radical militarism 1968
▢ Sendero Luminoso from 1980
◯ Return to civil rule 1980
President Fujimori suspends constitution 1992
▢ Bolivian revolution 1952-64
▢ Che Guevara (killed 1967)
▽ Military 1980; democratization 1982

◇ Eduardo Frei 1964-70

▢ Salvador Allende (Popular Unity) 1970-73

▽ Pinochet 1973 -88

◯ Democratization 1989

Military dictatorship Stroessner 1954 ▽
Rodriguez 1989 ▽

Batllismo 1903-33 ◯

Tupamaros ⬡

Military 1973 ▽

Civilian rule 1985; democratization 1986 ◯

Montoneros ⬡

Juan Domingo Perón 1943-55, 1973-4 ☆

Military 1976-83 ▽

Democratization and civilian rule 1983 ◯

2 Economic development

Direct US investment in Latin America
(figures in millions of US dollars)

1991
1979
1960
1943
1929

Chief exports of Latin America 1955-90
coffee   chief exports 1955
coffee   chief exports 1990
▲   represents over 50 per cent of
total exports
●   represents over 25 per cent of
total exports

Africa since 1945

After World War II, although some French and British liberals sympathetic to African claims for advancement initiated programmes of social improvement and political reform, these soon ran into difficulties in territories where they threatened the interests of white settler populations. Moreover, the need to exploit every asset in order to assist metropolitan recovery led to attempts to reassert colonial control. Nevertheless in the 1950s both the British and the French began to transfer responsibility to elected governments in their West African colonies.

In Muslim North Africa, longer-established nationalist movements received great stimulus from the overthrow of the Egyptian monarchy in 1952 and the subsequent rise to power of Gamal Abdel Nasser. In 1953-4 Britain agreed to withdraw its troops from the Suez Canal Zone; and in 1956 France granted independence to her protectorates of Tunisia and Morocco. But in Algeria, with a large white population, the government attempted to maintain control and incorporate the colony into metropolitan France. In 1954 the Front de Libération Nationale began a war which continued with increasing ferocity until in 1962 independence was finally granted.

At the other end of the continent, a Nationalist government dedicated to policies of racial separation ('apartheid') came to power in South Africa in 1948. Meanwhile, white settlers in East Africa also hoped to maintain their ascendancy: in Kenya, where British troops arrived to suppress the Mau-Mau insurrection directed against the settlers; and in Central Africa, where a federation of Nyasaland and Rhodesia aimed to preserve the dominance of Rhodesian whites. But in 1963 Kenya achieved independence and the Federation collapsed. Southern Rhodesia's white settlers created their own independent state in 1965, but had to accept black majority rule in 1980. Portugal retained her colonies longest, but in all of them guerrilla warfare eventually forced her ignominious withdrawal in 1974-5.

The political and economic structures of the newly independent African states remained fragile. Most possessed borders drawn by European governments in the 19th century with insufficient attention to ethnic rivalries, and almost immediately those rivalries began to tear them apart. In 1960, tribal and regional factions in Zaire (formerly the Belgian Congo) led to demands for a federal constitution at independence and, when these were refused, the army mutinied and the mineral rich province of Katanga seceded. United Nations intervention reunited the country in 1963, but two years later the army seized power. A similar pattern occurred in Nigeria, where the secession of Biafra in 1967 led to a three-year civil war which restored central control, but delivered power to the army. Elsewhere, ethnic violence caused enormous casualties – in the small state of Rwanda, Hutu-Tutsi violence

1984 major rioting
1987 Bourguiba ousted

MOROCCO

1976 Western Sahara jointly occupied by Morocco and Mauritania; Polisario guerrilla resistance backed by Algeria
1991 cease-fire between Morocco and Polisario

WESTERN SAHARA

1976-79 war with Polisario
1978 military rule
1991 multi-party elections

MAURITANIA

1968 civilian government overthrown
1974-85 border conflicts with Burkina

BURKINA

1957 first Black African country to gain independence
1966 Nkrumah deposed
1967-85 series of military coups

1989 outbreak of civil war
1993 pan-African peace-keeping force (Ecomog) intervenes in attempt to halt civil war

LIBERIA

1966 military takeover led by Col. Bokassa, crowned emperor 1976
1980 republic restored
1981 military coup

1966 Obote expels Kabaka (King) of Buganda
1970 border dispute with Kenya
1971 Obote overthrown by Amin;
Asians expelled; large-scale repression
1979 invaded by Tanzania, Amin overthrown;
Obote restored (1980), overthrown (Jan 1986)
1986 Yoweri Museveni president

left between 500,000 and 1 million dead in 1994 – while repeated droughts (compounded by government inefficiency and corruption) caused famine and massive refugee problems in many areas of East Africa. Some states found short-term relief through the exploitation of oil and other minerals, though often at the cost of diverting resources from producing food.

By the 1980s, only the Republic of South Africa maintained white supremacy in Africa. It sought to protect itself by tightening its illegal control of Namibia, by military incursions into neighbouring states, and by conceding to the impoverished labour reserves known as 'Bantustans' a spurious independence. But, under siege economically and subject to international condemnation, the apartheid system could not last. In 1990 the government freed Nelson Mandela, leader of the outlawed African National Congress, and began talks about a new political settlement. In 1994, after the first multi-racial elections in South African history, Mandela peacefully gained control of the richest state in the continent.

TUNISIA

ALGERIA
*1960s border conflicts with Morocco
1965 Ben Bella deposed by Col. Boumedienne
1990 election of Islamic fundamentalist-dominated chamber of deputies
1991 election results nullified; anti-government terrorist campaign by Islamic Fundamentalists*

LIBYA
*1969 King Idris deposed; replaced by military junta under Col. Gadhafi
1986 US bomb Tripoli in retaliation for terrorist attacks*

Aozou Strip

EGYPT
*1952 King Farouk deposed by army officers led by Neguib
1954-70 Nasser president
1956 Suez crisis
1967, 1973 wars with Israel
1981 Mubarak president on assassination of Sadat
1991 forces join US-led war against Iraqi occupation of Kuwait*

*1952 federated with Ethiopia
1962 Union
1961-91 armed resistance to Ethiopian rule in both Eritrea and Tigre
1991 Eritrean and Tigrean forces victorious
1993 independence*

ERITREA

CHAD
*1960 civil war; FROLINAT guerrillas supported by Libya
1973, 1981 Libyan invasion and withdrawal
1984 border war with Libya*

MALI   NIGER

GHANA

NIGERIA
*1967-70 Nigerian civil war
1981 civilian rule restored
1984, 1985, 1993 military coups
1993 elections declared void; riots; interim government ousted by military*

SUDAN
*1963-72 civil war
1969 General Numeiry takes power in military coup, intermittent civil war in South since independence
1984 severe famine
1985 Numeiry overthrown (civil war continues)
1989 military coup; National Islamic Front in effective control
1994-5 ceasefire between feuding southern anti-government forces*

ETHIOPIA
*1961- war against Eritrea secessionists
1974 Emperor Haile Selassie overthrown by army junta
1984-88 severe famine, aid from West
1991 Mengistu's Communist regime overthrown after civil war*

CENTRAL AFRICAN REPUBLIC

UGANDA   KENYA
1970s border disputes with Uganda and Somalia

SOMALIA
*1964, 1970 border disputes with Ethiopia and Kenya
1976-78 occupation of Ogaden and war with Ethiopia
1993 UN military intervention to halt civil war and famine*

ZAIRE
*1960-69 civil war
1978 invasion of Shaba province by anti-Mobutu dissidents, repelled with French assistance*

RWANDA
BURUNDI

*1962 independence; -1965 civil war, massacre of Tutsi (in Rwanda and Burundi)
1994 tribal violence/civil war; mass exodus of refugees to Rwandan borders
Large scale UN humanitarian assistance*

TANZANIA

1962 independence followed by civil war/tribal violence, massive refugee movement to neighbouring countries

ANGOLA
*1975- Marxist MPLA government in conflict with UNITA guerrillas aided by South Africa
1991 peace agreement between MPLA and UNITA breaks down after elections: civil war renewed
1992 renewed fighting
1994 agreement between UNITA and government*

ZAMBIA
*support for black nationalists in Angola, Namibia and Rhodesia
1991 Kaunda defeated in democratic election*

*1975-1993 civil war between Frelimo government and Renamo guerrillas
1980- South African intervention in support of Renamo
1994 multi-party elections following Renamo-Frelimo peace accord*

MOZAMBIQUE

1 Africa: post-independence wars and revolutions

✸ civil war

➜ invasion

✊ guerrilla activity

✶ border dispute

ZIMBABWE (RHODESIA)

MADAGASCAR
1972 military takeover

NAMIBIA
*South African presence resisted by SWAPO to 1990
1991 fully independent from South Africa*

*1965-80 independent as Rhodesia under white-minority rule
1980 black majority rule established; increasing steps towards one-party state*

*1948 implementation of apartheid
1975 invasion of Angola
1976 mounting black urban unrest
1976-81 African homelands (Bantustans) established in Transkei, Bophuthatswana and Ciskei
1984 new constitution, limited representation for Indians and coloureds
1985-87 growing African resistance and civil unrest
1986 commando raids on neighbouring countries
1990 Mandela released President de Klerk starts to dismantle apartheid
1993 multiracial council paves way to free elections
1994 election victory for ANC; Mandela president
1996 National party leaves governing coalition*

SOUTH AFRICA

South and South-East Asia since 1945

The history of southern Asia since independence has been dominated by three factors. First, the seizure of power by military leaders (Pakistan 1958, Indonesia 1967), with the aim – rarely successful – of abolishing corruption and stabilizing the economy; second, the resurgence of long-standing regional, tribal and religious conflicts (Naga and Sikh unrest in India; nationalist uprisings among the Mons, Shans and other 'hill people' in Thailand and Burma); finally, intervention by the Great Powers (Russia in Afghanistan; China and the United States in Vietnam).

Wars between states also characterized certain areas. The partition of the Indian subcontinent in 1947 left numerous points of friction between the new states of India and Pakistan, particularly Punjab, Kashmir and Bengal, and these erupted into war in 1965 and again in 1971 (in connection with the secession of East Pakistan to form the separate state of Bangladesh). Indian forces also expelled the Portuguese from their coastal enclaves (1961), fought China over a frontier dispute (1962), and intervened in Sri Lanka to protect the Hindu Tamil minority (1986-90). Civil wars, however, proved far more common (map 1). Malaya suffered a communist insurrection, led by ethnic Chinese, between 1948 and 1960; the Philippines experienced rebellions by both communists and Muslims from the 1960s; Cambodia was devastated by the civil war between the communist Khmer Rouge and its non-communist opponents.

The most savage conflict, however, occurred in Vietnam (map 2). After the Japanese collapse in 1945 Ho Chi Minh established a communist regime in Hanoi while the French recreated their colonial empire in the south. In 1946 armed conflict began, continuing until a humiliating defeat at Dien Bien Phu in 1954 forced the French to withdraw. Although this left Cambodia and Laos as independent states, it did not create a unified Vietnam: at the Geneva Peace Conference in 1954 Ho accepted a 'temporary' partition of the country at the 17th parallel until nationwide elections, mandated for 1956, took place. However an anti-communist regime in the south, backed by America, refused to hold elections. In 1959 Ho therefore attacked, and the US immediately provided munitions and advisers to the south, with regular troops and air strikes after 1965. Despite saturation bombing and the commitment of 500,000 US ground troops, the communists (supported by both Russia and China) held their own and in 1968 negotiations began between Hanoi and Washington. In 1973 American forces withdrew, although the US continued to supply the south on a massive scale. When the communists launched an orthodox military offensive in 1975, however, the south's army collapsed. Vietnam was now unified, under Hanoi, although its economy was ruined and its invasion of Cambodia in 1978 led to ostracism by the West.

Elsewhere in Asia, however, rapid development occurred. Following the path of Japan (page 142), Taiwan, Malaysia, Singapore, Thailand and eventually Indonesia achieved rapid rates of growth from the late 1960s. Even during the world recession of the 1980s, each experienced an annual growth rate of well over 5 per cent. Various factors were responsible: all except Singapore possessed large pools of cheap labour; all created a substantial industrial base oriented towards export markets throughout Asia, Europe and North America; all the governments sought to attract substantial foreign investment through tax incentives and infrastructural development. A major part of that investment came from Japan (map 3). Finally, political stability – Lee in Singapore; Mahathir in Malaysia; Suharto in Indonesia – underpinned the economic

1955 supports Baluchistani separatists in Pakistan
Dec. 1979 invaded by USSR; Amin killed, Karmal installed as president; continued resistance by Islamic guerrillas
1988 USSR withdraws
1992 post Soviet-backed regime defeated by Islamic guerrillas

AFGHANISTAN

PAKISTAN

1958 military coup by Ayub Khan
1965 border clashes with India in Rann of Kutch
1965 war with India over Kashmir
1971 war with India over Bangladesh
1972 ceasefire lines established
1977 military coup by Zia ul-Haq
1988 democratic elections;. Benazir Bhutto prime minister (deposed 1990)
1993 Benazir Bhutto returns as prime minister (deposed 1996)

1 Post-independence wars and revolutions

✵ civil war

➡ invasion

✊ guerrilla activity

✴ border dispute

2 Vietnam, 1966-8

Areas of control, early 1966

- controlled by the Vietcong
- under Vietcong influence
- controlled by the Government
- under Government influence
- heavily contested areas

— front lines, 1966-7

✴ Tet offensive, 1968

Vinh

LAOS

Dong Hoi

Vinh Linh

Ho Chi Minh trail

Hue

Phu Bai

Da Nang

THAILAND

Chu Lai

Qui Nhon

SOUTH VIETNAM

CAMBODIA

Phnom Penh

Saigon

7th US fleet 1964

South China Sea

Kurile Islands incorporated in USSR; claimed by Japan
1951 peace treaty with USA and end of occupation
1956 agreement with USSR, ending state of war; cession of
territories (including S. Sakhalin) taken from Russia in 1905
1960 widespread demonstrations against security treaty,
granting US military bases in Japan and Okinawa
1972 normalization of relations with China
1974 beginning of incipient trade disputes with US and EC
1990 agreements with USSR formally ending 1945 war
1995 Kobe earthquake

NORTH KOREA

1948 Democratic People's Republic
of Korea proclaimed
1950 invasion of South Korea
1994 death of dictator Kim Il Sung.
His son, Kim Jong Il succeeds

SOUTH KOREA

J A P A N

1950 invasion of Tibet
1953-57 first Five-Year Plan
1958-60 Great Leap Forward; abandonment of
Soviet model and beginning of Sino-Soviet dispute
1960- border conflicts with India and USSR
1966-68 Cultural Revolution; mobilization of Red Guards
1969-75 stabilization and economic progress
1971 China admitted to United Nations
1972 Nixon's visit to Peking and normalization of
Sino-American relations
1976 death of Mao Tse-tung; political reorientation under
Hua Guofeng and Deng Xiaoping, leading to a limited
revival of private sector trade and production
1989 demonstration for democracy by
Peking students crushed
1990- economic liberalization accompanies
new wave of political repression

C H I N A

1948 Republic of Korea proclaimed
1950 Korean War
1961 military coup followed by dictatorship
of Park Chung Hee (assassinated 1979);
mounting opposition from 1974
1979 martial law (relaxed 1981)

OKINAWA

occupied by US after 1945,
reverted to Japan 1972

TIBET

NEPAL

INDIA

spasmodic unrest among Nagas,
Sikhs and Tamils
1962 Sino-Indian border war
1975-77 state of emergency proclaimed
1980 further emergency measures
1984 Sikh separatist uprising suppressed;
Indira Gandhi assassinated
1991 Rajiv Gandhi assassinated

BANGLADESH

1971 secession from Pakistan;
civil war followed in 1975 by
murder of Sheikh Mujib
and military control

seat of Chinese Nationalist government
under Chiang Kai-shek since 1949
1958 territorial dispute with mainland
China over Quemoy and Matsu
1996 China attempts military intimidations.
as Taiwan holds first free elections

TAIWAN

1954 French withdrawal followed by civil war
1956-73 US backed South Vietnam and the
communist-backed North engaged in
escalating conflict (see map 2)
1973 US withdraws all forces
1976 North and South Vietnam reunified
under Viet-Minh rule
1978 invasion of Cambodia and border
clashes with China
1979 Chinese invasion

BURMA

VIETNAM

LAOS

1953-73 civil war
1975 monarchy abolished;
Pathet Lao seizes power

continuing guerrilla activity since
independence (1948) by Communist and
minority groups, united in 1975-76 into
Federal National Democratic Front
1958, 1962 military coups
1974 Socialist People's Republic inaugurated
May 1990 pro-democracy protests lend to free
elections; military refuse to recognise result
1995 opposition leader Aung San Suu Kyi
released from house arrest

THAILAND

1947 military takeover,
guerrilla activity by Communist
and minority groups since 1960
1976 border clashes with Cambodia
1978 Cambodian refugee camps in
E. Thailand become bases for
anti-Vietnamese factions
1987 border clashes with Laos

PHILIPPINES

Communist and Muslim insurgency since 1968,
eruption into civil war 1972-78
1986 Marcos regime ousted following
general election. Aquino president
1992 Ramos succeeds as president

CAMBODIA

1970 monarchy abolished
1970-74 civil war; victory of Khmer
Rouge who conduct massacre of
civilians 1978 Vietnamese invasion
overthrows Khmer Rouge
1989 Vietnamese forces withdraw
1991 peace agreement leads to
May 1993 elections, boycotted by
Khmer Rouge which carries on
civil war

Mindanao

1958, 1961 fighting between Sinhalese and Tamils
1971 government assumes emergency powers after
rural guerrilla uprisings; 1984 intercommunal rioting
1986-90 Indian intervention to crush Tamil rebellions
May 1993 President Ranasinghe killed in rebel Tamil
attack

SRI LANKA

1969 rising by Chinese minority groups
1975-78 Communist guerrilla activity
1978- renewed racial and religious conflict

M A L A Y S I A

IRIAN JAYA

I N D O N E S I A

1967 Sukarno ousted by military coup;
suppression of Communists
1976- resistance to Indonesian
rule in E. Timor
1977-79 secessionist rising in Irian Jaya

E. Timor

SOVIET UNION

Sea of
Okhotsk

MONGOLIA

40

Peking

N. KOREA

S. KOREA 606
Seoul

Tokyo

Osaka

C H I N A 438

Shanghai

Bonin Is.

**3 Japan, Australia
and Asia to 1989**

631 — Japanese direct investment,
1989 (US$ million)

Bangkok
1978 — major Japanese transport/
infrastructure project, with date

▲ — pilot Japanese transport/
infrastructure projects

✈ — major international airports

— principal air routes

/// — development corridors

Canton

Hanoi

Chiangmai

Taipei

TAIWAN 494

Hong
Kong 1,898

Rangoon

THAILAND 1,276

Bangkok
1978

PHILIPPINES 202

Phnom
Penh

Kota Kinabulu

Caroline Is.

**PACIFIC
OCEAN**

1971
Port
ang

673

Medan
1978

MALAYSIA
Johor Baharu 1,182

SINGAPORE
1,302

Kuala
Lumpur

Sumatra

Borneo

Celebes

631

I N D O N E S I A

PAPUA NEW GUINEA
New
Guinea

KIRIBATI

Bismarck Arch.

SOLOMON IS.

TUVALU

Jakarta

Bali

Timor
Sea

Cape York

Port
Moresby

Santa Cruz Is.

VANUATU

Darwin

Coral Sea

FIJI

New Caledonia

-20

Townsville

A U S T R A L I A

Brisbane

Perth

Adelaide

Sydney

Auckland

**NEW
ZEALAND**

Melbourne

Wellington

Hobart

Christchurch

90° 110° 130° 150° 190°

strategy of industrial development and
helped to attract foreign investment.

Increasingly, the pattern of trade
involved raw materials flowing to the Asian
economies in return for manufactured
goods (especially automobiles and electron-
ic goods). By the 1990s, the countries of the
Pacific Rim formed, together with North
America and the European Union, a 'triad'
of dominant economic trading blocs in the
world which between them attracted more
than four-fifths of worldwide direct foreign
investment, 70 per cent of it from other
triad states. Other parts of southern Asia
failed to share in the boom, creating new
divisions in the area (page 160).

153

The Cold War 1947-89

The defeat of Germany, Italy and Japan and the weakening of Britain and France in World War II left the USA and USSR as the only 'superpowers'. Their ideological and political confrontation expressed itself as the Cold War. Conflict between the two had already appeared before the final victory: The Western Allies had already agreed (reluctantly) at Yalta (February 1945) to allow Soviet control of eastern Europe after the end of the war. By 1949 Stalin had developed an atomic bomb, thus ending the US monopoly of nuclear weapons. In reply, the USA built up the defence of western Europe with the formation of the North Atlantic Treaty Organization (NATO) in 1949 (page 139). In 1952 the US tested a thermo-nuclear (hydrogen) bomb; Russia followed suit in 1953.

Although it started as a conflict over central Europe, the Cold War soon developed into a global confrontation. The US saw the Korean War (1950-3: page 142) as evidence of a world-wide communist conspiracy, and American policy now became the 'containment' of Communism by a series of encircling alliances. NATO was followed by the South-East Asia Treaty Organization (SEATO) in 1954 and the Baghdad Pact (1955); the US maintained over 1400 foreign bases, including 275 bases for nuclear bombers, in 31 countries around the Soviet perimeter (map 1). As long as nuclear devices could only be delivered by aircraft, possession of these bases conferred an enormous advantage on the US. But when in the early 1960s both sides began to deploy ballistic nuclear missiles capable of being launched from land silos and submarines, the odds altered: now, in the event of war, each of the two superpowers could attack the other's cities directly (chart 3).

In October 1962, this scenario was almost put to the test when, following an unsuccessful US attempt to unseat the communist regime, the USSR established nuclear missile sites in Cuba. President Kennedy proclaimed a 'quarantine' of the island and threatened that, if the missiles were fired, the US would immediately retaliate against the USSR. The Russians then agreed to their removal (map 2). In return, Kennedy agreed to remove some US missile sites from Turkey.

This crisis, with its real threat of nuclear holocaust, proved a turning point in the Cold War. Already both monolithic blocs had begun to show signs of strain, most seriously on the Soviet side: Hungary and Poland rebelled in 1956, and from 1960 China began to quarrel openly over territory and ideology. In western Europe, France rejected American political leadership after 1958 and left NATO. A desire to limit the spread of nuclear weapons led to the conclusion of a partial test-ban treaty in 1963 and a nuclear non-proliferation treaty in 1968, but not all nuclear or potential nuclear powers signed these agreements (notably France, China and India) while others (such

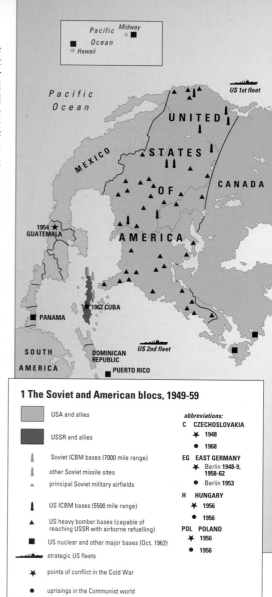

1 The Soviet and American blocs, 1949-59

▢	USA and allies
▨	USSR and allies
ⵑ	Soviet ICBM bases (7000 mile range)
ⵑ	other Soviet missile sites
▲	principal Soviet military airfields
ⵑ	US ICBM bases (5500 mile range)
▲	US heavy bomber bases (capable of reaching USSR with airborne refuelling)
■	US nuclear and other major bases (Oct. 1962)
⚓	strategic US fleets
✷	points of conflict in the Cold War
●	uprisings in the Communist world

abbreviations:
C CZECHOSLOVAKIA
✷ 1948
● 1968
EG EAST GERMANY
✷ Berlin 1948-9, 1958-62
● Berlin 1953
H HUNGARY
✷ 1956
● 1956
POL POLAND
✷ 1956
● 1956

3 The nuclear balance 1955-80

bombers   missiles   warheads

1955 1960 1965 1970 1975 1980

Map labels (main map):

Wake
Kwajalein
Pacific Ocean
Guam
Iwo Jima

JAPAN
US 7th fleet
Okinawa
PHILIPPINES
SOUTH KOREA
KOREA 1950-3
Formosa
Quemoy, Matsu
1954-5, 1958
SOUTH VIETNAM
1946-54, 1957-73
LAOS
INDO-CHINA
THAILAND
EAST PAKISTAN
Indian Ocean

ALASKA
Arctic Ocean
CHINA
MONGOLIA
SOVIET UNION
INDIA

GREENLAND
Iceland
PAKISTAN

NORWAY
HOLLAND
BELGIUM
DENMARK
IRELAND
UNITED KINGDOM
POL
EG
WEST GERMANY
H
ROM
YUGO 1948-53
BUL
Atlantic Ocean
FRANCE
ITALY
ALBANIA
GREECE 1946-9
TURKEY 1945-7
IRAN 1945-6, 1951-3
IRAQ 1958
LEBANON 1958
ISRAEL
SAUDI ARABIA
Azores
SPAIN
PORTUGAL
MOROCCO
LIBYA
US 6th fleet

2 The Cuban crisis, 1962

— American blockade zone

Soviet mobile missile and jet bomber bases

US Air Force base

US Naval base

as Iraq) later reneged on their commitment. The Cold War therefore continued and the superpowers created huge nuclear arsenals.

In the event, the economic and political difficulties of the USSR increased to the point where the Soviet leader Mikhail Gorbachev (1985-91) felt that only a dramatic reduction in the crushing burden of military expenditure could bring relief (page 158). First the Soviets withdrew their forces from eastern Europe (1989), then NATO and the Warsaw Pact declared that the other was no longer an enemy (1990), and finally the USSR itself began to disintegrate (1991). Further agreements on the reduction of nuclear and conventional forces soon followed, although the fate of the vast arsenal accumulated by the former USSR gave cause for concern.

FLORIDA
USAF and US Army build-up
Homestead AF
Miami
Key West
Guanajay
Havana
San Cristóbal
Candelaria
Bay of Pigs landing April 1961
Sagua la Grande
Remedios
Santa Clara
Bahama Islands
Task Force Screen (TF 136)
Air Patrol
CUBA
Santiago de Cuba
Guantánamo Bay
JAMAICA
HAITI
DOMINICAN REPUBLIC
Air Patrol
Caribbean Sea

Europe since 1973

The pre-war fascist regimes of the Iberian peninsula gave way to democracy in the 1970s: Portugal in 1974, following the failure of colonial wars in Africa; Spain in 1975, following the death of General Franco. Despite an attempted right-wing coup in 1981, Spain joined NATO in 1982 and in 1986 both countries joined the European Community (EC). 1974 also saw the restoration of democracy in Greece, where a right-wing military junta had seized power in 1967, and Greece too joined the EC in 1981 (map 1).

The Community thus expanded from six members in 1957 (page 138) to nine in 1973, and twelve in 1986, and further agreements linked it with Turkey, Malta and Cyprus. The first direct elections to the European Parliament took place in 1979, and in 1985 the EC agreed an agenda and timetable for the creation of a single European market. At Maastricht in 1991 the member states agreed in principle to work towards eventual economic and monetary union and the formation of a common European foreign and security policy. All members of the rival European Free Trade Association (EFTA), except for Switzerland and Iceland, applied for membership in 1994-5, as did most of the former socialist countries of eastern Europe. In January 1995, Austria, Finland and Sweden became full members of the European Union.

Whereas the original six members had all possessed a strong industrial base, combined with a powerful agricultural workforce in 1960, by 1993 their agricultural sector had shrunk dramatically (map 2). In the 'applicant' countries, by contrast, the percentage often stood far higher (almost 50 per cent in Turkey). Furthermore, the percentage of the EC workforce engaged in industry either remained stable or declined, with the service sector employing the largest number (over 70 per cent in Britain, Belgium and the Netherlands). This development reflected the industrial depression that followed the oil crisis of 1973 (chart 3) and helped to limit the EC's foreign policy – for example, towards the civil war in the former Yugoslavia (page 158).

2 Changes in economic structure 1960-93

percentage of employment in:

Services

Industry

Agriculture

1 The expansion of the European Union, 1981-96

- members of the EEC, Jan. 1981
- joined Jan. 1986
- admitted Oct. 1990
- joined Jan. 1995
- applied by June 1996 for EU membership, with date of application

The European Economic Area (EEA)

- members of the EEA, June 1996

3 European GDP growth 1950-92

(GDP per capita in 1990)

1950 — 1973 — 1992

$20,000

$15,000

$10,000

$5,000

0

Austria, Belgium, Denmark, Finland, France, W. Germany, Italy, Netherlands, Norway, Sweden, Switzerland, UK

The collapse of communism in Europe since 1989

From 1989, communism collapsed all over eastern Europe, culminating at the end of 1991 in the disintegration of the Soviet Union itself. The reasons for this startling transformation were as much economic as political. Throughout the 1970s and 1980s zero growth rates and immense external debts combined to bankrupt the communist economies of the region. Finally, unable any longer to guarantee the survival of its client states, the Soviet Union effectively abandoned them. The 'Brezhnev doctrine', formulated after the Soviet invasion to stop liberal reforms in Czechoslovakia in 1968, claimed for the Soviet Union the right to intervene in the affairs of any satellite country. But in a key speech delivered in 1987, Soviet leader Mikhail Gorbachev asserted that the 'The independence of each party, its responsibility to its people, the right to resolve questions of the country's development in a sovereign way – for us these are indisputable principles.' There could be no clearer hint to the leaders of eastern Europe – and their peoples – that they were now on their own.

The fall of communism in Europe began in August 1988 with strikes and demonstrations in Poland calling for the recognition of the free trade union Solidarity. In September 1989 a government led by Solidarity took office following partially-free elections. Shortly afterwards mass demonstrations in the German Democratic

Sep. 1989: mass exodus of political refugees reach the West via Hungary; communist leadership in crisis
Oct.-Nov. 1989: widespread demonstrations against leadership
9 Nov. 1989: Berlin Wall breached
Mar. 1990: free elections
July 1990: currency union with West Germany
Oct. 1990: reunified with West Germany

Dec. 1989: economic war between Belgrade government and Slovenia
Apr. 1990: free elections
June 1991: independence declared; Yugoslav army attempts to regain control of Slovenia
July 1991: Brioni Agreement ends fighting in Slovenia; Yugoslav army withdraws

Apr.-May 1990: free elections
Dec. 1990: Serbian-inhabited areas declare independence
June 1991: independence declared; fighting in Slovenia spreads to Croatia as Serbs attempt to extend territory in Croatia and Bosnia

2 The Yugoslav civil war, 1991-5

→ Croatian advances, Jan. 1993
→ Federation of Bosnia and Herzegovina advances, Oct.-Nov. 1994
--→ Croatian and Federation of Bosnia and Herzegovina advances, spring 1995
→ Bosnian Serb advances, summer 1995
→ Croatian and Federation of Bosnia and Herzegovina advances, Aug.-Oct. 1995

Croatia, June 1991
overrun by the Yugoslav army and Croatian Serb forces by Dec. 1991
Bosnia-Herzegovina, Mar. 1992
secured by Yugoslav army and Bosnian Serb forces by Dec. 1992
controlled by Bosnian Croat forces, Dec. 1992
under Bosnian government control , Dec. 1992
overwhelmingly or largely Muslim, 1991. No significant Muslim presence by 1996
Autonomous Province of Western Bosnia, Sep. 1993-Aug. 1994
remained under control of breakaway Serbian forces, Oct. 1995
to be returned to Croatian control by Nov. 1996 under Zagreb agreement
UN designated "safe areas"

1 The collapse of communism, 1985-91

Mar. 1990: Congress of Estonia formed, declares Soviet rule illegal
Mar. 1991: referendum endorses independence
Aug. 1991: independence declared
Sep. 1991: independence recognized by USSR

1989: mass anti-communist demonstrations
Mar. 1991: referendum endorses independence
Aug. 1991: independence declared
Sep. 1991: independence recognized by USSR

1989: mass anti-communist demonstrations
Mar 1991: independence declared
Apr.-June 1990: economic embargo imposed by USSR
Sep. 1991: independence recognized by USSR

Mar. 1985: Mikhail Gorbachev becomes leader of Communist Party; initiates perestroika and glasnost, loosens Soviet control of satellite states
June 1991: Boris Yeltsin elected president of Russian Federation
Aug. 1991: hard-line communist coup against Gorbachev fails
Nov. 1991: Communist Party declared illegal
Dec. 1991: USSR dissolved

from 1985: Solidarity leads opposition to communism
June 1989: partially free elections
Sep. 1989: Solidarity-led government takes office
Jan. 1990: Communist Party dissolved
Oct. 1991: free elections

June 1989: Popular Front founded.
Aug. 1991: independence declared
Dec. 1991: founder member of CIS

from 1988: anti-government demonstrations
Nov. 1989: mass demonstrations end communist rule
Apr. 1990: new constitution adopted; becomes a federation
June 1990: free elections

from 1987: communist regime relaxes control
Sep. 1989: allows East Germans to travel to the West
Oct. 1990: communist rule ends peacefully
Mar.-Apr. 1990: free elections

1989: opposition mass-movements emerge
Aug. 1991: independence declared
Dec. 1991: referendum endorses independence; founder member of CIS

TRANSNISTRIA

June 1989: Popular Front wins 75% of votes in election
Aug.1991: independence declared

GAGAUZIA

Dec. 1989: mass demonstrations lead to armed uprisings and overthrow of Ceaucescu regime
June 1991: free elections
Nov. 1991: new constitution adopted

Nov. 1989: President Zhivkov removed from office
June 1990: free elections
July 1991: fresh elections following adoption of new constitution

Nov. 1988: mass demonstrations against Russification
Mar. 1991: referendum endorses independence
Apr. 1991: independence declared

Nov. 1991: independence declared

CHECHENIA

Jan. 1990: state of emergency declared; Soviet troops intervene
Oct. 1991: independence declared

Jan.-May 1990: democratic reforms initiated by leadership
Mar. 1991: free elections

1987: mass strikes against wage freeze and falling living standards, growing Serb militancy against minorities
July 1990: provincial autonomies abolished
1990-1: increasing tension between Belgrade government and Slovenia and Croatia

Sep. 1989: economic embargo imposed by Azerbaijan
Sep. 1991: referendum endorses independence; independence declared

Sep. 1991: independence declared

NAGORNO-KARABAGH

Legend:
- Soviet-dominated Eastern Europe to 1989
- Soviet Union to 1991
- Yugoslavia to 1991
- other communist states to 1991
- united with the Federal Republic of Germany, 1990
- independent, 1991
- de-facto independent states, late 1991, on former territory of the Soviet Union, internationally unrecognized
- over-run by Yugoslav army, July-Dec. 1991

Republic resulted in the opening of the Berlin Wall (erected by the communist government in 1961). Almost immediately a massive wave of emigration led to the collapse of the east German economy and to re-unification (3 October 1990). By 1991, free elections had been held in every country in the region, including the Soviet Union (page 140). In Czechoslovakia, tensions between Czechs and Slovaks divided the country in 1993; but everywhere except in Romania the transition to democratic rule proved relatively peaceful (map 1).

Inevitably such rapid changes created problems: political instability, as former communists sought to reassert their authority; ethnic conflicts, as age-old nationalist sentiments revived; and economic dislocations. The fall-out from these sudden events was most extreme in former Yugoslavia (map 2). The fragility of the country's unity had become increasingly clear during the 1980s. Slovenia declared its independence in 1991. A vicious seven-month war broke out when Croatia, too, declared its independence the same year: Serbian forces intervened, using as an excuse their need to protect ethnic Serbs in Croatia (12 per cent of the population).

Similar developments occurred in Bosnia-Herzegovina, where 31 per cent of the population were Serbs, 17 per cent Croats, and 44 per cent Muslims (descendants of the Slavs who converted to Islam under Ottoman rule). War broke out there in 1992 as an army of Bosnian Serbs carried out 'ethnic cleansing' – the systematic removal and sometimes extermination of rival ethnic groups – which by 1994 had caused the death of at least 100,000 and displaced half of the region's 4 million inhabitants. In 1995 a renewed Serb offensive in Bosnia provoked NATO reprisals and in November a peace-settlement was signed at Dayton, Ohio. Bosnia was partitioned into seperate ethnic republics: a predominantly Muslim state based in Sarajevo; a Serb republic with strong ambitions to unite with Serbia; and a Croat area, notionally federated with the Sarajevo government.

The world in the 1990s

Despite unprecedented growth in prosperity after World War II, between 1960 and 1994 the economic gap separating the richest and poorest fifths of the world doubled. In part, the meagre economic performance of developing countries stemmed from rapid population growth unaccompanied by adequate increases in national income. The world population explosion slowed in the later 1980s, but long-term population increase remained a serious problem (chart 1). Improvements in health care reduced infant mortality rates and extended lifespans, except in areas where famine and disease (including AIDS) had become rife (chart 2).

In the later 1980s, the focus of economic competition between the three major trading blocs (North America, the European Union, and Japan) shifted from trade to capital. Between 1984 and 1989 the flow of foreign direct investment (FDI) rose at an annual rate of 29 per cent – three times faster than trade – to reach a total of $1500 billion.

4 Ozone depletion

Extent of ozone depletion in 1986

1992

1979

South Pole

Antarctic Circle

ANTARCTICA

3 The world in the 1990's

Gross National Product per capita in 1992

Below $300	$1001 – $2500
$300 – $600	$2501 – $10,000
$601 – $1000	Above $10,000

International Trade in Illicit Drugs in 1990

cocaine trade

opium trade

64,400t   quantity produced in metric tons

International terrorist incidents by region 1989-94

267   number of incidents in region

Metropolitan Areas in 1992

■ population over 10 million
● population over 5 million

Map labels:
CANADA
NORTH AMERICA 31
San Francisco
Los Angeles
USA
Chicago
New York
Mexico 62t
Mexico City
Guatemala 13t
Costa Rica
Colombia 32,100t
Bogota
Ecuador 120t
Peru 138,300t
Lima
Bolivia 64,400t
LATIN AMERICA 590
SOUTH AMERICA
Rio de Janeiro
São Paulo
Buenos Aires

Atlantic Ocean

St Petersburg
Moscow
London
Paris
EUROPE 715
Istanbul
Portugal $2123
Tehran
Lebanon 32t
Iran 300t
MIDDLE EAST 535
Cairo
ALGERIA
AFRICA
SUDAN
Nigeria $588
Lagos
SUB-SAHARAN AFRICA 136
ANGOLA
SOUTH AFRICA

Cocaine to North America via West Indies
Cocaine to Western Europe via Asia
Cocaine to Western Europe (some via Africa)
Opium to North America & Europe from the Golden Crescent* & Golden Triangle†
Opium to North America & Europe

160

Growth in world trade in goods, on the other hand, slowed from 8.5 per cent in 1988 to 3 per cent in 1991. Moreover, whereas in the earlier 1980s the proportion of world FDI in developing countries was 25 per cent, between 1985 and 1990 it shrank to a mere 17 per cent, making it increasingly difficult for those countries to finance their debts with export earnings.

However, developing countries did possess a clear competitive edge in the production and distribution of illicit drugs – opium from Asia; cocaine from South America – a $500-billion-a-year business second only to the world trade in arms. Drug production offered a vital source of hard currency and employment. Approximately 400,000 of Bolivia's 6.5 million population worked directly in the drug trade; in 1990, the gross income per acre of Peruvian coca farmers exceeded that of coffee farmers ten-fold; in 1991 Colombia alone exported an estimated 200 tons of cocaine to Europe (map 3). The UN declared the 1990s a 'decade against drugs'.

The UN also organized a conference on the Environment in Rio de Janeiro in 1992 which involved more governments (185) than any previous international gathering, and focused attention on issues such as the emission of pollution and 'greenhouse gases' (such as chlorine) that risked a potentially disastrous warming of the earth's climate by depleting the ozone layer which protects it against solar radiation (map 4). But although the economies of industrialized countries, which produced much of the existing contamination, seemed better able to adopt new, less deleterious technologies, developing countries, responsible for a growing proportion of the contamination, feared yet another expensive obstacle to their economic expansion.

Failure to tackle global problems seriously undermined confidence in the state and established institutions – whether in the former Soviet Union (page 140) or in the West, where evidence of institutionalized corruption in countries such as Japan and Italy, combined with prolonged economic recession, led some voters to favour more radical parties. But no one provided easy solutions.

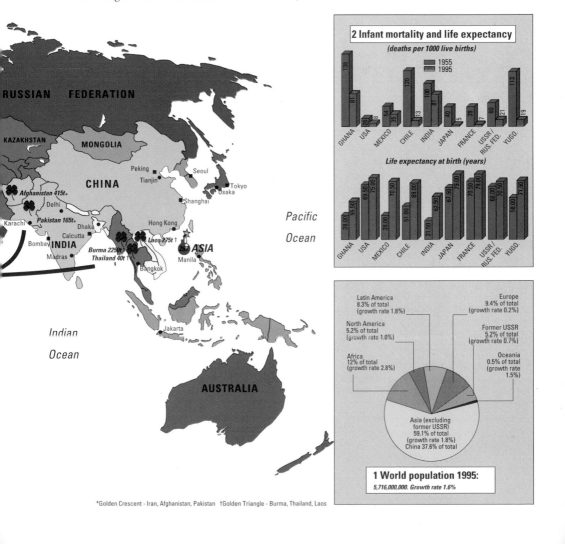

*Golden Crescent - Iran, Afghanistan, Pakistan †Golden Triangle - Burma, Thailand, Laos

INDEX

1 HISTORICAL PLACE NAMES

Geographical names vary with time and with language, and there is some difficulty in treating them consistently in an historical atlas, especially for individual maps within whose time span the same place has been known by different names. We have aimed at the simplest possible approach to the names on the maps, using the index to weld together the variations.

On the maps forms of names will be found in the following hierarchy of preference:

a English conventional names or spellings, in the widest sense, for all principal places and features, e.g., Moscow, Vienna, Munich (including those that today might be considered obsolete when these are appropriate to the context, e.g., Leghorn).

b Names that are contemporary in terms of the maps concerned. There are here three broad categories:
i names in the ancient world, where the forms used are classical, e.g., Latin or latinized Greek, but extending also to Persian, Sanskrit, etc.
ii names in the post-medieval modern world, which are given in the form (though not necessarily the spelling) current at the time of the map (e.g., St. Petersburg before 1914, not Leningrad).
iii modern names where the spelling generally follows that of *The Times Atlas of the World*, though in the interests of simplicity there has been a general omission of diacritics in spellings derived by transliteration from non-roman scripts, e.g., Sana rather than Şan'ā'.

2 THE INDEX

Where a place is referred to by two or more different names in the course of the atlas, there will be a corresponding number of main entries in the index. The variant names in each case are given in brackets at the beginning of the entry, their different forms and origins being distinguished by such words as *now, later, formerly* and others included in the list of abbreviations (*right*).

'Bizerta (*anc.* Hippo Zarytus)' means that the page references to that city on maps dealing with periods when it was known as Bizerta follow that entry, but the page references pertaining to it in ancient times will be found under the entry for Hippo Zarytus.

Places are located generally by reference to the country in which they lie (exceptionally by reference to island groups or sea areas), this being narrowed down where necessary by location as E(ast), C(entral), etc. The reference will normally be to the modern state in which the place now falls unless (a) there is a conventional or historical name which conveniently avoids the inevitably anachronistic ring of some modern names, e.g., Anatolia rather than Turkey, Mesopotamia rather than Iraq, or (b) the modern state is little known or not delineated on the map concerned, e.g., many places on the Africa plates can only be located as W, E, Africa, etc.

Reference is generally to page number/map number (e.g. 118/1) unless the subject is dealt with over the plate as a whole, when the references have been given sub-headings where possible, e.g., Civil War 129/4. Battles are indicted by the symbol **✕**.

Though page references are generally kept in numerical order, since this corresponds for the most part with chronological order, they have been rearranged occasionally where the chronological sequence would be obviously wrong, or in the interests of grouping appropriate references under a single sub-heading.

3 ABBREVIATIONS

a/c also called
AD Autonomous District
Alb. Albanian
anc. ancient
AR Autonomous Region
Ar. Arabic
a/s also spelled
ASSR Autonomous Soviet Socialist Republic
Bibl. Biblical
Bulg. Bulgarian
C Century (when preceded by 17, 18, etc.)
C Central
Cat. Catalan
Chin. Chinese
Cz. Czech
Dan. Danish
Dut. Dutch
E East(ern)
Eng. English
Est. Estonian
f/c formerly called
Finn. Finnish
form. former(ly)
Fr. French
f/s formerly spelled
Ger. German
Gr. Greek
Heb. Hebrew
Hung. Hungarian
Indon. Indonesian
Ir. Irish
Is. Island
It. Italian
Jap. Japanese
Kor. Korean
Lat. Latin
Latv. Latvian
Lith. Lithuanian
Mal. Malay
med. medieval
mod. modern
Mong. Mongolian
N North(ern)
n/c now called
Nor. Norwegian
n/s now spelled
NT New Testament
obs. obsolete
OT Old Testament
Pers. Persian
Pol. Polish
Port. Portuguese
Rom. Romanian
Russ. Russian
S South(ern)
s/c sometimes called
Som. Somali
Sp. Spanish
S.Cr. Serbo-Croat
SSR Soviet Socialist Republic
Sw. Swedish
Turk. Turkish
Ukr. Ukrainian
US(A) United States (of America)
var. variant
W West(ern)
Wel. Welsh
WW1 World War 1
WW2 World War 2

Aachen (*Fr.* Aix-la-Chapelle *anc.* Aquisgranum) W Germany Frankish royal residence 48/1; WW1 125/1
Abkhazia autonomous region of Georgia 140/1
Abyssinia (*now* Ethiopia) 112/2
Achaea (*a/s* Achaia) Roman province 35/1
Acragas (*Lat.* Agrigentum *mod.* Agrigento) Sicily Dorian colony 30/1
Acre (*OT* Accho *NT* Ptolemais *Fr.* St. Jean-d'Acre *Heb.* Akko) Palestine Levantine city 20/1
Addis Ababa Ethiopia Italian penetration 105/1
Aden S Arabia early town 74/1; Ottoman Empire 102/1; taken by British 112/2; British base 145/1
Aden Protectorate (*successively renamed* Protectorate of South Arabia, Federation of South Arabia, People's Republic of South Yemen, People's Democratic Republic of Yemen; *now part of* United Yemen)
Admiralty Islands S Pacific Japanese attack 134/1
Adowa N Ethiopia ✗105/1
Adrianople (*anc.* Adrianopolis *mod.* Edirne) W Turkey Byzantine Empire 44/1; Ottoman centre 67/1; occupied by Greece 128/1
Aegospotami (*Turk.* Karaova Suyu) NW Turkey ✗31/2
Aegyptus (*mod.* Egypt) Roman province 35/1
Afars and Issas, French Territory of (*form.* French Somaliland *now* Republic of Djibouti)
Afghanistan under Abbasid sovereignty 47/2; in Safavid Empire 58/1; independent sultanate 102/1; invaded by USSR 153/1; opium trade 161/1
Africa early man 11/1; agricultural origins 25/1; early cultures 25/1; early empires 54/1, 55/2; slave trade 54/1, 55/2; early European voyages of discovery 72/1; European expansion and trade 74/1, 75/2; 18C European trade 97/2; European penetration 105/1; colonial empires 112/2; anti-colonial resistance 145/1; modern political developments 150/1; economy 160/1; foreign direct investment 160/1
Africa (*mod.* Tunisia and Libya) conversion to Christianity 32/1; Roman province 35/1; Byzantine province 44/1
Aigun NE China treaty port 89/2
Ain Jalut Palestine ✗24/1, 47/2
Aix (*or* Aix-en-Provence *anc.* Aquae Sextiae) S France archbishopric 48/1; *parlement* 77/2
Ajnadain Palestine ✗47/1
Åland Islands (*Finn.* Ahvenanmaa) SW Finland neutralized 128/1
Alaska state of USA purchase from Russia 108/1
Albania Black Death 63/1; Ottoman province 102/1; principality 119/1; annexed by Italy 129/2; Cold War 154/1; employment 156; free elections 159/1

Albania ancient country of Caucasus 35/1
Albany (*form.* Fort Orange) NE USA seized by English 81/2
Alemannia SW Germany part of Frankish Empire 48/1
Aleppo (*anc.* Beroea *a/c* Yamkhad *Fr.* Alep *Ar.* Halab) Syria Mitannian city 20/1; Byzantine Empire 44/1; centre of European trade 97/2
Alessandria N Italy Lombard League 51/2
Aleutian Islands W Alaska to USA 108/1; attacked by Japanese 134/1; retaken by Americans 135/2
Alexandretta (*mod.* Iskenderun) E Turkey ceded to Turkey 128/1
Alexandria (*Ar.* Al Iskandariyah) Egypt taken by Alexander 30/3; spread of Christianity 32/1; Roman Empire 35/1; Christian centre 41/2; Arab conquest 47/1; trade 55/2; centre of European trade 97/2
Algeria Ottoman province 102/1; French invasion 105/1; French colonization 104/2, 105/1, 113/1; under Vichy control 132/1; independence 145/1; political development 150/1
Algiers (*Fr.* Alger *Sp.* Argel *Ar.* Al Jaza'ir *anc.* Icosium) N Algeria Corsair city 55/2; Ottoman rule 66/2; Habsburg Empire 87/1; Allied landing WW2 133/2
Alişar Hüyük C Anatolia Hittite city 20/1
Aljubarrota Portugal ✗63/1
Allenstein (*Pol.* Olsztyn) W Poland acquired by Germany after plebiscite 128/1
Alma-Ata (*until 1921* Vernyy; *n/s* Almaty) C Asia industry 126/2
Almanza Spain ✗76/3
Almohads Muslim dynasty and empire of North Africa 47/2; 54/1
Almoravids Muslim dynasty of Morocco 47/2
Alpes Cottiae Roman province, France/Italy 35/1
Alpes Maritimae Roman province, France/Italy 35/1
Alpes Poeninae Roman province, France/Italy 35/1
Alsace (*anc.* Alsatia *Ger.* Elsass) in German Empire 51/2; acquired by French 81/2; Habsburg Empire 87/1
Alsace-Lorraine (*Ger.* Elsass-Lothringen) region of E France annexed by German Empire 111/2; ceded to France 128/1
America, Central (*a/c* Mesoamerica) agricultural origins 14/1; early peoples 22/2, 23/1; early civilizations 23/1; Aztec Empire 68/2; colonial expansion 74/1; 18C Atlantic economy 96/1; foreign direct investment 160/1
America, North colonization 12/2; early cultures 23/1, 69/1; early voyages of discovery 72/1; colonial expansion 81/1,2; 18C Atlantic economy 96/1; industrialization 137/2; foreign direct investment 160/1. See also Canada, United States

America, South colonization 12/2; agricultural origins 14/1; early peoples 23/1; early civilizations 23/1; Inca Empire 68/3; early voyages of discovery 72/1; colonial expansion 74/1, 81/1; 18C Atlantic economy 96/1; independence 107/1; modern politics 107/1; foreign direct investment 160/1
American Samoa S Pacific 145/1 (inset)
Amoy (*n/s* Xiamen) S China treaty port 89/2; Japanese influence 89/2; occupied by Japanese 117/2; 143/2
Amphipolis N Greece ✗31/2
Anatolia early agriculture 16/1; incipient urbanization 18/1; Hittite cities 20/1; Black Death 63/1; Ottoman conquest 67/1. See also Asia Minor
Ancyra (*mod.* Ankara *obs. Eng.* Angora) W Anatolia Roman empire 35/1; Byzantine Empire 44/1
Andernach (*anc.* Antunnacum) W Germany ✗51/2
Angkor Cambodia Buddhist site 32/1
Angles tribe of NW Europe, migrations 39/1
Anglo-Egyptian Sudan condominium 104/2; Ottoman territory under British control 112/2
Angola SW Africa early Portuguese trade 74/1; source of slaves 74/1; Portuguese colonization 104/2, 105/1, 112/2; independence 145/1; political development 150/1
Angora (*anc.* Ancyra *mod.* Ankara) W Anatolia ✗57/2
Anguilla island of West Indies independence 145/1 (inset)
Anhwei (*a/s* Anhui) province of E China Manchu expansion 88/1; economy 143/2
Annam N Indo-China under T'ang control 42/1; annexed by Ming 64/1; expansion and early trade 82/2
Antarctica 84/1; ozone depletion 160/1
Antigua island of West Indies colony 107/1; independence 145/1 (inset)
Antioch (*Lat.* Antiochia *mod.* Antakya) NW Syria Roman Empire 35/1; archbishopric 40/1; Byzantine rule 44/1
Antipolis (*mod.* Antibes) SE France Ionian colony 30/1
Antung (*now* Dandong) Manchuria treaty port 89/2
Antwerp (*Fr.* Anvers *Dut.* Antwerpen) Belgium town of Spanish Netherlands 86/2; WW1 125/1; WW2 133/2
Aquileia (*med.* Aglar) N Italy Byzantine Empire 44/1
Aquincum (*mod.* Budapest) Hungary Roman Empire 35/1
Aquitaine (*anc.* Aquitania *mod.* Guyenne) region of SW France Black Death 63/1
Aquitania (*mod.* Aquitaine *later* Guyenne) Roman province of Gaul 35/1; Visigothic territory conquered by Franks 48/1

Arabia maritime trading 18/1; spread of Judaism 32/1; centre of Islam 47/1; 18C European trade 97/2
Arabia Petraea Roman province of N Arabia 35/1
Arabs territorial losses to Byzantine Empire 44/1; independence from Ottomans 102/1; emigration from Israel 146/2
Arachosia (*a/c* Harauvatish) Afghanistan ancient province of Persian and Alexander's Empires 26/1
Aragon (*Sp.* Aragón) region of E Spain rural uprisings 63/1; Muslim minorities 84/1; Habsburg Empire 87/1
Arakan district of SW Burma Islamic states 60/2; British control 82/2
Archangel (*Russ.* Arkhangelsk) N Russia founded 79/1; industry 126/2; Allied occupation 127/1
Arcole N Italy ✗93/1
Ardennes forest Belgium/France WW1 125/1; WW2 ✗133/2
Arelate (*mod.* Arles) S France Roman Empire 35/1,2
Argentina independence from Spain 107/1; political developments 149/1; industrialization and economy 149/2; 160/1
Arginusae islands of the Aegean ✗31/2
Armagnac region of SW France annexed to France 76/1
Armenia (*anc.* Urartu) country of Caucasus spread of Christianity 32/1; Roman province 35/1; Muslim conquest 47/1; Ottoman Empire 102/1; independence after WW1 128/1; SSR 140/1; independence 1991 159/1
Arras (*anc.* Nemetocenna) N France fort 77/2; WW1 125/1
Arretium (*mod.* Arezzo) C Italy Etruscan city 30/1
Artaxata Armenia Roman Empire 35/1
Artois region of NE France Burgundian possession 76/1; province of France 77/2
Ashur (*mod.* Sharqat) Mesopotamia Assyrian Empire 20/1; Mitannian city 20/1
Asia early man 11/1, 12/2, 14/1; colonization by hunters 13/1; Chinese expansion 37/1; tribal movements 39/1; early voyages of discovery 72/1, 74/1; Russian expansion 79/2; 18C European trade 97/2; colonial empires 112/2; anti-colonial resistance 145/1; foreign direct investment 161/1
Asia (*Byzantine name* Asiana) Roman province of Anatolia 35/1
Asia Minor conversion to Christianity 32/1; Ottoman control 67/1. See also Anatolia
Asir SW Arabia Ottoman Empire 102/1
Asoka's Empire India 26/1
Aspern/Essling Austria ✗93/1

Assyria Empire 20/1; Roman province 35/1
Astrakhan S Russia occupied by Mongols 57/2; Tartar khanate 79/1; Bolshevik seizure 127/1; WW2 133/2
Asturias region of N Spain kingdom 48/1
Athens (*Lat.* Athenae *mod. Gr.* Athinai) Greece Mycenaean palace 28/2; Greek parent state 30/1; war with Sparta 31/2; invaded by Huns 39/1; Byzantine Empire 44/1; WW2 133/2
Augusta Rauricorum (*mod.* Augst) W Germany Roman Empire 35/1
Augusta Treverorum (*mod.* Trier *Eng.* Treves) W Germany Roman Empire 35/1
Augusta Vindelicorum (*mod.* Augsburg) S Germany Roman Empire 35/1
Augustodunum (*mod.* Autun) C France Roman Empire 35/1
Augustów NE Poland WW1 125/1
Aulon (*later* Avlona *mod.* Vlorë) Albania Dorian colony 30/1
Austerlitz (*mod.* Slavkov) Czechoslovakia ✗93/1
Australia (*originally called* New Holland) early man 11/1; before the Europeans 24/2; settlement and development 100/1; emergence of Commonwealth 113/1; WW2 135/2; Pacific trade 153/3; foreign direct investment 161
Austrasia the eastern Frankish Empire 48/1
Austria (*Ger.* Österreich) German settlement 51/2; acquired by Habsburgs 62/2; Black Death 63/1; attacked by Ottomans 66/2; War of the Spanish Succession 76/3; Habsburg Empire 87/1; opposition to Napoleon 93/1; annexed by Germany 129/2; Allied occupation zones 139/1; employment 156; EFTA 159/1
Austro-Hungarian Empire (*a/c* Austria-Hungary) Industrial Revolution 95/2; European alliances 118/2; world trade 1860-1913 120/3; overseas trade 121/1; WW1 125/1; dismantled 128/1
Avignon (*anc.* Avenio) S France in Great Schism 63/1; Papal enclave 77/2
Azerbaijan (*anc.* Atropatene) country of the Caucasus Mongol Empire 24/1; Muslim conquest 47/1; Ottoman conquest 58/1, 66/2; acquired by Russia 79/1, 102/1; independence after WW1 128/1; SSR 140/1; independence 1991 159/1
Azores (*Port.* Açores) islands of N Atlantic trade 74/1; Portuguese colony 112/2
Aztec Empire Mexico 68/2; 1492 70/1
Babylon Mesopotamia Sumerian city 20/1; taken by Alexander 30/3
Badajoz SW Spain ✗93/1
Badr W Arabia ✗ 47/1
Baetica S Spain Roman province 35/1
Baffin Island N Canada discovery 72/1

Baghdad Mesopotamia Mongol attack 24/1; Mongol conquest 57/2; under Ottoman rule 67/1; Gulf War 147/3
Baghdad Pact 147/1
Bahamas islands of N Caribbean discovery 72/1; British colony 81/1 107/1, 112/2; independence 145/1 (inset)
Bahrain (*f/s* Bahrein *Ar.* Al Bahrayn) island of Persian Gulf independent sheikhdom 102/1; independence 145/1; Gulf War 147/3
Bailén S Spain ✗93/1
Baku (*n/s* Baki) Azerbaijan conquered by Ottomans 58/1, 66/2; industry 126/2; British occupation 127/1
Balagansk *s/c* Siberia founded 79/2
Balearic Islands W Mediterranean Byzantine Empire 44/1; attacked by Saracens 50/1; to Spain 76/3
Balikpapan E Borneo recaptured from Japanese 135/2
Balkans alliances 118/2; rise of nationalism 119/1
Balkh (*anc.* Bactra *a/c* Zariaspa) Afghanistan Mongol attack 24/1; conquest 47/1
Baluchistan region of NW India district of Mughal Empire 59/1; tribal agency 91/3
Bandjarmasin (*n/s* Banjarmasin) S Borneo trade centre 82/2
Bangkok (*Thai.* Krung Thep) S Thailand early trade centre 82/2; captured by Japanese 135/2; trade with Japan 153/3
Bangladesh (*form.* East Pakistan *or* East Bengal) 153/1
Bantam (*form.* Banten) Java early trade 60/2
Baqubah N Iraq oilfield 146/1
Bar region of NE France/W Germany Burgundian possession 76/1
Barbados island of West Indies British colony 107/1; independence 145/1 (inset)
Barcelona (*anc.* Barcino) NE Spain urban revolt 63/1; ✗93/1
Basque Republic N Spain autonomy 128/1
Bashkir ASSR W USSR 140/1
Basra (*Ar.* Al Başrah) Mesopotamia ✗47/1; Ottoman conquest 66/2; centre of European trade 97/2; Gulf War 146/1
Bassano N Italy ✗93/1
Basutoland (*now* Lesotho) S Africa British protectorate 104/2
Batavia (*form.* Sunda Kalapa, *since 1949* Jakarta *f/s* Djakarta) Java early trade 75/2; centre of European trade 97/2; occupied by Japanese 135/2
Batum (*n/s* Batumi) Caucasus industry 126/2; British occupation 127/1
Bautzen E Germany ✗9m3/1
Bavaria (*Ger.* Bayern) part of Frankish Empire 51/2; Reformation 84/1; German Empire 111/2
Bechuanaland (*now* Botswana) country of S Africa British protectorate 104/2

Beijing (*f/s* Peking) N China economy 1979-92 143/2
Belarus (*a/c* Belorussia) end of Communism 159/1
Belgian Congo (*form.* Congo Free State *now* Zaire) colony 104/2, 112/2; independence 145/1
Belgica Roman province of NE France 35/1
Belgium (*form.* Spanish Netherlands *or* Southern Netherlands) colonial empire 112/2; world trade 1860-1913 120/3; foreign investment 1914 121/2; WW1 125/1; acquisition of Eupen and Malmédy 128/1; economic and social development 1929-39, 130/1; WW2 132/2; EEC and NATO 138/2, 154/1; employment 156
Belgrade (*anc.* Singidunum *S. Cr.* Beograd) C Yugoslavia Ottoman conquest 66/2; WW1 125/1; WW2 133/2
Belize (*form.* British Honduras) independence 145/1 (inset)
Belleau Wood NE France WW1 125/1 (inset)
Belorussia (*n/c* Belarus, *f/c* White Russia) independence after WW1 128/1; SSR 140/1; 1993 159/1
Benevento (*anc.* Beneventum) C Italy dukedom under Byzantine Empire 44/1
Bengal country of E India district of Mughal Empire 59/1; under British rule 90/1,2, 91/3
Benghazi (*anc.* Berenice *Ar.* Banghazi) Libya Italian occupation 105/1; WW2 132/1
Berbers attack Roman Africa 39/1; people of NW Africa 52/1
Berenice (*mod.* Benghazi) Libya city of Roman Empire 35/1
Berezina river W Russia ✗93/1
Besançon (*anc.* Vesontio) E France archbishopric 48/1; fort 77/2
Beshbalik W Mongolia Mongol attack 24/1
Bessarabia region of Romania/Russia acquired by Russia 79/1; Ottoman province 102/1; regained by Russia 127/1; lost to Romania 128/1
Bigorre region of SW France independent fief 76/1
Bihać Bosnia-Herzegovina civil war 158/2
Bithynia ancient country of NW Anatolia 31/1; Byzantine Empire 44/1
Bithynia and Pontus Anatolia Roman province 35/1
Bizerta (*anc.* Hippo Zarytus *Fr.* Bizerte *Ar.* Banzart) Tunisia under Abbasids 47/2; Habsburg Empire 87/1; WW2 133/2
Black Death 63/1
Blenheim (*Ger.* Blindheim) W Germany ✗(called Höchstädt by French and Germans) 76/3
Boğazköy (*anc.* Hattushash *Gr.* Pteria) C Anatolia Hittite city 20/1
Bohemia (*Ger.* Böhmen) W part of mod. Czechoslovakia kingdom within Holy Roman Empire 51/2; expansion 62/2; Black Death 63/1; Reformation 84/1, 86/3;

Habsburg Empire 87/1; Austro-Hungarian Empire 128/1
Bolgar (*a/c* Bulgar) C Russia Mongol city 24/1
Bolivia country of S America independence 107/1; 20C revolutions 149/1; economy 149/2
Bombay W India British settlement 75/2; British rule 90/2; industry 91/3; centre of European trade 97/2
Bona (*mod.* Annaba *Fr.* Bône) N Algeria acquired by Habsburgs 87/1
Bonin Islands (*a/c* Ogasawara Islands) N Pacific annexed by Japan 117/2; attacked by US forces 134/1
Borneo (*Indon.* Kalimantan) island of East Indies Dutch trade 82/2; Dutch and British colonization 113/1; occupied by Japanese 134/1; retaken by Allies 135/2
Bornhöved N Germany ✗51/2
Bornu Nigeria early state 55/2
Borobudur C Java Buddhist site 32/1
Borodino W Russia ✗93/1
Bosnia country of C Yugoslavia under Hungarian Kingdom 62/2; Black Death 63/1; vassal state of Ottoman Empire 67/1
Bosnia-Herzegovina (*S. Cr.* Bosna i Hercegovina) under Ottoman rule 102/1; part of Austria-Hungary 119/1; after WW1 128/1; independence and civil war 158/2
Bosporan Kingdom S Russia 35/1
Botswana (*form.* Bechuanaland) S Africa independence 145/1
Bougainville one of Solomon Islands, W Pacific recaptured from Japanese 135/2
Bourbonnais (*a/c* Bourbon) region of C France annexed to France 76/1
Brandenburg region of E Germany under Bohemian rule 62/2; Black Death 63/1; Reformation 84/1, 86/3; part of Prussia 111/2
Brazil discovered 72/1; early trade 74/1; Portuguese colony 81/1, 92/1; 18C Atlantic economy 96/1; independent empire 107/1; economy and political development 160/1
Breitenfeld E Germany ✗86/3
Brest (*a/c* Brest-Litovsk *Pol.* Brześć nad Bugiem) W Russia WW1 125/1
Breton March NW France 48/1
Brigantes Britain early tribe 35/1
Brihuega C Spain ✗76/3
Britain 18C Atlantic economy 96/1. See also England, United Kingdom
Britannia Inferior Roman province of N England 35/1
Britannia Superior Roman province of S England 35/1
British Bechuanaland S Africa 105/1
British Cameroons (*now part of* Cameroon)
British Central Africa (*later* Nyasaland) protectorate 105/1
British Columbia province of W Canada joins Confederation 113/1, 115/2
British East Africa (*now* Kenya) colony 105/1
British Empire 112/2

Commagene region of SE Anatolia Roman province 35/1

Comoro Islands E Africa spread of Islam 55/2; French colonization 112/2; independence 145/1

Concord NE USA ✗99/1

Confederate States of America 99/3

Confederation of the Rhine 92/2

Congo (form. Middle Congo or French Congo) region of Africa independence 145/1; economy 160/1

Congo Free State (later Belgian Congo now Zaire) 105/1, 112/2

Constance (anc. Constantia Ger. Konstanz) S Germany Frankish kingdom 51/2

Constantinople (anc. Byzantium mod. Istanbul) NW Turkey centre of early Christianity 32/1; Arab attack 39/1; patriarchate 40/1; Arab attacks 47/1; Ottoman conquest 66/1; WW1 125/1

Coral Sea S Pacific ✗134/1, 135/2

Corcyra (mod. Corfu Gr. Kerkira) island of NW Greece Donan colony 30/1

Córdoba (anc. Corduba) S Spain Muslim conquest 47/1; Umayyad Caliphate and Muslim city 50/1; Corduba (mod. Córdoba) S Spain Roman Empire 35/1

Corfu (anc. Corcyra mod. Gr. Kerkira) island of W Greece Byzantine Empire 45/3; Ottoman siege 66/2; under Venetian rule 67/1

Corinth (Lat. Corinthus Gr. Korinthos) C Greece parent state 30/1; Byzantine Empire 44/1

Corinthus (Gr. Korinthos Eng. Corinth) C Greece town of Roman Empire 35/1

Cork S Ireland Viking settlement 50/1

Corregidor C Philippines surrender to Japanese 134/1

Corsica island of W Mediterranean Byzantine Empire 44/1; Muslim conquest 47/1; Saracen attack 50/1; Genoese rule 87/1; annexed by France 110/1

Corunna (Sp. La Coruña) NW Spain ✗93/1

Cossacks S Russia attacked by Ottomans 79/1; anti-Bolshevik activity 127/1

Costa Rica country of C America independence 107/1; political development 149/1; economy 149/2; 160/1

Crete (Lat. Creta mod. Gr. Kriti) Byzantine Empire 44/1; Muslim conquest 47/1; Ottoman province 102/1; cession to Greece 119/1; German capture 133/2

Crimea (Russ. Krym) S Russia Mongol conquest 24/1; Ottoman vassal khanate 67/1; acquired by Russia 79/1

Croatia (S. Cr. Hrvatska) conversion to Christianity 40/1; under Hungarian Kingdom 62/2; Habsburg Empire 87/1; forms part of Yugoslavia 128/1; WW2 133/2; independence and civil war 158-159

Croton (mod. Crotone) S Italy Achaean colony 30/1

Crusades 45/2

Ctesiphon (a/c Tayspun) Mesopotamia Roman Empire 35/1

Cuba discovered 72/1; Spanish colony 74/1; 81/1; independence 107/1; US Protectorate 149/1; Cold War crisis 155/2

Cynossema W Anatolia ✗31/2

Cyprus Gr. Kypros Turk. Kibris anc. Alashiya) Greek and Phoenician colonization 30/1; Byzantine Empire 44/1; Muslim expansion 47/1; acquired by Turks 66/2; independence 145/1

Cyrenaica region of N Africa Roman province 35/1; Muslim conquest 47/1; Ottoman rule 55/2; Italian conquest 105/1

Cyrene (It. Cirene) N Libya Dorian colony 30/1; spread of Christianity and Judaism 32/1; centre of Roman province 35/1

Cythera (a/c Cerigo mod. Gr Kithira) island S Greece colonization 28/2; captured by Athens 31/2

Cyzicus NW Anatolia Ionian colony 30/1; taken by 30/3; ✗31/2

Czechoslovakia created 128/1; territory lost to Germany and Hungary 129/2, 133/2; Comecon and Warsaw Pact 138/3; employment 156; end of Communist rule 159/1

Czechs post-War migration to West 139/1

Czernowitz (now Russ. Chernovtsy Rom. Cernăuţi) E Austro-Hungarian Empire WW1 125/1

Dacia (mod. Romania) Byzantine Empire 44/1

Dagestan ASSR Caucasus 140/1

Daghestan region of Caucasus acquired by Russia 102/1

Dahomey (n/c Benin) country of W Africa early state 55/2; French colony 105/1, 112/2; independence 145/1

Dairen (n/s Dalian Russ. Dalny) Manchuria ceded to Russia and Japan 89/2; 143/2

Dai Viet kingdom of N Indo-China 61/1

Dalmatia region of E Adriatic Byzantine Empire 45/2; civil war 143/2

Daman (Port. Damão) NW India Portuguese settlement 91/3

Damascus (Fr. Damas Ar. Ash Sham or Dimashq) Syria Levantine city 20/1; Byzantine Empire 44/1; Muslim conquest 47/1; revolt against Ottoman rule 66/2; Ottoman Empire 67/1

Damietta (Ar. Dumyat) N Egypt Byzantine Empire 44/1

Da Nang (Fr. Tourane) C Indo-China Vietnamese war 152/2/3

Danzig (Pol. Gdańsk) N Poland Free City 128/1

Dardanelles (Turk. Çanakkale Boğazi anc. Hellespont) straits, NW Turkey demilitarized and remilitarized 128/1

Dar es Salaam E Africa occupied by the Germans 105/1

Darfur region of W Sudan stone age culture 25/1; early state 54/1, 55/2

Dauphiné region of SE France province of France 77/2

Dego N Italy ✗93/1

Deira ancient kingdom of N England 48/2

Delaware state of E USA settled by Swedes 81/1; British colony 99/1; Depression 131/2

Delhi city and region of N India district of Mughal Empire 59/1; Indian Mutiny 90/2

Delian League Greece 31/2

Delium E Greece ✗31/2

Denain N France ✗76/3

Denmark conversion to Christianity 40/1; Reformation 84/1; Industrial Revolution 95/2; war with Prussia and Austria 111/2; WW1 125/1; N Holstein acquired by plebiscite 128/1; WW2 133/2; EEC and NATO 138/2, 154/1; employment 156

Diu NW India 59/1; Portuguese settlement 75/1, 75/2, 112/2; centre of European trade 97/2

Diyarbakir SE Anatolia revolt against Ottoman rule 66/2

Djerba island Tunisia ✗67/2

Djibouti (s/c Jibuti) NE Africa occupied by French 105/1

Dobruja (a/s Dobrudja) region of Romania/Bulgaria Ottoman Empire 67/1, 119/1, 128/1

Dodecanese (Gr. Dhodhekanisos) islands of SE Aegean occupied by Italy, ceded to Turkey 119/1

Dominica island of West Indies British colony 107/1; independence 145/1 (inset)

Dominican Republic Caribbean independence 107/1; US intervention 149/1

Dorchester-on-Thames S England ✗48/2

Dorestad (a/c Duurstede) Netherlands Viking invasion and settlement 50/1

Douala Cameroon W Africa German occupation 105/1

Dresden E Germany ✗93/1; WW1 125/1; WW2 133/2

Dristov Romania ✗52/1

Dubai (Ar. Dubayy) SE Arabia 147/3

Dublin (Ir. Baile Atha Cliath) Ireland Scandinavian settlement and control 50/1; WW1 125/1

Dunkirk (Fr. Dunkerque) N France fortification 77/2; WW2 132/1

Dura-Europos (mod. Salahiyeh) Syria Mithraic site 32/1; Roman Empire 35/1

Durazzo (anc. Epidamnus later Dyrrhachium mod. Durrës) Albania WW1 125/1

Durocortorum (mod. Rheims) N France Roman Empire 35/1

Dushanbe (1929-1961 Stalinabad) Russ. C Asia industry 126/2

Dutch East Indies (now Indonesia) early Dutch trade 75/2; early Dutch possessions 82/2; occupied by

Japanese 134/1; independence 145/1 (inset)

Dutch Guiana (now Surinam) S America 79/1, 112/2

Dutch New Guinea (later West Irian n/c Irian Jaya) East Indies transferred to Indonesia 145/1

Dutch Republic (or United Provinces or Holland) in War of Spanish Succession 76/3; revolt against Spain 86/2

Dyrrhachium (earlier Epidamnus mod. Durrës It. Durazzo) Albania Roman Empire 35/1; Byzantine Empire 44/1

Eastern Rumelia region of Balkans Ottoman province 102/1; ceded to Bulgaria 119/1

Eastern Turkestan C Asia Chinese protectorate 88/1

East Indies agricultural origins 16/1; early kingdoms 61/1; early trade 82/2; 18C European trade 97/2. See also Dutch East Indies, Indonesia

East Prussia (Ger. Ostpreussen) region of E Germany WW2 132/1; divided between Poland and Russia 159/1

Eckmühl/Ebersberg S Germany ✗93/1

Ecuador independence 107/1, 149/1; political development 149/1; economy 149/2; cocaine trade 160/1

Edessa (mod. Urfa) SE Anatolia First Crusade 45/2

Egypt (officially Arab Republic of Egypt form. United Arab Republic Lat. Aegyptus Ar. Misr) 15/1; centre of urban civilization 18/1; ancient 20/1; Old Kingdom 21/2; early settlement 25/1; campaigns of Alexander 30/3; spread of Christianity and Judaism 32/1; Arab conquest 44/1; Byzantine Empire 44/1; Fatimid Caliphate 54/1; conquered by Turks 55/2; Ottoman province 102/1; expansion into Sudan 105/1; independence 145/1; wars with Israel 146/2; political development 150/1; Anglo-French attack (Suez War) 150/1; economy 160/1; Gulf War 147/3

El Agheila Libya WW2 133/2

El Alamein Egypt ✗WW2 133/2

England Scandinavian settlement 50/1; expansion of Christianity 40/1; Black Death and religious unrest 63/1; possessions in France 76/1; Reformation 84/1; WW1 124-5. See also Britain, Great Britain, United Kingdom

Ephesus (Turk. Efes) W Anatolia early trade 20/1; Roman Empire Byzantine Empire 44/1

Epidamnus (later Dyrrhachium It. Durazzo mod. Durrës) Albania Dorian colony 30/1

Epirus ancient country of NW Greece 30/1; Roman province 35/1; Byzantine Empire 44/1; to Greece 119/1

Equator, Confederation of the E Brazil 107/1

Equatorial Guinea (*form.* Spanish Guinea *a/c* Rio Muni) country of W Africa independence 145/1; economy 160/1

Eritrea region of NE Ethiopia Italian rule 103; Italian colony 104/2, 129/2; political development 145/1

Estonia country of the Baltic acquired by Russia 79/1; Reformation 84/1; independence from Russia 128/1; constituted SSR 139/1, 140/1; independence 159/1

Ethiopia expansion of Christianity 32/1; 16C state 55/2; Italian invasion 105/1, 129/2; independence regained 145/1; economy 160/1

Etruscans ancient people of Italy 30/1

Eupen E Belgium ceded by Germany 128/1

Europe early man 11/1; colonization by hunters 12/1; agricultural origins 15/1; amber trade 28/1; agricultural settlement 28/1; Hun and Avar invasions 39/1; Germanic and Slavonic invasions 39/1; expansion of Christianity 40/1; Viking, Magyar and Saracen invasions 50/1; Black Death 63/1; 19-20C alliances 118/2; WW1 124-5; post-war territorial changes 139/1; economic blocs (EEC, EFTA, Comecon) 138/3; employment 156; economic blocs from 1957 157; collapse of Communist power 159/1; foreign direct investment 160

Eylau (*a/c* Preussisch-Eylau *now* Bagrationovsk) E Prussia ✕93/1

Faeroe Islands (*a/s* Faroes) Norse settlement 50/1

Falkland Islands (*Span.* Islas Malvinas) islands of S Atlantic 107/1; claimed by Argentina 145/1; war 149/1

Fanning Island C Pacific British possession 145/1 (inset)

Faroe Islands (*a/s* Faroes) Norse settlement 50/1

Fars (*a/c* Persis, Parsa) Persia Muslim conquest 47/1

Fashoda S Sudan British/French confrontation 105/1

Fatimids Muslim dynasty of Egypt 47/2, 54/1

Federated Malay States (*now* Malaysia) independence 145/1

Feodosiya (*a/c* Kefe, Kaffa *anc.* Theodosia) Crimea acquired by Пиззia 79/1

Ferghana region of C Asia Chinese protectorate 42/1; Muslim expansion 47/1

Fernando Po (*Sp.* Fernando Poó *form.* Macias Nguema Biyogo) island of Equatorial Guinea Dutch and Spanish settlement 55/2; Spanish colony 112/2; 145/1

Fez (*Fr.* Fès *Ar.* Al Fas) Morocco early trade 55/2; occupied by French 105/1

Fezzan (*anc.* Phazania) region of C Libya occupied by Italians 105/1

Fihl Palestine ✕47/1

Fiji S Pacific Melanesian settlement 24/2; British colony 112/2; independence 145/1 (inset)

Finland Reformation 84/1; WW1 125/1; independence 127/1; employment 156; EFTA 159/1

Finns post-war migration from Karelia 139/1

Flanders (*Fr.* Flandre *Dut.* Vlaanderen) region of N Belgium Black Death 63/1; WW1 125/1 (inset)

Florida British rule 81/1, 99/1; annexed by USA 98/2; Depression 131/2; base for invasion of Cuba 155/2

Foix region of S France acquired by France 76/1

Foochow (*a/s* Fu-Chou *n/s* Fuzhou) SE China treaty port 89/2

Formosa (*n/c* Taiwan) cession to Japan 117/2; air attack by US 134/1; US bases 154/1

Fort Amsterdam (*later* New Amsterdam *now* New York) Dutch post 81/2

Fort Lamy (*now* N'Djamena) C Africa occupied by French 105/1

Fort William (*n/c* Thunder Bay) C Canada growth 115/2

Fouta Djallon (*a/s* Futa Jallon) W Africa early state 105/1

France (*anc.* Gaul *Lat.* Gallia) conversion to Christianity 32/1; Arab invasion 47/1; Viking and Saracen invasions 50/1; Scandinavian settlement 50/1; Black Death 63/1; 15C-16C reunification 76/1; War of Spanish Succession 76/3; administrative system under Louix XIV 77/2; Vauban fortresses 77/2; Industrial Revolution 95/2; 18C Atlantic economy 96/1; trade with Africa and Asia 97/2; European alliances 118/2; world trade 1860-1913 120/3; foreign investment 1914 121/2; overseas trade and investment 121/1; WW1 124-5; EEC, NATO 154/1, 159/1; economy 156, 160/1

Franche-Comté region of E France Habsburg Empire 87/1

French Cameroons (*now* part of Cameroon) W Africa independence 145/1

French Congo (*a/c* Middle Congo *now* People's Republic of the Congo) W Africa colony 105/1, 112/2

French Equatorial Africa union of French colonies 145/1

French Guiana S America 107/1

French Guinea (*now* Guinea) W Africa colony 105/1

French Indochina (*now* Cambodia, Laos and Vietnam) colonized 89/2; occupied by Japanese 117/2, 134/1; independence 145/1

French Somaliland (*Fr.* Côte Française des Somalis *later* French Territory of the Afars and Issas *now* Republic of Djibouti) 105/1

French Sudan (*now* Mali) W Africa colony 105/1

French Territory of Afars and Issas (Djibouti)

French West Africa former union of French colonies 104/2, 112/2

Friedland (*now* Pravdinsk) E Prussia ✕93/1

Friedlingen W Germany 76/3

Fukien (*n/s* Fujian) province of SE China Ming province 65/1; Japanese influence 89/2, 117/2, under Nanking control 122/1; economy 143/2

Gagauzia minority area of S Moldova 159/1

Galatia country of C Anatolia Roman province 35/1

Galich (*mod.* Galicia) region of SW Russia Kievan principality 53/2

Galicia (*Russ.* Galich) in Austria-Hungary during WW1 125/1

Gallipoli (*anc.* Callipolis *Turk.* Gelibolu) W Turkey Ottoman centre 67/1; WW1 125/1

Gambia country of W Africa British settlement 55/2; independence 145/1

Gandara (*a/s* Gandhara) region of E Afghanistan Indian kingdom 26/1

Gansu (*f/s* Kansu) province of NW China economy 1979-92 143/2

Gascony (*Fr.* Gascogne) region of SW France part of Frankish Empire 48/1; province of France 77/2

Gaza Palestine Philistine city 30/1; Levantine city 20/1; Byzantine Empire 35/1; Roman Empire 44/1

Gaza Strip Palestine autonomy 146/2

Georgia state of S USA colony 99/1; industry 114/1; population 115/3; Depression 131/2

Georgia country of the Caucasus Mongol Empire 24/1; acquired by Russia 79/1; kingdom 102/1; independent after WW1 128/1; SSR 140/1; independence 1991 159/1

Germania Inferior province of Roman Empire 35/1

Germania Superior province of Roman Empire 35/1

Germantown E USA ✕99/1

Germany (*Lat.* Germania *Ger.* Deutschland *now* Federal Republic of Germany and German Democratic Republic) conversion to Christianity 40/1; Magyar invasion 50/1; Thirty Years' War 86/3; Reformation 84/1; fragmentation 93/1; Industrial Revolution 95/2; expansion in Africa 102/3; unification 111/2; colonial empire 112/2; 19C alliances 118/2; world trade 1860-1913 120/3; overseas trade and investment 121/1; foreign investment 1914 121/2; WW1 124-5; territorial changes after WW1 128/1; occupation 1934 41 129/2; territorial losses to Poland 138/2; Allied control zones 139/1; East and West reunited 159/1

Germany, East (German Democratic Republic *or* DDR) 138/2; Warsaw Pact 138/3, 154/1; employment 156

Germany, West (German Democratic Republic *or* FDR) EEC 138/2; NATO 154/1; employment 156

Germiyan Turkoman principality of W Anatolia 67/1

Ghana (*form.* Gold Coast) W Africa early kingdom 25/1; independence 145/1, 150/1

Goa district of W India 59/1; early trade 74/1, 75/2; Portuguese

settlement 90/1, 91/3; centre of European trade 97/2

Golan Heights Syria occupied by Israel 146/2

Gold Coast (*now* Ghana) slave trade 96/1; early European settlement 105/1 (inset); British colony 105/1, 112/2

Golden Horde Khanate of the Mongol Empire 24/1

Goražde Bosnia-Herzegovina civil war 158/2

Gorlice SE Poland ✕125/1

Goths invasions 39/1

Granada city and region of Spain Muslim minority 84/1; Habsburg Empire 87/1

Great Britain opposition to Napoleon 92-3; trade with Africa and Asia 97/2; 19C European alliances 118/2; WW1 124-5; WW2 132-3. See also England

Great Khan, Empire of the E Asia Mongol state 24/1

Greece (*anc. Gr.* Hellas *mod. Gr.* Ellas) Levantine ports 20/1; campaigns of Alexander 30/1; invaded by Visigoths 39/1; Black Death 63/1; conflict with Bulgaria and Turkey 102/1; independent kingdom 119/1; WW1 124-5; WW2 133/2; Cold War 154/1; employment 156; infant mortality and life expectancy 160

Grenada island of W Indies British colony 107/1; self-government 145/1 (inset); US invasion 149/1

Guadalcanal island of Solomons, S Pacific ✕135/2

Guadeloupe island of W Indies 81/1; French territory 107/1, 145/1 (inset)

Guam island of W Pacific occupied by US 115/2; occupied by Japanese 134/1; recaptured by US 135/2; US base 154/1 (inset)

Guangdong (*f/s* Kwangtung) province of S China economy 1979-92 143/2

Guangxi (*f/s* Kwangsi) province of S China economy 1979-92 143/2

Guantánamo Bay E Cuba US naval base 155/2

Guatemala country and city of C America founded 74/1; 18C Atlantic economy 96/1; independence 107/1; US involvement 154/1; opium trade 160

Guiana region of S America colonized by Dutch and French 81/1; 18C Atlantic economy 96/1. See also Surinam, French Guiana, Guyana

Guinea (*form.* French Guinea) independence 145/1

Guinea-Bissau (*form.* Portuguese Guinea) W Africa independence 145/1

Guizhou (*f/s* Kweichow) province of S China economy 1979-92 143/2

Gujerat (*n/s* Gujarat) region of W India district of Mughal Empire 59/1; under British rule 90/1, 90/2

Gupta Empire India 27/3; destroyed by White Huns 39/1

Gurgan (*a/s* Gorgan *anc.* Hyrcania) city and region of N Persia Muslim conquest 47/1

Lindisfarne (a/c Holy Island) N England Viking attack 50/1

Lindsey early kingdom of E England 48/2

Lindum (mod. Lincoln) E England Roman Empire 35/1

Lisbon (Port. Lisboa anc. Olisipo) Portugal Muslim conquest 40/1, 47/1; colonial trade 74/1; ✗93/1

Lithuania country of the Baltic conversion to Christianity 40/1; early expansion 62/2; Black Death 63/1; acquired by Russia 79/1; Reformation 84/1; independence 128/1; loses Memel territory to Germany 129/2; Soviet Socialist Republic 139/1, 140/1; retaken by Russia 159/1; independence 159/1

Livonia region of NW Russia occupied by Teutonic Knights 62/2; conquered by Russia 79/1; Reformation 84/1

Locarno Switzerland 1925 Conference 128/1

Lodi N Italy Lombard League 51/2; ✗93/1

Lombardy region of N Italy Habsburg Empire 87/1; unification of Italy 110/1

Lonato N Italy ✗93/1

Londinium (mod. London) S England Roman Empire 35/1

London (anc. Londinium) S England Vikings 50/1; urban unrest 63/1; Industrial Revolution 95/2; WW1 125/1

Lorraine (Ger. Lothringen) region of NE France part of medieval German Empire 51/2; acquired by Habsburgs 76/1; Habsburg Empire 87/1; German Empire 111/2

Louisiana state of S USA French rule 81/1,2; purchased by USA 98/2; Spanish rule 99/1; population 115/3; Depression 131/2

Lo-yang (als Luoyang) N China sacked by Hsiung-nu 39/1; industry 143/1

Luanda Angola Portuguese settlement 55/2; early trade 74/1; centre of European trade 97/2

Luang Prabang SE Asia early political centre 61/1

Lucknow N India Indian Mutiny 90/2; industry 91/3

Lungchow SW China treaty port 89/2

Lusatia (Ger. Lausitz) region of E Germany acquired by Habsburgs 62/2; Habsburg Empire 87/1

Lutetia (mod. Paris) N France Roman Empire 35/1

Lutter W Germany ✗86/3

Lützen C Germany ✗86/3, 93/1

Luxembourg (Ger. Luxemburg) EEC and NATO 138/2

Luzon island of N Philippines Spanish control 74/1; US landings 135/2

Luzzara N Italy ✗76/3

Lycia country of SW Anatolia 31/1; Roman Empire 35/1

Lydia country of W Anatolia Byzantine Empire 44/1

Macao (Port. Macau) S China early Portuguese trade 74/1; Portuguese settlement 75/2; centre of

European trade 97/2; Portuguese colony 89/2, 112/2, 145/1

Macassar (Indon. Makasar) East Indies Dutch settlement 75/2, 82/2

Macedonia SE Europe 31/1; Roman province 35/1; Byzantine Empire 44/1; Ottoman province 102/1; divided between Serbia, Greece and Bulgaria 119/1; Greek-Bulgarian conflict 128/1

Madagascar (form. Malagasy Republic) Indonesian settlement 25/1, 54/1, 3; settlement from Africa 55/2; French penetration 105/1; French colony 105/1, 112/2; independence 145/1; political development 150/1; economy 160/1

Madeira island of E Atlantic Portuguese territory 112/2, 145/1

Madras (now Tamil Nadu) state and city, S India British settlement 75/2; under British rule 90/2; trade and industry 91/3

Madrid C Spain captured by French 93/1; Industrial Revolution 95/2

Magenta N Italy ✗110/1

Maginot Line E France defence system 132/1

Magna Graecia the Greek colonies of S Italy 31/1,2

Maine state of NE USA British settlement 81/2; population 115/3; Depression 131/2

Malaca (mod. Málaga) S Spain Roman Empire 35/1

Malacca (Mal. Melaka) district of S Malaya early sultanate 61/1; European discovery 72/1; early trade 74/1; captured by Dutch 75/2; under Portuguese rule 82/2; centre of European trade 97/2; British possession 113/1

Málaga (anc. Malaca) S Spain ✗76/3

Malatya (anc. Melitene) E Turkey Hittite city 20/1; revolt against Ottoman rule 66/2

Malawi (form. Nyasaland) country of C Africa independence 145/1; political development 150/1; economy 160/1

Malaya spread of Islam 60/2; British control 112/2; occupied by Japanese 134/1. See also Malaysia

Malaysia (state formed by amalgamation of Malaya, Sarawak and Sabah) independence 145/1; economy 160/1; Pacific trade 153/3

Maldives islands of N Indian Ocean protectorate 112/2; independence 145/1

Mali (form. French Sudan) country of West Africa independence 145/1; political development 150/1; economy 160/1

Mali Empire early state of W Africa 54/1; 70/1

Malindi Kenya Muslim colony 54/1; early Portuguese trade 55/2

Malmédy E Belgium ceded by Germany 128/1

Maloyaroslavets W Russia ✗93/1

Malplaquet N France ✗76/3

Malta island of C Mediterranean British colony 112/2; WW2 133/2; independence 145/1

Mamelukes (a/s Mamluk) 47/2

Manchouli N China treaty town 89/2

Manchukuo (name given to Manchuria as Japanese puppet state)

Manchuria (called 1932-45 Manchukuo) region of NE China Manchu homeland 88/1; occupied by Russia 89/2; Russian and Japanese spheres of influence 117/2; Japanese puppet state 117/2, 122/1; 134/1; reoccupied by Russia 135/2

Manchus people of NE China, under the Ming 65/1; homeland expansion 88/1

Mandalay C Burma trade 82/2; terminus of Burma Road 117/2; occupied by Japanese 134/1; retaken 135/2

Manhao SW China treaty town 89/2

Manila C Philippines early trade 74/1; Spanish settlement 75/2; Spanish trade 97/2; captured by Japanese 134/1

Manitoba province of C Canada joins Confederation 113/1; economic development 115/2

Manus Island W Pacific Allied base 135/2

Manzikert E Anatolia ✗44/1

Marcomanni early tribe of C Europe 35/2

Marengo N Italy ✗93/1

Mari people of C Russia 53/2, 79/1; ASSR 140/1

Marianas (form. Ladrones) islands of W Pacific German colony 112/2; US occupation 135/2

Marienwerder (Pol. Kwidzyn) N Poland 1920 plebiscite 128/1

Maritime Provinces (Russ. Primorskiy Kray) Russ. Far East acquired from China 89/2

Marne river NE France ✗125/1

Marquesas Islands S Pacific Polynesian dispersal centre 24/2; French colony 145/1 (inset)

Marseilles (Fr. Marseille anc. Massilia) S France galley port 77/2

Marshall Islands C Pacific German colony 112/2; occupied by US 135/2

Martinique island of W Indies French settlement 81/1; French territory 107/1, 112/2, 145/1 (inset)

Maryland state of E USA colony 81/2, 99/1; population 115/3; Depression 131/2

Massachusetts state of NE USA British colony 99/1; population 115/3; Depression 131/2

Massachusetts Bay NE USA British colony 81/2

Massawa N Ethiopia Ottoman settlement 105/1; Italian attack 105/1

Matsu island SE China Nationalist outpost 154/1

Mauretania region of NW Africa conversion to Christianity 32/1

Mauritania country of NW Africa independence from France 145/1; political development 150/1; economy 160/1

Mauritius (Fr. Maurice) island Indian Ocean early trade 75/2; British colony 113/1

Maya people and civilization of C America 22/2, 23/1, 68/2

Mecca (Ar. Al Makkah) W Arabia birth of Islam 47/1; Ottoman Empire 66/2

Media (a/c Mada) ancient country of NW Persia campaigns of Alexander 30/3

Medina (Ar. Al Madinah) W Arabia centre of Islam 47/1; Ottoman Empire 66/2

Mediolanum (mod. Milano Eng. Milan) N Italy Roman Empire 35/1

Mediterranean Sea Greek colonization 30/1; Phoenicians 30/1; Saracen invasions 50/1

Melanesia region of W Pacific early settlement 24/2

Melilla (anc. Rusaddir) N Morocco Habsburg Empire 87/1

Melitene (mod. Malatya) E Anatolia spread of Mithraism 32/1; Roman Empire 35/12

Memel Territory (Ger. Memelgebiet or Memelland) region of SW Lithuania annexed by Germany 129/2

Memphis Lower Egypt city of Ancient Egypt 20/1,21/2; campaigns of Alexander 30/3; Roman Empire 35/1; Byzantine Empire 44/1

Mengtze (Fr. Mong-tseu) SW China treaty port 89/2

Mercia early kingdom of C England 48/2

Merv (since 1937 Mary anc. Alexandria) Russ. C Asia spread of Christianity 32/1; Muslim conquest 47/1

Mesoamerica classic period 22/2, 23/1

Mesopotamia (mod. Iraq) early agriculture 16/1; centre of urban civilization 18/1; Alexander's Empire 31/2; spread of Mithraism 32/1; Roman Empire 35/1; Muslim conquest 47/1

Mexico Aztec Empire 68/2; imperial trade 74/1; population 98/2; political development 107/1; independence 149/1; US intervention 149/1; Zapatista revolt 149/1; economy 160/1; opium trade 160; infant mortality and life expectancy 160

Middle East (a/c Near East) Cold War 147/1

Midway island of C Pacific WW2✗ 134/1; US base 135/2, 154/1 (inset)

Milan (It. Milano anc. Mediolanum) N Italy Lombard League 51/2

Miletus W Anatolia Levantine port 20/1; Mycenaean city 28/2; Greek parent state 30/1; Roman Empire 35/1; Byzantine Empire 44/1

Mindanao island of S Philippines Japanese occupation 134/1; retaken by US 135/2

Mindoro island of C Philippines US landings in WW2 135/2

Ming Empire China 65/1

Mocha (Ar. Al Mukhā) S Yemen centre of European trade 97/2

Modena (anc. Mutina) N Italy Lombard League 51/2; unification of Italy 110/1

Moesia region of Balkans district of Byzantine Empire 44/1

Moesiae late Roman province of Greece 35/2

Moesia Inferior Roman province of the Balkans 35/1

Moesia Superior Roman province of the Balkans 35/1

Mogadishu (n/s Muqdisho It. Mogadiscio) Somalia Muslim colony 54/1; Italian occupation 105/1

Mohács Hungary ✗67/2

Moldavia (Turk. Boğdan Rom. Moldova) region of Romania/Russia Hungarian 62/2; under Ottoman control 67/1; occupied by Russia 93/1; part of Romania 119/1; SSR 140/1; independence (Moldova) 159/1

Moluccas (Indon. Maluku Dut. Molukken form. Spice Islands) islands of E Indies Muslim expansion 60/2; early Portuguese trade 74/1; Dutch control 82/2

Monastiraki Crete palace site 28/2

Mondovi NW Italy ✗93/1

Monemvasia (It. Malvasia) S Greece Byzantine Empire 45/2; Ottoman conquest 66/2

Mongol Empire 24/1

Mongolia (form. Outer Mongolia) nomadic pastoralism 19/1; Mongol Empire 24/1; under Turkish Empire 39/1; Chinese incursions under Ming 65/1; Chinese protectorate 88/1; autonomy 89/2; Russian sphere of influence 112/2; limit of Japanese expansion 117/2

Montenegro (S. Cr. Crna Gora) region of S Yugoslavia under Ottoman rule 102/1; 19C alliances 118/2; independent state 119/1; WW1 125/1; forms part of Yugoslavia 128/1; WW2 133/2

Montenotte N Italy ✗93/1

Montereau N France ✗93/1

Montmirail N France ✗93/1

Montreux Switzerland 1936 conference 128/1

Montserrat island West Indies British colony 145/1 (inset)

Moravia (Czech. Morava Ger. Mähren) region of C Czechoslovakia medieval German Empire 51/2; occupied by Poland 61/1; acquired by Bohemia 62/2; Hussite influence 63/1; Reformation 84/1; Habsburg Empire 87/1; forms part of Czechoslovakia 128/1

Mordvinian ASSR W USSR 140/1

Morea (a/c Peloponnese) region of S Greece Byzantine Empire 45/2; conquered by Ottomans 67/1

Morocco (Fr. Maroc Sp. Marruecos) under Almohads 54/1; Sharifian dynasties 55/2; independent sultanate 102/1; Spanish conquest 105/1; French and Spanish protectorates 112/2; independence 145/1; conflict with Algeria 150/1; US bases 154/1; economy 160/1

Morotai island N Moluccas, E Indies captured by Allies 135/2

Moscow (Russ. Moskva) W Russia early bishopric 40/1; city of Vladimir-Suzdal 53/2; captured by Napoleon 93/1; Industrial Revolution 95/2; industrial development 126/2; Bolshevik seizure of power 127/1; military district 141/1

Mossi early states of W Africa 60-61

Mostar Herzegovina, Yugoslavia civil war 158/2

Mosul (Ar. Al Mawsil) Iraq Muslim conquest 47/1; Ottoman Empire 67/1; oilfield 146/1

Mozambique (form. Portuguese East Africa Port. Moçambique) early trade 75/2; Portuguese settlement 75/2; centre of European trade 97/2; Portuguese colony 105/1; 113/1; independence 145/1; political development 150/1; economy 160/1

Mughal Empire India 66/2

Mukden Manchuria capital of Manchuria 88/1; treaty town 89/2; Japanese occupation 117/2

Muscat and Oman (now Oman) SE Arabia British protectorate 102/1

Muscovy early principality of W Russia 66/2, 79/1

Muslims minority in Bosnia and Serbia 158/2

Mwenemutapa early state of SE Africa 55/2

Mycenae ancient city of S Greece 28/2

Mysore (now Karnataka) region of S India district of Mughal Empire 59/1

Mytilene (a/s Mitylene) island of Aegean ceded to Greece 119/1

Nagasaki W Japan early European trade 74/1, 75/2; industry 83/1; Dutch trade 97/2; bombed by US 135/2

Nagorno-Karabakh Caucasus 140/1; 159/1

Namibia (form. South West Africa earlier German South West Africa) German colony 105/1, 112/2; independence from South Africa 145/1, 150/1; economy 160/1

Nanking (n/s Nanjing) N China Ming provincial capital 65/1; treaty port 89/2; occupied by Japan 117/2; economy 143/2

Nanning S China treaty port 89/2

Nantes NW France Scandinavian settlement 50/1

Naples, Kingdom of Black Death 63/1; to Austria 76/3; Habsburg Empire 87/1; satellite of France 93/1; unification of Italy 110/1

Narbonensis (a/c Gallia Narbonensis) Roman province of S France 35/1

Narbonne (anc. Narbo) S France Muslim conquest 47/1

Naroch lake W Russia WW1 ✗125/1

Nations, Battle of the (Leipzig) E Germany ✗93/1

Naucratis Egypt Greek colony 30/1

Nauru island W Pacific independence 145/1 (inset)

Navarre (Sp. Navarra) region of N Spain/SW France acquired by France 77/2; Habsburg Empire 87/1

Navas de Tolosa S Spain ✗47/2

Neapolis (mod. Napoli Eng. Naples) S Italy Greek colony 30/1, 31/2; Roman Empire 35/1

Nehavend (anc. Laodicea in Media) W Persia ✗47/1

Nepal tributary state of Chinese Empire 88/1; 89/2; economy 160/1

Nerchinsk, Treaty of 88/1

Netherlands (a/c Holland form. Dutch Republic United Provinces) agriculture and land reclamation 26/2; Habsburg Empire 87/1; Industrial Revolution 95/2; 18C Atlantic economy 96/1; trade with Africa and Asia 97/2; colonial power 112/2; EEC and NATO 138/2; economy 160/1. See also Belgium, Flanders, Holland

Netherlands, Austrian (mod. Belgium) revolt against Emperor 92/1

Netherlands East Indies (now Indonesia) occupied by Japanese 134/1. See also East Indies, Borneo, Java, Moluccas, Sumatra

Netherlands, Spanish (later Holland or United Provinces; and Belgium) Reformation 84/1; Dutch revolt 86/2

Neustria the Frankish lands of N France 48/1

Nevis island W Indies British colony 107/1; self-government with St. Christopher 145/1 (inset)

New Amsterdam (earlier Fort Amsterdam now New York city) colonized by Dutch 81/2

New Britain island Papua New Guinea early Melanesian settlement 24/2; retaken from Japanese 135/2; to New Guinea 145/1 (inset)

New Brunswick province of E Canada joins Confederation 113/1; 115/2

New Caledonia islands S Pacific early Melanesian settlement 24/2; French colony 112/2, 145/1; US base 134-5

Newchwang Manchuria treaty port 89/2

New England NE USA British settlement 81/2

Newfoundland province of E Canada rediscovered 72/1; British colony 81/1; British settlement 81/2; joins Dominion 115/2

New France French possessions in Canada 81/2

New Galicia Spanish colony of C Mexico 74/1

New Granada (mod. Colombia) Spanish colony 74/1, 81/1; vice-royalty in rebellion against Spain 92/1, 107/1; 18C Atlantic economy 96/1

New Guinea (now part of Papua New Guinea) early settlement 24/2; Dutch/German/British control 112/2; attacked by Japanese 134/1; retaken by Allies 135/2. See also West Irian

New Hampshire state of NE USA colony 81/2; 99/1; population 115/3, Depression 131/2

New Hebrides (Fr. Nouvelles Hébrides now Vanuatu) islands S Pacific early Melanesian settlement 24/2; British/French condominium 112/2; US base 134/1; independence 145/1 (inset)

New Ireland island Papua New Guinea early Melanesian settlement 24/2; occupied by Japanese 134/1

New Jersey state of E USA colony 81/2, 99/1; population 115/3; Depression 131/2

New Mexico state of SW USA ceded by Mexico 107/1; population 115/3; Depression 131/2

New Orleans S USA French/Spanish occupation 81/1

New Sarai S Russia Mongol city 24/1

New South Wales state of SE Australia settlement and development 100/1; statehood 113/1

New Spain (mod. Mexico, C America and Caribbean) Spanish vice-royalty 74/1; early voyages of discovery 81/1; rebellion against Spain 92/1

New Territories S China acquired by Britain 89/2

New York City (1653-64 called New Amsterdam earlier Fort Amsterdam) 81/2; industry 114/1; population 114/1; economic growth 137/2

New Zealand early Polynesian settlement 24/2; settlement and development 101/2, 113/1; pacific trade 153/3; foreign direct investment 161

Nicaea (mod. Iznik) W Anatolia Roman Empire 35/1; Byzantine Empire 45/2

Nicaragua country of C America early exploration 72/1; independence 107/1; US protectorate 107/1; Sandinista revolution 149/1

Nicephorium (mod. Rakka) Syria Roman Empire 35/1

Nicobar Islands Indian Ocean territory of British India 91/3

Nicomedia (mod. Izmit) W Anatolia Roman Empire 35/1; Byzantine Empire 44/1

Nicopolis W Greece Byzantine Empire 45/2

Niger country of W Africa French colony 105/1; independence 145/1; economy 160/1

Nigeria country of W Africa British colony 104/2, 105/1, 112/2; independence 145/1; political development 150/1; economy 160/1

Nineveh Mesopotamia early farming village 16/1; 20/1; Assyrian Empire 20/1; Mitannian city 20/1

Ningpo (n/s Ningbo) E China treaty port 89/2

Ningxia (f/s Ningxia) province of N China economy 1979-92 143/2

Nippur C Mesopotamia Sumerian city 20/1

Samara (*1935-91* Kuybyshev) C Russia founded 79/1; on railway to east 108/1; Bolshevik seizure 127/1

Samarkand (*anc.* Maracanda) C Asia Mongol attack 24/1; Muslim conquest 47/1; Timur's Empire 57/2; Soviet Union 126/2

Samoa islands S Pacific early settlement 24/2; German colony 112/2 . See also Western Samoa

Samogitia (*Lith.* Ṛemaitija) region of NW Russia occupied by Lithuania 37/1, 62/2

San Agostín (*now* St. Augustine) SE USA Spanish fort 74/1

Sandinista revolt Nicaragua 149/1

San Francisco (*form.* San Francisco de Asís) W USA Spanish settlement 81/1; economic growth 137/2

Santa Cruz (*n/c* Ndeni) Solomon Islands WW2 ✕135/2

Santa Fé de Bogotá (*n/c* Bogotá) Colombia Spanish capital of New Granada 74/1

Santo Domingo (*now* Dominican Republic) W Indies Spanish colony 74/1; 81/1

Santuao E China treaty port 89/2

São Tomé and Príncipe islands W Africa united as independent republic 145/1

Saracens invasion of S Europe 50/1

Saragossa (*anc.* Caesaraugusta *mod.* Zaragoza) N Spain bishopric 40/1; ✕93/1; captured by French 93/1

Sarajevo C Yugoslavia captured by Ottomans 67/1; Ottoman administrative centre 67/1; WW1 125/1; WW2 133/1; civil war 158/2

Saratoga NE USA ✕99/1

Sardinia (*It.* Sardegna) island W Mediterranean Muslim conquest 47/1; Byzantine Empire 44/1; Muslim conquest 47/1; Saracen attacks 50/1; Habsburg Empire 87/1; Kingdom 110/1

Sardis (*a/s* Sardes) W Anatolia Roman Empire 35/1; Byzantine Empire 44/1

Sarkel S Russia ✕52/1

Sarmatians (*Lat.* Sarmatae) tribe of Caucasus and S Russia 30/1, 35/1

Sarmizegetusa Romania Roman Empire 35/1

Sasanian Empire Western Asia 27/3

Saudi Arabia Gulf War 147/3

Savoy (*Fr.* Savoie *It.* Savoia) region of France/Italy medieval state 63/1; Calvinism 84/1; Habsburg Empire 87/1; ceded to France 110/1

Saxon March 48/1

Saxony region of N Germany Frankish Empire 48/1; Black Death 63/1; Reformation 84/1

Scandinavia (*anc.* Scandia) Viking invasions of Europe 50/1; world trade 1860-1913 120/3. See also Denmark, Sweden, Norway

Scapa Flow N Scotland WW1 125/1

Schleswig-Holstein region of N Germany unification of Germany 111/2

Scotland (*anc.* Caledonia) Scandinavian settlement 50/1;

Black Death 63/1; Reformation 84/1

Scupi (*mod.* Skoplje *Mac.* Skopje *Turk.* Üsküb) Byzantine Empire 44/1

Scythians ancient tribe of S Russia 30/1

Sebastopol (*Russ.* Sevastopol) Crimea. S Russia 1905 Revolution 109/2; WW1 125/1

Sedan N France ✕111/2; WW2 132/1

Seleucia (*a/c* Seleucia Tracheotis) SE Anatolia Byzantine Empire 44/1

Selinus (*mod.* Selinunte) Sicily Greek colony 30/1, 31/2

Seljuks Turkish Muslim dynasty of Middle East 45/2, 47/2

Senegal W Africa French colony 105/1, 112/2; independence 145/1; economy 160/1

Senegambia region of W Africa source of slaves 55/2; slave trade 96/1

Seoul (*Jap.* Keijo) S Korea Korean war 143/1; population 160/1

Septimania ancient region of S France, part of Frankish Empire 48/1

Serbia (*now part of* Yugoslavia) country of SE Europe conversion to Christianity 40/1; Byzantine Empire 45/2; empire under Stephen Dushan 62/2; Black Death 63/1; Ottoman province 67/1; Industrial Revolution 95/2; independence 102/1, 119/1; WW1 125/1; forms part of Yugoslavia 128/1; WW2 133/2

Serdica (*a/s* Sardica *mod.* Sofia) Bulgaria Roman Empire 35/1; Byzantine Empire 44/1

Sevastopol (*Eng.* Sebastopol *med. Turk.* Akhtiar) Crimea acquired by Muscovy 79/1

Seville (*Sp.* Sevilla *anc.* Hispalis) S Spain Emirate of Cordoba 50/1

Shaanxi (*f/s* Shensi) province of N China economy 1979-92 143/2

Shanghai E China treaty port 89/2; occupied by Japanese 117/2; Nationalist control 122/1; industry 122/2; economy 143/2, 153/3

Shansi (*n/s* Shanxi) province of N China Ming province 65/1; Manchu expansion 88/1; economy 143/2

Shan State(s) Burma part of India 91/3

Shandong (*f/s* Shantung) province of E China economy 1979-92 143/2 special economic zone 143/2

Shantung (*n/s* Shandong) province of E China under Ming 65/1; Manchu expansion 88/1; Japanese influence 122/1; economy 143/2

Shanxi (*f/s* Shansi) province of N China economy 1979-92 143/2

Shensi (*n/s* Shaanxi) province of N China under Ming 65/1; Manchu expansion 88/1; economy 143/2

Shenzhen S China special economic zone 143/2

Shetland (*form.* Hjaltland) NE Scotland Norwegian settlement 50/1

Shias Muslim minority of S Iraq 147/3

Siam (*now* Thailand) spread of Buddhism 32/1, 60/2; conquests 82/1; under Japanese influence

117/2; occupied by Japanese 134/1

Sian (*n/s* Xi'an) China Ming provincial capital 64/1

Siberia Russian expansion 79/2

Sichuan (*f/s* Szechwan) province of W China economy 1979-92 143/2

Sicily (*Lat. and It.* Sicilia) island C Mediterranean Greek colonization 30/1; Byzantine Empire 44/1; Saracen raids 50/1; German attacks 51/2; to Savoy 76/3; Habsburg Empire 87/1; Kingdom of the Two Sicilies annexed to Piedmont/Sardinia 110/1; WW2 133/2

Sidon (*mod.* Saïda *Ar.* Sayda) Lebanon Assyrian Empire 20/1; Levantine city 20/1; Phoenician city 30/1; taken by Alexander 30/3

Sierra Leone country of W Africa slave trade 96/1; British settlement 105/1; British colony 112/2, 113/1; independence 145/1; economy 160/1

Sikkim country of Himalayas British protectorate 89/2 dependency of India 91/3; annexed to India 145/1

Silesia (*Ger.* Schlesien *Pol.* Śląsk) region of Germany/Poland medieval German Empire 51/2; acquired by Habsburgs 62/2; Habsburg Empire 87/1; unification of Germany 111/2; divided between Germany and Poland 128/1

Silla (*Eng.* Korea *Kor.* Koryo) occupied by T'ang 42/1

Singapore (*earlier* Tumasik) S Malaya early trade 82/2; occupied by Japanese 134/1; independence 145/1; Pacific trade 152/2; economy 153/3, 160/1

Sinkiang (*n/s* Xinjiang) province of NW China part of Han Empire 88/1; cession of territory to Russia 89/2; economy 143/2

Sinope (*mod.* Sinop) N Anatolia Greek colony 30/1; Roman Empire 35/1; Byzantine Empire 44/1

Slovakia forms part of Czechoslovakia 128/1; occupied by Hungary in WW2 132/1

Slovenia in Yugoslavia 128/1; independence 159/1

Smolensk W Russia bishopric 40/1; principality 53/2; acquired by Lithuania 62/2; captured by Napoleon 93/1; Bolshevik seizure 127/1; industry 126/2

Smyrna (*mod.* Izmir) W Anatolia Roman Empire 35/1; Byzantine Empire 67/1; Ottoman Empire 67/1; centre of European trade 97/2

Socotra island Arabian Sea British control 103; acquired by Britain 112/2

Sofala Mozambique Portuguese settlement 55/2; early trade 75/2

Sofia (*anc.* Serdica *a/s* Sardica *med.* Sredets) Bulgaria Ottoman control 67/1; WW2 133/2

Sogdiana (*a/c* Sogdia, Suguda) ancient region of C Asia Chinese protectorate 42/1

Solferino N Italy ✕110/1

Solomon Islands SW Pacific British protectorate 113/1 (inset); occupied by Japanese 134/1; retaken by Allies

135/2; independence 145/1 (inset)

Somalia (*form.* British and Italian Somaliland) independence 145/1; political development 150/1; economy 160/1

Somaliland divided between British, Italians and French 103

Somme river NE France WW1 offensive 125/1 (inset)

Songhay (*a/s* Songhai) early empire of W Africa 55/2; 70/1

Soochow E China treaty port 89/2; industry 122/2

Sopron (*Ger.* Ödenburg) Hungary to Hungary after plebiscite 128/1

Sorbs Slavic tribe of C Europe 48/1

South Africa Union 112/2; Republic 145/1; political development 150/1

South Carolina state of SE USA colony 81/2, 99/1; population 115/3; Depression 131/2

South-East Asia early civilizations 26/2; Mongol attacks 61/1; post 1945 conflicts 153/1, 154/1

Southern Rhodesia (*now* Zimbabwe *f/c* Rhodesia) British colony 105/1, 112/2

South Ossetian AR Caucasus 140/1

South Tyrol (*Ger.* Südtirol *It.* Alto Adige) region of Austro-Hungarian Empire acquired by Italy 128/1

South Vietnam independence 145/1; war 152/2. See also Vietnam, Indo-China

South Yemen (*also called* People's Democratic Republic of Yemen *form.* Federation of South Arabia *earlier* Protectorate of South Arabia *earlier* Aden Protectorate) independence 145/1; union with north Yemen 145/1; political development 150/1; economy 160/1

Spa Belgium 1920 Conference 128/1

Spain (*anc.* Hispania) early invasions 39/1; conversion to Christianity 40/1; Muslim conquest 47/1; Umayyad caliphate 47/2; Reformation 84/1; War of the Spanish Succession 76/3; colonial empire 92/1; opposition to Napoleon 93/1; Industrial Revolution 95/2; 18C Atlantic economy 96/1; 19C alliances 118/2; world trade 1860-1913 120/3; US bases 154/1; economy 156, 160/1

Spanish Guinea (*now* Equatorial Guinea) W Africa colony 113/1

Spanish March 48/1

Spanish Sahara (*a/c* Western Sahara *includes* Rio de Oro) NW Africa 102; Spanish colony 105/1; partition between Morocco and Mauritania 145/1, 150/1; economy 160/1

Spanish Succession, War of the 76/3

Sparta (*a/c* Lacedaemon) S Greece Mycenaean palace site 28/2; Peloponnesian War 31/2; Roman Empire 35/1

Spartalos N Greece ✕31/2

Sphacteria S Greece ✕31/2

Srebrenica NE Herzegovina UN safe area 158/2

Srinagar N India capital of Kashmir 91/3

...aya E Indies early empire 61/1
...ngrad (until 1925 Tsaritsyn since ...Volgograd) S Russia WW2 132-3
...esa N Italy 1935 Conference 128/1
...ria (Ger. Steiermark) province of ...Austria acquired by Habsburgs ...2/2; Habsburg Empire 87/1
...udan (form. Anglo-Egyptian Sudan) ...British control 102/1; Mahdist state 105/1; Anglo-Egyptian condominium 105/1; independence 145/1, 150/1; economy 160/1
Sudetenland C Europe German annexation 129/2
Suez Canal N Egypt Egyptian-Israeli war 146/2; Anglo-French attack 150/1
Suifen NE China treaty port 89/2
Sukhothai C Thailand Buddhist site 32/1; major political centre 61/1
Sumatra (Indon. Sumatera) E Indies spread of Buddhism 32/1; Dutch possession 112/2; occupied by Japanese 134/1
Sumerians ancient people of Mesopotamia 21/2
Sung Empire China Mongol conquest 24/1
Süntel N Germany ✗48/1
Surabaya (Dut. Soerabaja) Java trading centre 82/2; occupied by Japanese 134/1
Swakopmund SW Africa German settlement 105/1
Swatow (n/s Shantou) S China treaty port 89/2; Japanese occupation 117/2; 143/2
Swaziland country of SE Africa British protectorate 113/1; independence 145/1; economy 160/1
Sweden conversion to Christianity 40/1; Viking expansion 50/1; Black Death 63/1; Reformation 84/1; Industrial Revolution 95/2; EFTA 138/3; economy 156, 160/1
Switzerland Reformation 84/1; Industrial Revolution 95/2; neutral in WW2 132/1; EFTA 138/3; economy 156, 160/1; infant mortality and life expectancy 160
Sydney SE Australia founded 100/1; Allied base in WW2 135/2
Syracusa (a/s Syracusae mod. Siracusa Eng. Syracuse) Sicily Greek colony 30/1; Roman Empire 35/1; Byzantine Empire 44/1
Syria Mitannian cities 20/1; Arab conquest 47/1; Ottoman province 102/1; WW2 132/1; independence 145/1; Gulf War 147/3
Szechwan (n/s Sichuan) province of W China under Ming 65/1; Manchu expansion 88/1; Nationalist control 122/1; economy 143/2
Szemao SW China treaty town 89/2
Tagliacozzo C Italy ✗51/2
Taiwan (a/c Formosa) Mesolithic sites 16/2; early settlements 16/2; contested by Dutch and Spanish 82/2; rising of aboriginals 88/1; acquired by Japan 89/2, 122/1, 117/2; seat of Chinese Nationalist government 153/1; Japanese investment 153/3

Taiyuan (a/s T'ai-yüan) N China T'ang city 42/1; Ming provincial capital 65/1; French railway 89/2
Tajiks people of C Asia 140/1
Talas river C Asia ✗47/1
Talavera C Spain ✗93/1
Tamanrasset S Algeria Saharan trade 55/2; French occupation 105/1
Tamsui N Taiwan treaty port 89/2
Tana S Russia Mongol conquest 57/2
Tanais S Russia Greek colony 30/1
Tananarive (n/s Antananarivo) Madagascar centre of Merina kingdom 105/1
Tanganyika (form. German East Africa now part of Tanzania) independence 145/1; political development 150/1
Tangier (a/c Tangiers Fr. Tanger Sp. Tánger Ar. Tanjah anc. Tingis) Morocco centre of European trade 97/2; international control 105/1
Tannenberg (Pol. Stębark) E Prussia ✗WW1 125/1
Tannu Tuva (now Tuvinskaya ASSR) C Asia Russian protectorate 89/2
Tanzania (formed by amalgamation of Tanganyika and Zanzibar) 150/1; infant mortality and life expectancy 160. See also German East Africa
Tarawa Gilbert Islands, S Pacific ✗135/2
Tarentum (mod. Taranto) S Italy Greek colony 30/1
Tarim Basin C Asia occupied by China 42/1, 88/1
Tarnopol (now Russ. Ternopol) E Austria-Hungary WW1 125/1; WW2 133/2
Tarquinii (later Corneto mod. Tarquinia) C Italy Etruscan city 30/1
Tarraco (mod. Tarragona) NE Spain Greek colony 30/1, 35/1
Tarraconensis Roman province of N Spain 35/1
Tarsus S Anatolia early trade 20/1; Assyrian Empire 20/1; Hittite city 20/1; Roman Empire 35/1; Byzantine Empire 44/1
Tartars (a/s Tatars) Turkic people of E Russia 79/2, 140/2
Tashkent Russ. C Asia Mongol conquest 57/2; industry 126/2
Tasmania (until 1856 Van Diemen's Land) island state of SE Australia settlement and development 100/1 (inset)
Tatar ASSR (n/c Tatarstan) W USSR 141/1, 159/1
Tengyueh SW China treaty town 89/2
Tenochtitlán Mexico Aztec capital 68/2
Teotihuacán early culture of C America 22/2
Tertry N France ✗48/1
Teschen (Cz. Těšín or Český Těšín Pol. Cieszyn) city and district divided between Poland and Czechoslovakia 128/1; Czech part retaken by Poland 129/2
Tete Mozambique Portuguese settlement 55/2
Teutonic Order Baltic 53/2
Texas state of S USA independent

107/1; population 115/3; Depression 131/2
Thailand (f/c Siam) Theravada Buddhism 60/2; political developments 153/1; US bases 154/1; economy 153/3, 160/1; opium trade 161. See also Siam
Thebes (mod. Gr. Thivai) C Greece Mycenaean palace 28/2
Thebes (Lat. Thebae earlier Diospolis Magna) Upper Egypt 20/1; Roman Empire 35/1
Theodosia (mod. Feodosiya) Crimea Greek colony 30/1
Thera (mod. Thira a/c Santorini) island of S Aegean Greek parent state 30/1
Thessalonica (a/c Salonika Gr. Thessaloniki) N Greece Roman Empire 35/1; Byzantine Empire 44/1
Thessaly (Gr. Thessalia) region of C Greece district of Byzantine Empire 44/1; ceded to Greece 119/1
Theveste (mod. Tebessa) Algeria Roman Empire 35/1
Thirteen Colonies N America 81/1, 92/1
Thrace (anc. Thracia) region of SE Europe divided between Bulgaria and Turkey 119/1; East occupied by Greece 128/1
Thracia (Eng. Thrace) SE Europe Roman province 35/1; Byzantine Empire 44/1
Thuringia (Thüringen) region of E Germany medieval German Empire 48/1; German unification 111/2
Tiahuanaco Empire C Andes site 23/1
Tianjin (f/s Tientsin) NE China economy 1979-92 143/2
Tibet (anc. Bhota Chin. Xizang) C Asia spread of Buddhism 32/1; early expansion 39/1; unified kingdom 42/1; Chinese protectorate 88/1; British sphere of influence 89/2; economy 143/2; absorbed by China 145/1
Tientsin (n/s Tianjin) NE China treaty port 89/2; Japanese occupation 117/2; economy 143/2
Tiflis (n/c Tbilisi) Caucasus Mongol attack 24/1; Muslim conquest 47/1; Mongol conquest 57/2; Timur's Empire 57/2; urban growth 141/1
Timbuktu (Fr. Tombouctou) W Africa occupied by French 105/1
Timor island of E Indies early Portuguese colony 75/2; Dutch/Portuguese control 112/2; occupied by Japanese in WW2 134/1
Timur's Empire Persia 57/2
Tingis (mod. Tangier) Morocco Roman Empire 35/1
Tingitana NW Africa region of Roman Empire 35/1
Tinian island Marianas, C Pacific occupied by US in WW2 135/2
Tippu Tib's Domain E Africa 105/1
Tirana Albania Ottoman Empire 102/1
Tobruk (Ar. Tubruq) N Libya WW2 132/1
Togo (form. Togoland) country of W Africa independence 145/1; economy 160/1
Togoland W Africa German colony 105/1, 112/2

Tokyo (form. Edo) C Japan industrialization 83/1; trade 153/3
Toledo (anc. Toletum) C Spain Muslim conquest 47/1
Toletum (mod. Toledo) C Spain Roman Empire 35/1
Tomi (now Constanta) Romania Greek Colony 30/1; Roman Empire 35/1
Tonga island kingdom of S Pacific early settlement 24/2; British protectorate 112/2; independence 145/1 (inset)
Tongking (Fr. Tonkin) region of N Indo-China Hindu-Buddhist state 82/2; tributary state of China 88/1
Toulouse (anc. Tolosa) S France Muslim conquest 47/1; parlement 81/2
Tours (anc. Caesarodunum later Turones) C France archbishopric 48/1; seat of intendant 77/2
Trafalgar S Spain ✗93/1
Transjordan country of N Arabia Ottoman province 102/1; British mandate 132/1
Transkei region of SE Africa independent Bantustan 150/1
Transnistria Russian-speaking region of E Moldova 159/1
Transoxiana ancient region of C Asia Muslim conquest 47/1
Transylvania region of Hungary/Romania part of Austro-Hungarian Empire 128/1
Trapezus (mod. Trabzon Eng. Trebizond) NE Anatolia Greek colony 30/1; Roman Empire 35/1
Trebizond (Turk. Trabzon anc. Trapezus) NE Anatolia Byzantine Empire 44/1
Trebizond, Empire of NE Anatolia 67/1
Trier (Eng. Treves Fr. Trèves anc. Augusta Treverorum) W Germany archbishopric 48/1
Trieste (anc. Tergeste S. Cr. Trst) WW1 125/1; WW2 133/2
Trinidad island of W Indies British colony 107/1; independence 145/1
Triple Alliance 118/2
Tripoli (Ar. Tarabulus al Gharb anc. Oea) N Libya trans-Saharan trade 55/2; Muslim conquest 66/2; centre of European trade 97/2; Italian occupation 105/1
Tripoli (Ar. Tarabulus ash Sham anc. Tripolis) Syria Roman Empire 35/1; Byzantine Empire 44/1
Tripolitania N Africa district of Byzantine Empire 44/1; under Almohads 54/1; Italian occupation 105/1
Troy (Lat. Ilium Gr. Troas) NW Anatolia 18/2
Trucial Coast (later Trucial Oman, Trucial States now United Arab Emirates) E Arabia British control 102/1
Truk Caroline Islands, C Pacific Japanese base in WW2 134/1, 135/2
Tsaritsyn (1925-61 Stalingrad now Volgograd) S Russia founded 79/1; urban growth 141/1; Bolshevik seizure 127/1